D0015691

ZOMBIE ECONOMICS

ZOMBIE ECONOMICS

HOW DEAD IDEAS STILL WALK AMONG US

JOHN QUIGGIN

PRINCETON UNIVERSITY PRESS

PRINCETON AND OXFORD

Published by Princeton University Press,
41 William Street, Princeton, New Jersey 08540
In the United Kingdom: Princeton University Press,
6 Oxford Street, Woodstock, Oxfordshire OX20 1TW

Library of Congress Cataloging-in-Publication Data

Quiggin, John.
Zombie economics : how dead ideas still walk among us / John Quiggin.
p. cm.
Includes bibliographical references and index.
ISBN 978-0-691-14582-2 (hbk. : alk. paper)
1. Economics—History—20th century.
2. Economic policy—History—20th century.
3. Economics. I. Title.
HB87.Q54 2010
330—dc22
2010023189

British Library Cataloging-in-Publication Data is available

This book has been composed in Sabon
Printed on acid-free paper.
press.princeton.edu
Printed in the United States of America

1 3 5 7 9 10 8 6 4 2

CONTENTS

PREFACE

The idea for this book began when I read this striking passage in *Animal Spirits* by George Akerlof and Robert Shiller:

> The economics of the textbooks seeks to minimize as much as possible departures from pure economic motivation and from rationality. There is a good reason for doing so—and each of us has spent a good portion of his life writing in this tradition. The economics of Adam Smith is well understood. Explanations in terms of small deviations from Smith's ideal system are thus clear, because they are posed within a framework that is already very well understood. But that does not mean that these small deviations from Smith's system describe how the economy actually works. Our book marks a break with this tradition. In our view, economic theory should be derived not from the minimal deviations from the system of Adam Smith but rather from the deviations that actually do occur and can be observed. (Akerlof and Shiller 2009, 4–5)

This passage motivated me to write about its implications for macroeconomics in the Crooked Timber blog. In comments, economist Max Sawicky, posting under the pseudonym MiracleMax, suggested that this, combined with some earlier posts on ideas refuted by the financial crisis, would make a good book. Brad DeLong of the University of California at Berkeley picked up the idea, and the next day Seth Ditchik of Princeton University Press e-mailed me to say he thought it was a great idea. The result is before you.

More than most books, this one has been improved by comments from others, not all of whom I can name. As I wrote draft chapters, I posted them on crookedtimber.org, and on my personal blog johnquiggin.com, then combined them in a draft on wikidot.com. I asked for comments and received, in total, several thousand, from well over a hundred different commenters, most of them pseudonymous.

I can't thank all those who commented, but I would like to mention "Alice," "Bert," "Bianca Steele," Martin Bento, Kevin Donoghue, Kenny Easwaran, John Emerson, "Freelander," Jim Harrison, "JoB," P. M. Lawrence, Terje Petersen, Donald Oats, Andrew Reynolds, "smiths," John Street, "Uncle Milton," Robert Waldmann, Tim Worstall, and "Zamfir."

I also received helpful comments from friends and colleagues, including George Akerlof, Chris Barrett, Brad DeLong, Joshua Gans, Paul Krugman, Andrew McLennan, and Flavio Menezes. Several anonymous reviewers for Princeton University Press went above and beyond the call of duty in providing extensive and valuable comments. My wife and colleague, Nancy Wallace, read the entire text and made many helpful editorial and substantive suggestions.

Thanks also to the editorial and production team at Princeton University Press. Seth Ditchik was a marvelous and supportive editor, ably assisted by Janie Chan. Debbie Tegarden, my production editor, was unfailingly cheerful and supportive, not to mention highly efficient in turning a manuscript into a book on a very tight time frame. Other production staff including Jack Rummel and Jim Curtis gave able support. The marvelous cover design by Karl Spurzem and Dimitri Karetnikov, drawing on an idea from Seth Ditchik, speaks for itself (it says, "Brraaaiiinnnsssss").

In addition, I must thank all my cobloggers at Crooked Timber, Chris Bertram, Michael Berube, Harry Brighouse, Daniel Davies, Henry Farrell, Maria Farrell, Eszter Hargittai, Kieran Healy, John Holbo, Scott McLemee, Jon Mandle, Ingrid Robeyns, Belle Waring, and Brian Weatherson. Without the lively and supportive environment they've provided, this book would never have happened.

ZOMBIE ECONOMICS

INTRODUCTION

> The ideas of economists and political philosophers, both when they are
> right and when they are wrong, are more powerful than is commonly
> understood. Indeed the world is ruled by little else. Practical men, who
> believe themselves to be quite exempt from any intellectual influences,
> are usually the slaves of some defunct economist. Madmen in authority,
> who hear voices in the air are distilling their frenzy from some academic
> scribbler of a few years back.
>
> —*J. M. KEYNES, The General Theory of Employment, Interest
> and Money*

Ideas are long lived, often outliving their originators and taking new and
different forms. Some ideas live on because they are useful. Others die
and are forgotten. But even when they have proved themselves wrong and
dangerous, ideas are very hard to kill. Even after the evidence seems to
have killed them, they keep on coming back. These ideas are neither alive
nor dead; rather, as Paul Krugman has said, they are undead, or zombie,
ideas. Hence the title of this book.

Before the Global Financial Crisis ideas like the Efficient Markets Hypothesis and the Great Moderation were very much alive. Their advocates
dominated mainstream economics. Their influence, acknowledged or not,
guided the thinking of the practical men and women whose decisions created a financial system without parallel in history. Tens of trillions of dollars of interlinked obligations were built on a foundation of speculative, or
entirely spurious, investments. The result was a global economy in which
both households and nations lived far beyond their means.

Today the Efficient Markets Hypothesis and the Great Moderation
look like defunct ideas. Commentators who were proclaiming, a year
or two ago, that the business cycle had been tamed, have admitted their

error or, more commonly, moved on to talk of other things. The claim that financial markets make the best possible use of economic information and can never be subject to irrational bubbles is rarely made overtly and usually hedged with all kinds of qualifications and escape clauses. In this zombie state, such claims continue to lumber around the intellectual landscape.

But habits of mind and thought are hard to change, especially when there is no ready-made alternative. The zombie ideas that brought the global financial system to the brink of meltdown, and have already caused thousands of firms to fail and cost millions of workers their jobs, still walk among us. They underlie the thinking of those who are responding to the crisis and, to a large extent, of the commentators and analysts who assess those responses.

If we are to understand the financial crisis, and avoid the kinds of responses that set the stage for a new and even bigger crisis in a few years time, we must understand the ideas that got us to this point. This book describes some of the ideas that have played a role in the crisis. They are

* the Great Moderation: the idea that the period beginning in 1985 was one of unparalleled macroeconomic stability;
* the Efficient Markets Hypothesis: the idea that the prices generated by financial markets represent the best possible estimate of the value of any investment;
* Dynamic Stochastic General Equilibrium: the idea that macroeconomic analysis should not concern itself with economic aggregates like trade balances or debt levels, but should be rigorously derived from microeconomic models of individual behavior;
* Trickle-down economics: the idea that policies that benefit the well-off will ultimately help everybody; and
* Privatization: the idea that any function now undertaken by government could be done better by private firms.

Some of these ideas, such as the Efficient Markets Hypothesis and Dynamic Stochastic General Equilibrium belong to the realm of technical economic theory. Others, such as privatization are policy prescriptions, derived from these abstract ideas. Still others, like the Great Moderation and trickle-down economics, are catchphrases for claims about how the economy works, or at least, how it worked in the thirty years or so before the current crisis.

Together these ideas form a package which has been given various names: "Thatcherism" in the United Kingdom, "Reaganism" in the United States, "economic rationalism" in Australia, the "Washington Consensus" in the developing world, and "neoliberalism" in academic discussions. Most of these terms are pejorative, reflecting the fact that it is mostly critics of an ideological framework who feel the need to define it and analyze it. Politically dominant elites don't see themselves as acting ideologically and react with hostility when ideological labels are pinned on them. From the inside, ideology usually looks like common sense. The most neutral term I can find for the set of ideas described by these pejoratives is *market liberalism,* and this is the term that will be used in this book.[1]

The book is organized in a way that I hope will help readers understand how market liberalism depends on ideas that have failed the test of the Global Financial Crisis. If these ideas continue to influence policy, they will ensure a repetition of the crisis.

Each chapter deals with a single idea and begins by describing the birth of the idea, followed by a section on its life, focusing on theoretical and policy implications. The next section describes the death of the idea brought about by the global crisis, but usually resulting from weaknesses that were evident well before the crisis. A brief section on reanimation looks at attempts to raise these dead ideas from the grave as undead zombies. The next section, entitled "After the Zombies," looks at alternatives to the ideas of market liberalism. Finally, there are some suggestions for further reading.[2]

---

[1] There is a similar problem of terminology on the other side of the debate. Market liberalism emerged as a reaction against a set of ideas and policies commonly referred to as "social liberalism" or "social democracy" in Europe and simply as "liberalism" in the United States. These ideas included a commitment to full employment, based largely on Keynesian economic management, and a major role for the state in the provision of income security and services such as health and education. I will generally use the term *social democracy* to avoid the ambiguities surrounding *liberal.*

[2] For ease of reading, I have dispensed with the traditional apparatus of endnotes, which force the reader to keep the book open in two places to follow notes, many of which turn out to be nothing more than academic citations. Instead, I've made sparing use of footnotes

The final chapter, "Economics for the Twenty-first Century" looks more generally at the theoretical and policy ideas that will be needed in the light of the failure of market liberalism. A simple return to traditional Keynesian economics and the politics of the welfare state will not be sufficient. It is necessary to develop both theories and policies that respond to the realities of the twenty-first century economy.

It is clear that there is something badly wrong with the state of economics. A massive financial crisis developed under the eyes of the economics profession, and yet most failed to see anything wrong. Even after the crisis, there has been no proper reassessment. Too many economists are continuing as before, as if nothing had happened. Already, some are starting to claim that nothing did happen, that the Global Financial Crisis and its aftermath constitute a mere "blip" that should not require any rethinking of fundamental ideas.

The ideas that caused the crisis and were, at least briefly, laid to rest by it are already reviving and clawing their way through up the soft earth. If we do not kill these zombie ideas once and for all, they will do even more damage next time.

---

like this one to cover points of tangential interest, notes about some of the economists whose work is discussed, and so on. The further reading section at the end of each chapter includes Harvard-style citations to books and journal articles that have been mentioned in the chapter, and detailed references are given in the bibliography.

CHAPTER 1

THE GREAT MODERATION

Stock prices have reached what looks like a permanently high plateau.
—*ATTRIBUTED TO IRVING FISHER, October 1929*

A zombie idea is one that keeps on coming back, despite being killed. In the history of economics, there can be no more durable zombie idea than that of a New Era, in which full employment and steady economic growth would continue indefinitely. Every sustained period of growth in the history of capitalism has led to the proclamation of such a New Era. None of these proclamations has been fulfilled.

As Irving Fisher's famous prediction, made only a few days before the Wall Street Crash of 1929, illustrates, the belief that the era of boom and bust has finally been put behind us is not new. In fact, ever since the emergence of industrial capitalism in the early nineteenth century, the global economy has been shaken, and stirred, by periodic booms and busts. And, in every intervening period of steady growth, optimistic observers have proclaimed the dawning of a New Economy in which the bad old days of the business cycle would be put behind us. Even the greatest economists (and Irving Fisher was a truly great economist, despite some spectacular eccentricities) have been fooled by temporary success into believing that the business cycle was at an end.[1]

In 1929, Irving Fisher's confidence was based in part on the development of the tools of monetary policy implemented by the U.S. Federal

---

[1] He was among other things a prohibitionist, health campaigner, and eugenicist. In his economic career though, he made fundamental contributions to the theory of interest rates and inflation and, ironically, to our understanding of the deflationary processes that deepen depressions.

Reserve, which had been established in 1913 and had dealt successfully with several minor crises. The central idea was that, in the event of a financial panic, the Fed would lower interest rates and release funds to the banking system until confidence was restored.

But the Fed proved unable or unwilling to produce an adequate response to the stock market crash of October 1929. The Great Crash was followed by four years of uninterrupted decline that threw as many as a third of all workers out of work, not only in the United States, but all around the world.

Economists are still arguing about the causes of the Great Depression, and the extent to which mistaken policies contributed to its length and depth. These disputes, once polite and academic, have taken on new urgency and ferocity in the context of the current crisis, which echoes that of 1929 in many ways.

In the aftermath of the Great Depression and World War II, the analysis that held sway over the great bulk of the economics profession was that of John Maynard Keynes.[2] Keynes argued that recessions and depressions were caused by inadequate effective demand for goods and services and that monetary policy would not always be effective in increasing demand. Governments could remedy the problem through the use of public works and other expenditure programs.

The rapid return to full employment in the war years seemed to confirm Keynes's analysis. As Australia's *White Paper on Full Employment*, published in 1945, put it:

> Despite the need for more houses, food, equipment and every other type of product, before the war not all those available for work were able to find employment or to feel a sense of security in their future. On the average during the twenty years between 1919 and 1939 more than one-tenth of the men and women desiring work were unemployed. In the worst period of the depression well over 25 per cent were left in unproductive idleness. By contrast, during the war

---

[2] As an economist, Keynes had a lot in common with Fisher, but in other respects he could scarcely have been more different. A *bon vivant* and member of the Bloomsbury Group of intellectuals, married to a glamorous Russian ballerina, Keynes was also a successful speculator, whereas Fisher lost much of his personal fortune in the Crash.

no financial or other obstacles have been allowed to prevent the need
for extra production being satisfied to the limit of our resources.
(Commonwealth of Australia 1945, 1)

In sharp contrast with previous wars, the full employment of the
war years was maintained after the return of peace. For most developed countries, the years from the end of World War II until the early
1970s represented a period of full employment and strong economic
growth unparalleled before or since. Referred to as the "Golden Age"
or "Long Boom" in English, "Les Trente Glorieuses" in French, and the
"Wirtschaftswunder" in German, this period saw income per person in
most developed countries more than double.

By the 1960s, many Keynesian economists were prepared to announce
victory over the business cycle. Walter Heller, chairman of the Council
of Economic Advisors under John F. Kennedy, hailed the switch to active fiscal policy in the 1960s, saying "We now take for granted that the
government must step in to provide the essential stability at high levels of
employment and growth that the market mechanism, left alone, cannot
deliver."[3] Attention turned to the more ambitious goal of "fine-tuning"
the economy so that even "growth recessions" (temporary slowdowns in
the rate of economic growth that typically produced a modest increase in
unemployment rates) could be avoided.

Pride goes before a fall. In the 1970s, the seemingly endless postwar
boom came to an abrupt halt. It was replaced by accelerating inflation
and high unemployment. Keynesian fiscal policies, aimed at eliminating unemployment, were abandoned. Restrictive monetary policies and
high interest rates allowed central banks to squeeze inflation out of the
system over the course of the 1980s. The pressure for price stability was
reinforced by globalization, and particularly by the growing size and influence of the global financial sector.

While price stability returned, the full employment of the postwar
era was gone, and has never truly returned. Economic growth returned
gradually, but, at least in developed countries, never regained the rapid
rates of the postwar boom.

---

[3] Heller (1966), 9.

It seemed that the idea of a New Era was dead, once and for all. But zombie ideas are not so easily killed.

BIRTH: CALM AFTER THE STORMS

If only by comparison with the dismal 1970s and 1980s, the 1990s were an era of prosperity for the developed world, and particularly for the United States. The boom of the late 1990s produced improvements in income across the board, after a long period of stagnation for those in the lower half of the income distribution. The boom in the stock market produced even bigger gains for the wealthy. House prices were slower to move, but because they are such a large part of household wealth, contributed even larger capital gains.

The long and strong expansion of the 1990s, combined with political events such as the collapse of the Soviet Union, produced a new air of optimism and, at least in the United States, triumphalism. The success of books like Francis Fukuyama's *The End of History* and Thomas Friedman's *The Lexus and the Olive Tree* reflected the way they matched the popular mood.

Fukuyama argued that the great conflicts that made history something more than the passing of time were over, and that the end of the Cold War marked "the end point of mankind's ideological evolution and the universalization of Western liberal democracy as the final form of human government."[4] Fukuyama assumed that "Western" implied "capitalist." However, he showed some ambivalence about the meaning of "capitalism." Fukuyama's use of this term implied a triumphant market liberalism. But in defending the factual claim of a universalized social order, his use of "capitalism" encompassed the whole range of political and economic systems observed in Western societies, from Scandinavian social democracies to the winner-take-all society then emerging in the United States.

Friedman dispenses with such nuance. In a book full of cute phrases and memorable metaphors, the most prominent was the "Golden

---

[4] Fukuyama (1992), 4.

Straitjacket." This was Friedman's way of saying that, in a globalized economy, adherence to the principles of market liberalism would guarantee golden prosperity. On the other hand, any deviation from those principles would bring down the wrath of the "Electronic Herd" of interconnected global financial markets.

Fukuyama's celebration of the new order made him an intellectual superstar. His books were widely cited, if not quite so widely read. Friedman's breezy boosterism, by contrast, did not earn him so much intellectual credit, but it put him on the bestseller lists. Everyone wanted to be part of the new Lexus-owning world.

Economists were a little late to the party. Well into the 1990s, they worried about weak productivity growth, the possibility of resurgent inflation, and unemployment rates that remained high by the standards of the postwar boom.

By the early 2000s, however, it was possible to look at the U.S. data and discern a pattern that was the very opposite of a lost golden age. Rather, the data could be read as showing a decline in the volatility of output and employment. Most economists saw the decline in volatility as a once-off dropping that took place in the mid-1980s, after the early 1980s "Volcker" recession, so called because it was induced by the restrictive anti-inflation policies of Fed chairman Paul Volcker.[5]

Although most attention has been focused on the volatility of output, the most important impact of recessions is the variability of employment, which is best measured by the employment/population ratio. As with measures of GDP volatility, the standard measures of employment volatility declined noticeably after 1985.

This apparent decline in volatility largely coincided with the chairmanship, lasting nearly twenty years, of Volcker's successor, Alan Greenspan. Whether deservedly or not, Greenspan, rather than Volcker, got the credit. Greenspan's status as the source of all economic wisdom was symbolized in the ultimate Washington accolade, a biography (or rather, hagiography) from Bob Woodward, entitled *Maestro*.

---

[5] The cigar-chewing, six-foot seven Volcker literally towered over the economic scene in his day and remains active (at 81, he's an adviser to President Obama) but has been almost entirely displaced in popular memory by Alan Greenspan.

Greenspan's successor, Ben Bernanke, graduated *summa cum laude* from Harvard in 1975, and completed a Ph.D. at MIT in 1979. He is, therefore, a leading figure in the generation of economists whose careers began after the breakdown of the long postwar boom, and coincided with the Greenspan era. Unsurprisingly perhaps, Bernanke was among those who did most to promote the idea of a New Era of economic stability.

Bernanke also popularized the use of the term the *Great Moderation* to describe the New Era. This term was originally coined by James Stock of Harvard University and Mark Watson of Princeton University. Bernanke used it as the title of a widely publicized speech given in 2004.

The Great Moderation was hailed, like previous periods of prosperity, as representing the end of the business cycle. As Gerard Baker wrote in *The Times of London* in 2007:

> Economists are debating the causes of the Great Moderation enthusiastically and, unusually, they are in broad agreement. Good policy has played a part: central banks have got much better at timing interest rate moves to smooth out the curves of economic progress. But the really important reason tells us much more about the best way to manage economies.
>
> It is the liberation of markets and the opening-up of choice that lie at the root of the transformation. The deregulation of financial markets over the Anglo-Saxon world in the 1980s had a damping effect on the fluctuations of the business cycle. These changes gave consumers a vast range of financial instruments (credit cards, home equity loans) that enabled them to match their spending with changes in their incomes over long periods. (Baker 2007)

A couple of years later, writing his farewell column for *The Times*, Baker wrote an unusually candid admission of error, saying,

> My biggest intellectually missed opportunity was the one that essentially informed so much of my economic commentary in the past couple of years. And one, I suppose in my defence, I could say was shared by quite large number of economists more qualified than I. It was a faith in the idea called the Great Moderation. (Baker 2009)

The economic crisis that began in 2007, and is still continuing, marks a dramatic end to "moderation" in economic outcomes. And, as we will see, it represents the failure of the set of ideas to which Baker and others attributed the supposed New Age. To understand both the widespread appeal and the ultimate failure of these ideas, it is necessary to understand the birth and death of the "Great Moderation" theory.

The simplest way to understand why so many economists saw a Great Moderation in the macroeconomic data is to look at recessions and expansions. Before doing this, it's worth taking a moment to discuss how economists use the term *recession*.

It is common to describe the occurrence of two successive quarters of negative economic growth as the "technical" definition of a recession. However, economists rarely use this definition except as a rough guide to the current state of the economy. Rather, economists in the United States generally rely on the assessments made by the Business Cycle Dating Committee of the National Bureau of Economic Research (NBER).

The NBER defines a recession as "a significant decline in economic activity spread across the economy, lasting more than a few months, normally visible in real GDP, real income, employment, industrial production, and wholesale-retail sales." The Dating Committee issues judgments as to when recessions have begun and ended. Similar bodies in other countries make the same kind of judgment, though none has quite the authority of the NBER.

These judgments typically take place a year or so after the event, which is one reason so much attention is paid to the "technical definition." A great deal of energy was expended in 2008, arguing that, despite obvious signs of economic distress, the required two successive quarters of negative growth had not been observed. But in December 2008, the NBER announced that a recession had begun a year earlier, in December 2007. The announcement of the end of a recession takes place with a similar delay.

Whatever the definition, in the years before 1981 (the end of the Volcker recession) recessions in the United States were relatively frequent, about one every five years. The NBER committee defined nine recessions between 1945 and 1981, two of which (those of the early 1970s and the double-dip recession of 1980–81) were both long and severe.

By contrast, the period from 1981 to 2007 was one of long expansions and short recessions. In the entire period, there were only two recessions, in 1990–91 and 2001, and each lasted only eight months. In the light of past experience of failed claims, it might seem premature to proclaim the end, or at least the taming, of the business cycle on the strength of two good cycles. However, history teaches us that we rarely learn from history. The prevailing atmosphere of triumphalism ensured a positive reception for statistical analyses that seemed to show that the business cycle had been tamed.

The dating decisions of the NBER are inevitably somewhat subjective and do not lend themselves to statistical analysis. As result, economists seeking statistical confirmation of the idea that the business cycle had been tamed focused on quarterly economic data. This approach was consistent with the popular idea of a recession as two quarters of negative growth.

The focus on the volatility of quarterly growth also fitted neatly with the prevailing approach to the assessment of macroeconomic policy, called the Taylor rule, after John Taylor who first formalized it in 1993.[6] Taylor argued that central banks should (and mostly did) seek to minimize the variance of the rates of output growth and inflation about their long-run average values.

A variety of statistical tests suggested that the volatility of economic growth rates in the United States had declined sharply beginning in the early 1980s. The apparent moderation was not confined to U.S. output growth. A similar decline was observed in both the average rate of inflation and the volatility of inflation, and in the volatility of employment and unemployment rates. Broadly similar patterns were observed in other developed economies.

The big exception was Japan, where a decades-long bubble in real estate and stock prices burst at the end of the 1980s. The crash paved the way for a long period of stagnation. Occasional brief expansions were punctuated by renewed downturns. At the time, though, Japan's problems were regarded as specifically Japanese. Similarly, the financial crisis of the late 1990s was seen as a specifically Asian problem of "crony capitalism."

---

[6] Taylor has been a leading figure in the New Keynesian school of macroeconomics, discussed in chapter 3, and also a prominent Republican economist.

The discovery of the Great Moderation, and even more, Bernanke's imprimatur, spawned an instant academic industry. Hundreds of studies dissected the Great Moderation from every possible angle, considering alternative interpretations, causal hypotheses, and projections for the future. Participants in the industry displayed the disagreements for which economists are notorious. But, as is commonly the case with specialists in any field, disputes over details concealed broad agreement on fundamentals. In particular, few, if any, writers on the Great Moderation suggested that it was approaching an abrupt end.

LIFE: THE GREAT RISK SHIFT

During its brief lifetime, the Great Moderation appeared to represent empirical confirmation of the success of market liberalism. The apparent stabilization of the business cycle offered market liberals the pragmatic justification that, whatever the inequities and inefficiencies involved in the process, the shift to market liberalism since the 1970s had delivered sustained prosperity. The Great Moderation seemed to show that, in macroeconomic terms, market liberalism had succeeded where Keynesianism had failed.

The stagflation of the 1970s and the decade of economic disruption that followed it had, it seemed, paved the way for sustained and broad-based growth. Similar improvements in economic stability, observed in a number of English-speaking countries, could be attributed to the radical reforms implemented by such leaders or finance ministers as Margaret Thatcher in the United Kingdom, Roger Douglas in New Zealand, and Paul Keating in Australia. The European Union was generally seen as a laggard, with little choice but to follow the lead of the "Anglosphere."

Causes

Central bankers, and particularly Alan Greenspan and Ben Bernanke, were happy to take the credit for the positive outcomes of the Great Moderation, while, for the most part, ignoring or downplaying the evidence of unsustainable imbalances and unmanaged risks. For Greenspan in particular, the Great Moderation appeared to be an enduring legacy.

The claim of improved monetary policy did not rest entirely on the supposed genius of Greenspan and his fellow central bankers. The more serious claim was that, thanks to financial liberalization, the economy could be stabilized using only a single policy instrument. This magic lever was a short-term interest rate determined by the central bank. In the United States this is the Federal Funds rate.

Most economic analysis of the Great Moderation focused primarily on the role of monetary policy and central banks. But the Great Moderation idea also fitted naturally into broader triumphalist stories about market liberalism and globalization. In particular whereas Keynesianism required national governments to manage macroeconomic risk, the rise of global financial markets allowed such risk to be spread around the world. Since, it was assumed, national economic fluctuations would largely cancel each other out, risk could be moderated without government intervention. All that was required was for investors to hold diversified portfolios, and for capital to flow freely where its return was highest.

A third possibility was that the Great Moderation was just a run of good macroeconomic luck. Random luck might have generated a couple of cycles where the expansion went on a little longer than usual and the recessions were relatively mild. Academic studies tended to mention this possibility, but mostly only to dismiss it. Popular promoters like Gerard Baker ignored the question.

The econometric tests reported in studies of the Great Moderation showed a statistically significant change occurring in the mid-1980s. However, it is an open secret in econometrics that such tests mean very little, since the same set of time series data that suggests a given hypothesis must be used to test it. This is quite unlike the biomedical problems for which the statistical theory of significance was developed, where a hypothesis is developed first, and then an experiment is designed to test it.

A fourth possibility, not mentioned at all in most discussions of the Great Moderation, was that the apparent stability was actually a reflection of policies that were bound to fail in the end. Simply put, the prosperity apparently generated by market liberalism was a bubble waiting to burst. More precisely, it was a series of bubbles, each larger than the last, and each encouraged by a combination of financial deregulation and expansionary monetary policy.

The Great Risk Shift

Beyond giving market liberals bragging rights in their perennial disputes with social democrats, the Great Moderation supported a central tenet of market liberalism. This was the idea that individuals and businesses, rather than governments, were best placed to manage the risks associated with modern economic life. This idea found its expression in what Jacob Hacker has called the *Great Risk Shift*. Risks that had been borne by corporations or governments were shifted back to workers and households.

The Great Risk Shift represented a reversal of a long-term trend toward improved social protection. In his pathbreaking book, *When All Else Fails,* Robert Moss surveys two centuries of American history, in which he presents the state as "the ultimate risk manager." Moss shows how state management of risk began with the provision of greater security for business and moved to innovations such as limited liability and bankruptcy laws, introduced in the period before 1900.

Moss's second phase, "security for workers," was produced by the shift from an economy dominated by agricultural smallholdings to a economy based on manufacturing, in which most households depended on wage employment. Historically the phase includes Progressive initiatives such as workers' compensation and the core programs of the New Deal like unemployment insurance and social security. The third phase, "security for all," began after World War II and includes such diverse initiatives as consumer protection laws, environmental protection, and public disaster relief.

The Great Risk Shift in economic policy was part of a bigger backlash against social risk management, which has been equally ferocious when directed against action to mitigate environmental risks such as climate change. In economic policy, the Great Moderation and the Great Risk Shift went hand in hand.

Since aggregate employment was seen as more stable than ever, people who lost one job were presumed to be capable of finding another. Failure in this task was attributed to personal failings rather than to the workings of the economy. In these circumstances, companies felt the need to be "nimble" and "flexible" in their operations. These buzzwords translated into a willingness to fire large numbers of workers whenever doing so would yield a short-run increase in profitability. Similarly, there was seen to be less need for generous benefits for the unemployed. So these benefits were duly cut or frozen.

The Great Risk Shift extended to areas such as health care and retirement income. The "one size fits all" systems of single-payer health care and retirement income provision introduced in the aftermath of the Great Depression and World War II were attacked as bloated bureaucracies that crippled individual choice. Instead, it was argued, ordinary households should make their own provision for health insurance and retirement. The public sector "safety net" was reserved for the indigent and improvident, and soon began to fray.

Even during the Great Moderation, the wealthy elite showed much more enthusiasm for individual risk-bearing when it was undertaken by ordinary workers than they did when they were bearing the risk themselves. Great show was made of remuneration devices such as options, which gave senior executives the chance to benefit when their company did well and the share price rose. The other side of the coin was that, if share prices fell, executives were supposed to get nothing. But, one way or another, they always managed to get paid.

Economists such as Michael Jensen provided the theoretical basis for option schemes. Jensen argued that they aligned the interests of managers and shareholders and thereby, in the jargon of the time, "incentivized shareholder value maximization."

The benefits of incentivization were taken very happily during the boom years of the late 1990s, when almost all stock prices were going up, regardless of the quality of their management. But, once the bubble burst, enthusiasm for stock options declined. Large numbers of companies repriced the options they had already issued, setting the price low enough that their executives were once again "in the money." This is the equivalent of letting gamblers change their bets after the race has been run.

Of the institutions that were seen as obstacles to improved economic performance by market liberals, none has been more vilified than restrictions on dismissal of workers, or requirements for generous redundancy pay. The supposed sclerosis of the European economies was blamed, more than anything else, on the difficulty of firing workers, which, it was argued, acted as a disincentive to hiring.[7]

Arguments against rewarding failure were forgotten when it came to CEOs. In case after case, failed CEOs have been rewarded with payouts running into millions, or even tens of millions, of dollars. Meanwhile the workers whose jobs were lost due to the incompetence of these CEOs were lucky to receive a few weeks' pay.

The upshot was that, despite their vastly greater capacity to absorb financial shocks, senior executives as a group faced no more risk, relative to their average income, than ordinary workers. Relative to their wealth, senior executives faced much less risk than most people. The most disastrous failures among CEOs rarely end up poor, or even back in the middle class. As long as the Great Moderation continued, inconsistencies like this were disregarded. Companies abandoned any pretense of a social contract with their workers. At an early stage in this process, employees were relabeled as "human resources."

Risk has both an upside and a downside. In the later years of long expansions, the balance of bargaining power in labor markets shifts toward workers, resulting in improved wages and conditions for some. But over the course of the Great Moderation, the downside predominated. Faced with the ever-present risk of job loss, employees accepted a faster pace of work and reduced working conditions as the price of continued employment.

---

[7] This faith has been shaken by the experience of the financial crisis, where U.S. unemployment rates rapidly reached and surpassed those of the EU, in part because it was so easy to fire people. Undeterred, Charles Murray of the American Enterprise Institute, delivering the Irving Kristol Lecture at that body's 2009 annual dinner, assured his audience that yet-to-be-made discoveries in genetics and neuroscience would prove that the European model was unnatural and unsustainable.

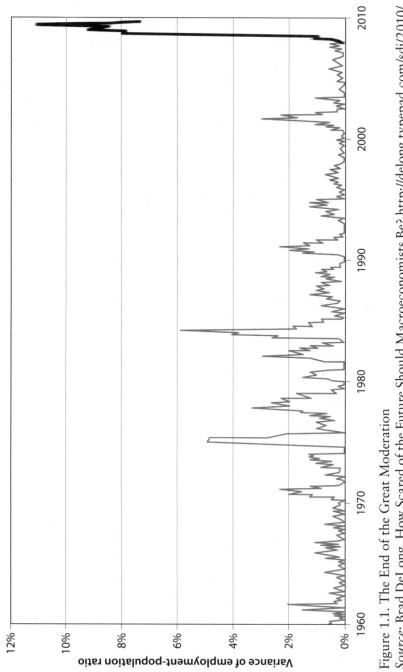

Figure 1.1. The End of the Great Moderation
Source: Brad DeLong, How Scared of the Future Should Macroeconomists Be? http://delong.typepad.com/sdj/2010/01/how-scared-of-the-future-should-macroeconomists-be.html

Governments also sought to get out of the business of risk management. Throughout the years of the Great Moderation, market liberals railed against the social protections of the welfare state, which they saw as inefficient and outdated. They had some successes, most notably with welfare reform in the United States. But on the whole the welfare state proved surprisingly resilient. Core programs like Social Security in the United States and the National Health Service in Britain enjoy deep and broad popular support.

DEATH: THE DISSENTERS AND THEIR VINDICATION

Whether it was a real economic phenomenon or a statistical illusion, the Great Moderation, considered as a pattern of long expansions punctuated by brief and mild recessions, is clearly dead now. The global recession has been long and deep by postwar standards, and the current recovery is slow and fragile. As shown in figure 1.1, the end of the Great Moderation jumps out of the data on employment volatility.

In retrospect, the Great Moderation was dead by the time its discovery was announced in the early 2000s. The recovery from the 2001 recession was not, as advocates of the Great Moderation supposed, the beginning of a third long expansion in the United States. Rather, it was weak, short lived, and overwhelmingly driven by the unsustainable bubble in housing prices and the expansionary monetary policies of Greenspan and Bernanke. The expansion lasted only six years. It was four years old before total employment regained the prerecession peak. All of the employment gains of the expansion, and more, were wiped out in the first few months of the Global Financial Crisis.

The U.S. experience was typical of the developed countries. While some, such as Australia and Canada, did better, others such as Ireland and Iceland suffered economic meltdowns with output losses of more than 10 percent.

It is not sufficient to point out the obvious fact that the Great Moderation is finished. The thinking that led so many economists to claim that the business cycle had been tamed by financial liberalization remains influential and is implicit in many arguments about policy responses to the crisis. So, it is important to understand why the Great Moderation hypothesis was so badly wrong.

The Dissenters

While the boom persisted, the view that the Great Moderation was the product of unsustainable policies received little attention. It was espoused only by old-style Keynesians, a relatively marginal group on the left of the economics profession, and members of the Austrian School, a fringe group on the right. While the two groups agreed in offering a negative prognosis, they differed radically regarding both diagnosis and proposed cure.

The major contributions of the Austrian School were made in the early twentieth century by Ludwig von Mises and Friedrich von Hayek. Mises and Hayek put forward a theory of the business cycle based on financial markets. According to the theory, the business cycle unfolds in the following way.

First, the money supply expands either because of an inflow of gold, printing of fiat money, or financial innovations. The result is lower interest rates. Low interest rates stimulate borrowing from the banking system. The artificially stimulated borrowing seeks out diminishing investment opportunities. This leads to an unsustainable boom. This boom causes capital resources to be misallocated into areas that would not attract investment if price signals were not distorted. A correction, or credit crunch, occurs when credit creation cannot be sustained. Markets finally clear, causing resources to be reallocated to more efficient uses.

The standard classical theory suggested that depressions should not occur and, if they did, would rapidly fix themselves. The Austrian theory showed that protracted depressions could take place as a result of monetary shocks. But it lacked a number of key elements.

Austrian business cycle theory was a big advance at the time it was put forward. But, by focusing on misallocation of capital, it ignored the most obvious feature of the business cycle, namely the massive unemployment of labor.

Equally important, Austrian business cycle theory had radical implications that were largely overlooked by its proponents. If considered carefully, Austrian business cycle theory implied that financial markets were not efficient. That in turn implied that government intervention could be beneficial in offsetting the fluctuations in investment demand associated with the business cycle.

Unfortunately, both Hayek and Mises were dogmatic supporters of laissez-faire. As a result, having taken the first steps in the direction of a serious theory of the business cycle, Hayek and Mises spent the rest of their lives running hard in the opposite direction. They took a nihilistic "liquidationist" view in the Great Depression, arguing that businesses that had made bad investments in the boom should be left to fail. This mistake has hardened into dogma in the hands of their successors.

The Austrian School was at the forefront of business cycle theory in the 1920s. Sadly, it has not developed in any positive way since then and is now largely occupied with dogmatic internal disputes and arguments about methodology.

It was left to Keynes and his followers to produce the first really convincing theory of the business cycle, and the first effective policy response to severe economic crises. Keynesians argued that, without adequate regulation, financial instability was inevitable. This view was part of the assumed background for Keynesians of all kinds. For example, Nobel Laureate James Tobin, one of the leaders of mainstream Keynesianism, argued for a global tax on financial transactions that would "throw sand in the gears" of the global financial system, and thereby discourage destabilizing speculation. Tobin's proposal, first put forward in the 1970s, is finally gaining some attention in the wake of the Global Financial Crisis.

Although Keynesians of all kinds worried about financial instability, this phenomenon was particularly emphasized by the post-Keynesian school associated with Hyman Minsky. Minsky focused on the instability of credit and investment processes in a market economy and argued that capitalist financial systems are inherently unstable because large swings in investor expectations tend to occur over the course of the economic cycle.

In Minsky's model there are three classes of financial enterprises: conservative "hedge" financiers whose operations generate sufficient income to service their capital costs; "speculative" financiers who rely on rising asset prices to service debt and who drive the market further upward; and "Ponzi financiers," who do not cover their losses in either the short term or the long term, but who can conceal their insolvency long enough to reap substantial gains.

Minsky's account of the business cycle goes like this. The cycle starts in a recession, where expectations are subdued. As the recovery gathers pace, profits rise and balance sheets are restored. Caution remains for a period, reflecting memories of the previous downturn. As the economy continues to grow, perhaps spurred further by technological breakthroughs, profits are rebuilt and expectations of future growth begin to rise. Caution begins to recede. Increasingly, "animal spirits" are stirred, banks begin lending more freely and credit expands.[8] Even cautious investors are encouraged to join the upward surge for fear of forfeiting profit opportunities.

At this point the boom phase begins. Momentum builds behind what Minsky referred to as the "euphoric economy." In this phase, speculative financiers make large profits, encouraging an influx of Ponzi financiers. Increasingly, the market is dominated by speculation about sentiments and movements in the market rather than about fundamental asset values.

Ponzi financiers fail from time to time, but in periods of growth, these failures are seen as isolated events of no general significance. However, in the later stages of a bubble, when a large proportion of economic activity has been devoted to speculative finance, the failure of a Ponzi financier can bring about a sudden shift in sentiment, as investors fear that the associated corruption is widespread. The rush to withdraw extended credit brings about more failures, not only of Ponzi financiers but of the speculative finance firms that relied on continued growth. The economy

---

[8] The term *animal spirits* was introduced by Keynes (1936, 161–62), who observed "a large proportion of our positive activities depend on spontaneous optimism rather than mathematical expectations, whether moral or hedonistic or economic. Most, probably, of our decisions to do something positive, the full consequences of which will be drawn out over many days to come, can only be taken as the result of animal spirits—a spontaneous urge to action rather than inaction." The term refers in part to the role of emotional factors such as optimism and pessimism, and in part to the practical impossibility of calculating the mathematical expectations that are typically assumed by economists to determine investment and other economic decisions.

undergoes a sudden crash, ending in recession and a (temporary) return to caution and conservatism.

Minsky's work became a standard name check for Keynesians writing about financial crises past, present, and future. For example, Charles Kindleberger used Minsky's model as the basis for his study *Manias, Panics, and Crashes*, declaring that "the model lends itself effectively to the interpretation of economic and financial history." But Minsky had little influence on the development of macroeconomic theory.

Whatever their disagreements and theoretical limitations, Keynesians and Austrians mostly got it right as regards the bubble economy of the decade leading up to the Global Financial Crisis. This is not to say that they predicted the timing and course of the crisis in detail. It is in the nature of bubbles that their bursting is unpredictable and has unpredictable consequences. Even the most accurate prophets, such as Nouriel Roubini of the Stern School of Business, focused more on international imbalances and unsustainable house prices than on the largely opaque superstructure of financial transactions that financed and magnified these imbalances.

Was There Really a Great Moderation?

The abrupt end to the Great Moderation raises anew the question of whether it was a real phenomenon or an overoptimistic interpretation of the data. Even when the standard story of the Great Moderation was generally accepted, it was not the only interpretation put forward. In a paper published by the Brookings Institute in 2001, Olivier Blanchard of MIT and John Simon of the Reserve Bank of Australia argued that the data implied a long-term decline in volatility since the 1950s, interrupted temporarily in the 1970s and early 1980s.

Although this interpretation fitted the data as well as the standard view, it was not widely accepted. A statistical test suggesting that the economy was more volatile in the 1950s and 1960s than in the 1990s is hard to accept in view of the actual experience of the postwar boom as a period of strong growth and low unemployment. If measures of volatility contradict this experience, the obvious response is to suggest that they must not be measuring the right thing.

If data on quarterly volatility lends itself to such a problematic interpretation, this must cast doubt on its use to support the standard Great Moderation story. It is therefore worth looking more closely at the measures and their interpretation.

The first difficulty with a focus on the volatility of output growth is that it takes no account of changes in the average rate of economic growth. Looking at U.S. growth rates, for example, the standard deviation of the rate of economic growth was 2.0 percentage points in the 1960s, as compared to 1.5 percentage points in the 1990s. This seems to support the usual story suggesting a decline in the volatility of output growth.

But the average rate of output growth was 4.3 percent in the 1960s, and only 3.0 percent in the 1990s. So, expressed relative to the average growth rate, volatility was actually lower in the 1960s. In particular, the implied probability of negative growth was lower.

A second problem is that quarterly volatility measures are sensitive to relatively short-term fluctuations.[9] The same is true of the NBER measure that defines a recession as a downturn lasting a few quarters. These measures have their advantages, but they miss some critical features of the cycle.

Although the postwar boom was characterized by relatively frequent recessions, these recessions were not as severe. Postwar recessions were typically followed by rapid and strong recoveries: they had to be, to sustain the high average rate of economic growth.

The recoveries following the recessions of 1990–91 and 2001 were different, so different that the term *jobless recovery* was coined to describe them. Well after output had begun to recover, employment kept falling and unemployment kept rising. In each case the recovery in output was sufficient to constitute a recovery according to the popular "negative growth" definition, and also according to the somewhat broader criteria used by the NBER. But, to the average person, the early years of these expansions felt much like recessions.

President George H.W. Bush was among the first casualties of the new-style business cycle. By the time of the 1992 U.S. election, the economy

---

[9] In the statistical jargon, this is called high-frequency volatility.

was about eighteen months into an expansion, according to the standard measures. Bill Clinton, whose campaign was summarized by the catch-phrase "It's the economy, stupid," was able to capitalize on the actual experience, which was that of continuing depressed conditions. The same experience was repeated after the 2000 recession.

The jobless recovery phenomenon was not confined to the United States. In Australia, for example, the economy went into recession in 1989 and, on the standard measures, began a renewed expansion in 1990. But unemployment peaked at 11 percent in 1994 and did not re-gain its 1989 levels until after 2000, more than a decade into one of the longest expansions on record. The defeat of the Keating government in 1996 was largely attributed to the continued impact of the recession.

The standard measures of quarterly volatility did not match the ex-perience of workers in general, but they fitted very neatly with that of participants in financial markets. For these groups, the recessions were periods of severe losses in profitability and sharp cuts in employment, but all these losses, and more, were regained as the economy recovered. Even the weak recovery after the 2000 recession was sufficient to propel incomes in the financial sector to stratospheric heights, unheard of at any time in the past. For this group, The Great Moderation was a reality.

Individual and Aggregate Volatility

Economic analysis of the Great Moderation showed a striking paradox. Even though economic aggregates appeared to be more stable than at any time in the past, individuals and families experienced ever increas-ing risk, volatility, and instability. Risk has, it seems, increased in every dimension. Income inequality has grown substantially, in part because income mobility has increased, but also because lifetime income has be-come more risky. Short-term variability in income has also increased.

The consequence, as Peter Gosselin observes in his book *High Wire: The Precarious Financial Lives of American Families,* is that even as the United States as a whole has become richer, individuals and families have become less secure. The result is that "a comparatively few enjoy great wealth at almost no risk, while the great majority must accept the possibility that any reversal—whether of their own or someone else's making—can destroy a lifetime of endeavor" (2009, 324).

This seems like a paradox. Since aggregate income is the sum of all individual incomes, an increase in individual risk should translate into an increase in the riskiness of aggregate income, even allowing for the fact that some gains and losses will cancel out.

Economic analysis of the paradox showed that the development of financial markets had weakened links between economic variables such as income and consumption. Faced with a decline in income, households could borrow to maintain their consumption levels. As a result, the flow-on impact for consumer demand of a shock in one sector of the economy was reduced. This meant that high levels of volatility in individual incomes could coexist with aggregate stability.

Is such a pattern sustainable? If variations in income are transitory, then borrowing to maintain living standards through a rough patch makes sense. On the other hand, responding to a permanent decline in income by going into debt is a recipe for disaster. Since it's difficult to tell in advance whether an income decline is going to be temporary or permanent, using borrowing to smooth consumption is a risky option.

Not surprisingly, as income volatility increased, so did the number of people who got into trouble by borrowing. The most direct measure is the number of people filing for bankruptcy. This has increased in most English-speaking countries, but nowhere more than in the United States. Reliance on access to credit to manage income risk was encouraged by relatively liberal bankruptcy laws, which acted as a kind of substitute for a more redistributive tax-welfare system. Within the United States, the states with the least progressive tax systems have typically had the most generous bankruptcy laws.

In the early years of the twenty-first century, more than 2 million people declared bankruptcy in the United States every year.[10] In fact, in these years, Americans were more likely to go bankrupt than to get divorced. The commonest immediate causes of bankruptcy were job losses and

---

[10] Because married couples file jointly, the number of people who go bankrupt is greater than the number of filings for personal bankruptcy, which averaged around 1.4 million per year.

unexpected health care costs. But the underlying cause was a culture of indebtedness, which meant that most people who experienced financial stress rapidly ran into trouble meeting existing commitments.

In 2005, the credit card industry hit back at the rising bankruptcy rates by successfully pressing for the passage of the Bankruptcy Abuse Prevention and Consumer Protection Act. This law put a number of obstacles in the path of people seeking to resolve their debt problems through bankruptcy.

In the year before the law came into effect, more than 2 million households rushed to file. In the months immediately following "reform," bankruptcies dropped almost to zero, and remained well below those of the prereform period for several years. But the pressures of increasing debt meant that many people had no choice but to negotiate the newly established obstacles. Over the first few years of the new law, the number of bankruptcies rose slowly.

The onset of the financial crisis was initially reflected more in foreclosures than in bankruptcies. Most mortgages in the United States are (legally in some states and *de facto* in others) nonrecourse, which means that, after foreclosing on the house offered as security, creditors cannot go after the other assets of the borrower. Even if a foreclosure yields far less than the amount owed, the borrower's obligations are discharged.

So, as long as the crisis was primarily confined to housing markets, the number of bankruptcies rose only gradually. But, with the onset of high unemployment and the end of easy access to credit of all kinds, bankruptcies have soared. In 2009, there were 1.4 million consumer bankruptcy filings, comparable to the prereform level, and the number is expected to pass 1.5 million in 2010.

Despite the volatility of individual income, and the risks of relying on credit markets, economists continued to celebrate the Great Moderation throughout 2007. The events of 2008 came as a rude shock.

The Global Financial Crisis

The Great Moderation vanished with surprising rapidity.

Bernanke's Great Moderation hypothesis was not the first claim that the business cycle had been tamed, and it is unlikely to be the last. But, even by the unexacting standards of past economic projections, the Great Moderation has been one of the more spectacular failures.

The Golden Age of Keynesianism lasted three decades and delivered big increases in living standards throughout the developed world. By contrast, the Great Moderation didn't really begin until the end of the first Bush recession in the early 1990s, and almost collapsed in the dot-com crash of 2000. Only Alan Greenspan's reckless monetary expansionism kept the bubble economy of the 1990s afloat. That expansion paved the way for an even more disastrous crash a few years later.

The global economy has undergone a severe recession, which will generate a substantial increase in the volatility of output. Even if the economy makes a strong recovery, which seems unlikely at the time of writing (March 2010), crucial elements of the Great Moderation hypothesis have already been refuted. Over the period of the Great Moderation, all the major components of aggregate output (consumption, investment, and public spending) became more stable. By contrast, the current recovery is the result of a massive fiscal stimulus, a huge increase in public expenditure (net of taxes) offsetting large reductions in private sector demand.

The crisis has also invalidated most of the popular explanations for the Great Moderation. The idea that improvements in monetary policy have been a force for economic stabilization looks rather silly now. A crisis generated within the financial system has brought about a crisis against which the standard tools of monetary policy, based on adjustments to interest rates, have proved ineffective.

It is to the credit of central banks that, when their standard tools failed, they were willing to adopt more radical measures. The most important was quantitative easing, that is, printing money and using it to purchase securities such as government bonds and corporate paper. Such radical steps, which contrast sharply with the passive response to the financial shocks of the Great Depression, have helped to prevent a complete meltdown of the financial system. But willingness to abandon failed policies does not change the fact of failure.

If the pretensions of central banks have been shaken, those of financial markets have been utterly discredited. There is now no reason to accept the claim that financial markets provide individuals and households with effective tools for risk management. Rather, the unrestrained growth of financial markets has proved, as on many past occasions, to be a source of instability.

The collapse of the Great Moderation has destroyed the pragmatic justification that, whatever the inequities and inefficiencies involved in the process, the shift to market liberalism since the 1970s delivered sustained prosperity. If anything can be salvaged from the current mess, it will be in spite of the policies of recent decades, and not because of them.

China and India

In the wake of the Global Financial Crisis, some advocates of market liberalism have sought to shift the grounds of debate. These advocates have argued that, whatever the impact of market liberalism on developed countries, it has been hugely beneficial for India and China. Since, between them, these two countries account for a third of the world's population, market liberalism can still be called a success. This argument, or excuse, does not stand up to scrutiny.

Strong growth in China and India offers little support for market liberalism. Neither China nor India come anywhere near the liberal ideal of a free market economy. China still has a huge state-owned enterprise sector, a tightly restricted financial system, and a closely managed exchange rate. These factors have allowed the Chinese government to undertake a massive stimulus to the economy in response to the global crisis, producing a rapid recovery in economic activity. India began its growth spurt before the main period of market liberalization and retains a large state sector. In both countries, as earlier in Japan, Korean, Taiwan, and Singapore, the state has played a major role in promoting particular directions of development.

The development success stories of China and India, and, before them of Japan and the East Asian tigers, may have some useful lessons for countries struggling to escape the poverty trap. But they can tell us nothing about the relative merits of market liberalism and social democracy.

REANIMATION: A GLOBAL CRISIS OR A TRANSITORY BLIP?

With unemployment still above 10 percent in many countries, aggregate budget deficits in the trillions, and bankruptcy and foreclosure taking place on a massive scale in the United States and elsewhere, you might think that the idea of the Great Moderation would be, not just dead, but buried once and for all. You would be wrong.

This zombie idea was never really killed and it is already climbing out of the grave. In a blog post entitled "Does the Great Recession Really Mean the End of the Great Moderation?" Olivier Coibion and Yuri Gorodnichenko answer this question with a resounding "No." Coibion and Gorodnichenko present a series of graphs on the variability of real GDP growth in the United States to support the conclusion that "we are experiencing a particularly severe business cycle that nonetheless pales in comparison to the volatility experienced in the 1970s."[11]

Such a claim looks convincing if you look only at the absolute variability of GDP. But that variability reflects the net impact of a massive fiscal stimulus from the public sector and massive contraction in private sector demand. Any moderation in total demand is not evident in its components.

Not only have the components of GDP fluctuated wildly, but so have all sorts of other macroeconomic variables. Brad DeLong points out that the variance of the employment/population ratio has shown the biggest spike since at least the Korean War.

More fundamentally, the idea that we are still in a "Great Moderation" in which stability is the result of good policy fails the laugh test. The story used to be that the "good public policy" that gave us stability consisted of the judicious adjustment of interest rates in line with a Taylor rule based on inflation rates and output growth. The response to the Global Financial Crisis started out that way, but the policymakers rapidly threw the rulebook out the window. Interest rates were cut all the way to zero. Then huge amounts of liquidity were pumped into banks and Wall Street firms through "quantitative easing" and opening of the

---

[11] See Coibion and Gorodnichnenko (2010).

discount window. Then there was the trillion dollar bailout of late 2008, and the massive fiscal stimulus package of 2009.

Many words could be used to describe these responses, but "judicious" and "moderate" would not be among them. It could plausibly be said that, massive as they were, the responses were still inadequate. But that just goes to point up the magnitude of the crisis.

Why then would anyone make such a claim? The answer can be sought in the internal dynamics of the economics profession. The Great Moderation vanished in 2008 and 2009, but the academic industry built to analyze it did not. Research projects based on explaining, measuring, and projecting the Great Moderation were not abandoned. The intellectual commitments on which those projects are based have proved tenacious.

Coibion and Gorodnichenko are proponents of the view that the Great Moderation was the product of good public policy. They are the authors of a forthcoming paper in the *American Economic Review* making precisely this case. The paper is theoretically elegant and uses some impressive econometrics, reflecting the years of work that go into the production of such a piece. But, if the Great Moderation is indeed over, such a paper becomes an exercise in economic history, and the "good policy" explanation is clearly false.

Unsurprisingly, then, Coibion and Gorodnichenko are attracted to the opposite view. A crisis that had destroyed whole national economies, bankrupted millions, doubled the U.S. unemployment rate, and threatened to bring down the entire financial system becomes, in their telling of the story, a "transitory volatility blip in 2009."

We will be hearing a lot more of this kind of thing in the future. But, if we are to avoid repeating the mistakes of the last couple of decades, we must first recognize them for what they are. The Great Moderation is a dead idea, and it should be buried once and for all.

AFTER THE ZOMBIES: RETHINKING THE EXPERIENCE OF THE TWENTIETH CENTURY

The failure of the Great Moderation has implications for a wide range of government policies. The central implications of the end of the Great

Moderation relate to the need to reverse the Great Risk Shift. That can only be done by reinvigorating the social and collective risk management institutions that constitute the social democratic welfare state.

The end of the Great Moderation has already produced a massive increase in the economic risk faced by individuals, families, and businesses. In the United States, as many as 10 million households are expected to face foreclosure by 2012. Over the same period, and despite laws designed to make bankruptcy less accessible, it is likely that between 5 and 10 million households will face bankruptcy.[12]

The sharp decline in stock market values, which are still below the levels of a decade ago, has eaten away the life savings of many workers. More fundamentally, it has undermined the idea of a shareholding democracy. The promise that most households would have sufficient financial wealth, earning good returns, to be capable of financing their own retirement, has not been fulfilled.

Around the world, tens of millions of workers have lost their jobs, and millions more will do so before the economy recovers fully. And even though economic growth has resumed, at least for the moment, the impacts will be felt for a long time to come. In the absence of positive government action, unemployment will remain high for years. The unstable state of the global financial system, and the lack of any significant movement toward more effective regulation, suggests there will be more shocks to come.

The increase in inequality that produced this increase in risk is most evident in the United States, but it has occurred, with a shorter or longer time lag, in many other countries, both developed and developing. Where the social democratic welfare state has remained strong, growth in inequality has been less marked. But it is no longer possible to suppose that simply slowing the pace of market liberalization will prevent growth in inequality, and the growth in risk and insecurity it implies.

Rethinking the Experience of the Twentieth Century

The failure of the Great Moderation calls for a rethinking of the macroeconomic experience of the twentieth century, and in particular, the

---

[12] The two groups will overlap.

crisis of the 1970s. Considered as a whole, the performance of developed economies in the era of market liberalism looks considerably less impressive than that of the postwar period of Keynesian social democracy.

Yet the Keynesian era ended in the chaos and failure of the 1970s. Until the current crisis, that failure was taken as conclusive. Whatever its merits, Keynesian economic management had proved unsustainable in the end, while the methods of market liberalism seemed to promise the continuing stability of the Great Moderation.

That view can no longer be sustained. The Great Moderation has ended in a failure at least as bad as that of the postwar boom. If there is a recovery, it will be due to the very measures that market liberalism was supposed to have rendered obsolete. How then, should we think about the Keynesian era and its failure?

One possible interpretation, a pessimistic one, is that business cycles are so deeply embedded in the logic of market economics, and perhaps of all modern economies, that they cannot be tamed. Success breeds hubris, and hubris leads us to ignore the lessons of the past: that resources are always constrained, that budgets must ultimately balance, that wages and other incomes cannot, for long, exceed the value of production, and so on. In the 1960s and 1970s, this hubris manifested itself in unsustainable budget deficits and the wage-price spiral. In the 1990s and 2000s, it was seen in the speculative frenzy unleashed by the self-styled Masters of the Universe in the financial sector.

But this is not the only possible interpretation. Perhaps the failures of the 1970s were the result of mistakes that could have been avoided with a better understanding of the economy and stronger social institutions. If so, the current crisis may mark a return to successful Keynesian policies that take account of the errors of the past.

The end of the Great Moderation has forced policymakers to relearn the basic lessons of Keynesian economics. Economies can collapse to a point where only large-scale monetary expansion and fiscal stimulus can revive them. But having revived the economy, can Keynesian policies restore and sustain full employment in a system that is inherently prone to crisis? An answer to this question will require radical new directions in macroeconomics. As I will argue in this book, that means the abandonment of yet more dead or obsolete ideas.

FURTHER READING

It is hard to understand the current debate without some knowledge of the history of the business cycle and particularly of the Great Depression. Kindleberger (2000) provides a useful, if now incomplete, history of panics and crashes. Galbraith (1969) is an accessible account of the Great Crash, and his idea of the "bezzle" anticipates Minsky's story of Ponzi finance. To understand how economists explain recessions and depressions, it is essential to read Keynes (1936), whose ideas still form the starting point for debate (and, often enough, the endpoint as well). Fisher's (1933) discussion of debt deflation is also relevant, as are the earlier works of Hayek and Mises, collected in Mises, Rothbard, Haberler, and Hayek (1996). More modern analyses include Bernanke (2004b) and Temin (1991).

The long postwar boom and its collapse are discussed by Marglin and Schor (1990). Judt (2005) offers a broader historical perspective on the postwar period in Europe.

The Tobin tax is advocated by Tobin (1978, 1992). Palley (1999) gives a good supporting analysis.

The Great Moderation ended not long after it was discovered, having given rise to a huge number of journal articles and conference papers exploring different aspects of the supposed moderation, but little in the way of broad overview. Crucial papers include Bernanke (2004a, b), Blanchard and Simon (2001), Dynan et al. (2006), and Stock and Watson (2002). The publications of the NBER Cycle Dating Committee can be found at http://www.nber.org/cycles/main.html.

To recall the euphoric atmosphere of the 1990s, which encouraged acceptance of the Great Moderation hypothesis, it is worth looking at books like Glassman and Hassett (1999) and Luttwak (1999), as well as Friedman and Fukuyama.

Dissenting views on the sustainability of the Great Moderation include Bell and Quiggin (2006), Quiggin (2004), Setser and Roubini (2005), and from an Austrian perspective, Schiff and Downes (2007).

The general point that Asian development models give little support to the advocates of market liberalism has been made most effectively by Wade (1990), whose analysis of the "East Asian tiger" economies in the 1980s is equally applicable to China and India today.

The best work on bankruptcy in America is that of Elizabeth Warren and her coauthors (Sullivan, Warren, and Westbrook 2006; Himmelstein, Thorne, Warren, and Woolhandler 2009). The case for creditors, unconvincing in my view, can be found in Zywicki (2005).

The term *risk society* is due to Beck (1992). The analysis draws on Barr (2001), Giddens (2002), Hacker (2006), Moss (2002) and my own work, including Bell and Quiggin (2006), Quiggin (2007), and Quiggin (2009b).

Other works cited in this chapter include DeLong (2010), Coibion and Gorodnichenko (2008, 2010), Friedman and Heller (1969), and Woodward (2001). A detailed reference to each work cited can be found in the back of this book.

CHAPTER 2

THE EFFICIENT MARKETS HYPOTHESIS

> When the capital development of a country becomes a by-product of
> the activities of a casino, the job is likely to be ill-done.
> **—J. M. KEYNES,** *General Theory of Employment, Interest,*
> *and Money*

Unlike other monsters like werewolves and vampires, zombies always come in mobs. Individually, they seem easy enough to kill, but in a group their strength can be overwhelming. So it is with the ideas underlying market liberalism. Factual claims like the Great Moderation may seem relatively unconvincing in isolation, and abstract economic theories may appear obviously unrealistic to those not inculcated in the appropriate modes of thought, but taken together, and combined with a policy program, they have proved almost irresistible.

The Efficient Markets Hypothesis is the central theoretical doctrine of market liberalism, born just as the Keynesian era was drawing to a close. It was finally killed, in terms of intellectual credibility, by the Global Financial Crisis. The Efficient Markets Hypothesis says that financial markets are the best possible guide to the value of economic assets and therefore to decisions about investment and production. This requires not only that financial markets make the most efficient possible use of information, but that they are sufficiently well-developed to encompass all economically relevant sources of risk.[1]

---

[1] For this reason, the hypothesis would more properly be called the Completely Efficient Financial Markets Hypothesis. I will discuss the implications of incomplete financial markets in more detail in chapter 5.

Although economists since Adam Smith have pointed out the virtues of markets in general, the Efficient Markets Hypothesis, with its focus on financial markets, is specific to the era of finance-driven capitalism that emerged from the breakdown of the Keynesian Bretton Woods system in the 1970s. The Efficient Markets Hypothesis justified, and indeed demanded, financial deregulation, the removal of controls on international capital flows, and a massive expansion of the financial sector. These developments ultimately produced the Global Financial Crisis, from which the world economy is still recovering.

BIRTH: FROM CASINO TO CALCULATING MACHINE
Keynes and the Casino

Few economists have been successful investors, and quite a few have been disastrous failures. John Maynard Keynes was one of the successes. After a narrow escape from disaster early in his investing career, Keynes made a fortune for his Cambridge college by speculating in futures markets. Surprisingly (or perhaps not) given his close acquaintance with financial markets, Keynes was among the most scathing of all economists in his assessment of their performance.

Keynes's views were reflected in the systems of financial regulation adopted as governments sought to rebuild national economies and the global economic system in the wake of World War II. The international negotiations undertaken at a meeting in Bretton Woods, New Hampshire, in 1944, where Keynes represented the British government, established an international framework in which exchange rates were fixed and movements of capital were tightly controlled. National governments similarly adopted policies of stringent financial regulation. They also established a range of publicly owned financial institutions in response to the failures of the private market.

During the decades of the long Keynesian boom following World War II, financial markets were tightly regulated. As a result, financial crises disappeared almost entirely from the experience and memory of the developed world. In the United States, a host of regulatory bodies were established to control financial institutions. The Glass-Steagall Act established the Federal Deposit Insurance Corporation (FDIC) and prohibited bank holding companies from owning other financial companies. The Federal National Mortgage Association (Fannie Mae) was established to support the mortgage market.[2]

Although the details of intervention varied from country to country, the effect was the same everywhere. Banking in the 1950s and 1960s was a dull but secure business, resembling a public utility in many respects. Parents scarred by the Great Depression urged their children to look for "a nice safe job in a bank."

The Efficient Markets Hypothesis changed all that.

Random Walks

At the margin, substantial profits could be made by finding ways to work around the regulations, while relying on governments to maintain the stability of the system as a whole. Not surprisingly, there was a warm reception for theoretical arguments that presented a more favorable view of financial markets.

The rise of the Efficient Markets Hypothesis began relatively modestly with the argument that the prices of assets such as stocks cannot be predicted from their past movements in the way claimed by "chartists" and "technical analysts." In the popular terminology, prices follow a "random walk." This idea had been put forward as early as 1900 in a neglected paper by a French statistician, Louis Bachelier, but it was not rediscovered until the 1950s.

The idea behind the random walk hypothesis was simple. Since everyone in the market can see the history of prices, any predictable pattern will soon be exploited. The very process of trying to exploit a pattern (say, prices falling on Fridays) would eliminate it. The random walk hypothesis went against the powerful human tendency to find patterns in

---

[2] Later quasi-privatized as Fannie Mae, and then renationalized during the early stages of the Global Financial Crisis.

data, whether they exist or not. Nevertheless, it stood up well to initial statistical testing and has done so ever since.

None of the patterns typically analyzed by students of stock market charts, such as trends, reversals, and support levels, appear to be of any use in predicting stock price movements. There remains some dispute about whether subtler features of the behavior of stock prices are consistent with the possibility of a profitable trading strategy based solely on observation of past prices.

Among economists, the random walk hypothesis, now referred to as the "weak form" of the Efficient Markets Hypothesis, is fairly generally accepted. Some, like Andrew Lo, director of the MIT Laboratory for Financial Engineering, have argued that because of investor irrationality, asset prices display some momentum over time. But this claim remains controversial, as does the performance of algorithmic trading strategies designed to exploit such patterns. Even the skeptics agree that any violations of the weak form of the hypothesis are subtle and hard to exploit.

In a striking instance of the inefficiency of financial markets, however, investment banks continue to employ "technical analysts" using charting methods, decades after such methods have been shown not to work. The human desire to believe that there must be a way to beat the odds is reflected in the continuing prevalence of "systems" guaranteed to make you a winner at the roulette table.

The "Strong" Form of the Efficient Markets Hypothesis

The argument underlying the random walk hypothesis was that the existence of predictable price patterns in efficient markets with rational and well-informed traders was logically self-contradictory. Empirical tests showed that a random walk model fitted the data very well, suggesting that real markets were indeed efficient, at least in this limited sense.

It wasn't long before economic theorists realized that the same argument applied to other kinds of information, such as information about the likely future earnings of companies. If this information is publicly available, then traders should take it into account, just as they do with the past history of the stock price. So, the stock price will be the best available estimate of the future value of the stock, taking account of all available information.

The key steps in the discovery of the strong Efficient Markets Hypothesis were taken independently by two leading economists. One was Paul Samuelson, the leading economic theorist of the postwar era, and a prominent Keynesian. The other was Eugene Fama, the father of modern finance theory, and an adherent of the free market Chicago school. As we will see, they took the idea in rather different directions.

There was one more subtle distinction to make before the Efficient Markets Hypothesis assumed its modern form. The arguments so far concerned publicly available information. What about information that was only available to some people, such as company insiders, or customers? Some theorists argued that such information would inevitably be reflected in market trades. Others stuck with the traditional focus on publicly available information.

Fama proposed a three-part distinction between the weak form of the Efficient Markets Hypothesis, which excluded profitable trading based on price history; the semistrong form, which extended the claim to cover publicly available information; and the strong form, which claimed that the stock price incorporates all information held by traders, whether it is public or private.[3]

LIFE: BLACK–SCHOLES, BANKERS, AND BUBBLES

Black-Scholes and the Rise of Finance-driven Capitalism

The Efficient Markets Hypothesis made a big difference to the way economists viewed financial markets. Initially, though, it had much less impact on financial markets themselves. In *The Money Game*, an entertaining and economically literate description of the stock market scene in the 1960s, "Adam Smith" (a pseudonym for George Goodman) describes

---

[3] Since the weak form of the Efficient Markets Hypothesis is relatively uncontroversial and mostly unimportant, I will use the term Efficient Markets Hypothesis to refer to the strong and semistrong versions from now on. Where the distinction between the two is important, I will try to make it clear which one I mean.

"a random walk professor choking on his ice-cream at the thought that there are people called 'technicians' who claim to forecast the stock market." "Smith" makes it clear that the vast majority of Wall Streeters believed the technicians more than the economists.

The economic theory that really changed thinking in financial markets was the model of pricing options developed by Fischer Black and Myron Scholes in 1973 and subsequently formalized by Robert Merton.[4] The model was named Black-Scholes, but Merton got his share of the glory when he shared the 1997 Nobel Memorial Prize in economics with Scholes, two years after Black's death.

The Black-Scholes model showed that, under plausible assumptions, it was possible to duplicate the payoff from an option by a combination of trades in the original stock and in riskless bonds. So, the "right" option price could be calculated by looking at the interest rate on bonds and the variability of the stock price. If the market price differed from the Black-Scholes price, traders could make money, with little or no risk, by combining trades in the two markets.

There was something of a paradox here. The Black-Scholes pricing rule shows how an option price ought to be determined in an efficient market. But traders can only make a profit using Black-Scholes and similar rules to value derivatives if the market price deviates from the "correct" price, that is, if the Efficient Markets Hypothesis is not satisfied. This paradox was given a rigorous formulation by Sanford Grossman and Joseph Stiglitz, in one of the contributions that later earned Stiglitz the Nobel Memorial Prize in economics.

Economists have wrestled with the Grossman-Stiglitz paradox for a long time without working out a completely satisfactory solution. The most common view was one that seemed to preserve the Efficient Markets Hypothesis while justifying the huge returns reaped by financial market professionals. This is the idea that the market is just close enough to perfect efficiency that the returns available from exploiting any inefficiency are equal to the cost of the skill and effort that goes into discovering it.

---

[4] An option is one of the simplest kinds of financial derivatives, that is, assets derived from other assets. An option gives you the right to buy (or sell) a given stock at a given price and on a given date.

With this accommodation, the Efficient Markets Hypothesis, which now formed the basis of the dominant approaches to financial economics, could coexist with a large and expanding financial sector devoted to finding, exploiting, and thereby eliminating, opportunities for profitable trades.

Although Paul Samuelson and Eugene Fama were jointly responsible for the formulation of the Efficient Markets Hypothesis, they had very different views of how it should be interpreted.

Samuelson maintained a characteristically Keynesian distinction, between microeconomics, where a standard competitive market analysis was applicable, and macroeconomics, where a Keynesian analysis was needed. He argued that while tests of the Efficient Markets Hypothesis showed that financial markets were micro-efficient, the experience of bubbles and busts showed that they were "macro-inefficient." That is, the Efficient Markets Hypothesis works better for individual stocks than it does for the aggregate stock market.

Samuelson's position means, for example, that it is difficult, if not impossible, to outperform the stock market by examining the price history of individual stocks, or by poring over company reports. On the other hand, it is possible to identify bubbles in the stock market as a whole, and to propose policies to stabilize asset markets.

Writing in 1998, as the "dotcom" bubble was approaching its peak, Samuelson called for increased interest rates to deal with the "quasi-bubble" on Wall Street. And, repeating Keynes's response to the idea that rational speculators would always prevent such bubbles getting out of hand, Samuelson wrote, "We have no theory of the putative duration of a bubble. It can always go as long again as it has already gone. You cannot make money on correcting macro inefficiencies in the price level of the stock market."[5]

By the 1990s, Samuelson was in the minority, and his view that the Efficient Markets Hypothesis was consistent with macro-inefficiency commanded little support. The alternative interpretation, more logically consistent (if less consistent with reality), was that the financial market

[5] Samuelson (1998), 36.

price of an asset was not merely the best estimate of its value relative to other assets of the same kind, but was the best possible estimate, given available information.

This maximal interpretation of the Efficient Markets Hypothesis was espoused in academic works by Fama and his many students and followers. By the 1990s, it was accepted by most finance theorists, and nearly all policymakers. The hypothesis was popularized by such writers as Thomas Friedman, whose *The Lexus and the Olive Tree* warned governments that they could not possibly hope to resist the collective financial wisdom embodied in the "Electronic Herd" of global financial traders,[6] and more directly, by James Surowiecki in *The Wisdom of Crowds*.

The implications of the Efficient Markets Hypothesis go well beyond financial markets. The Efficient Markets Hypothesis provides a case against public investment in infrastructure and implies that macroeconomic imbalances, such as trade and current account deficits should not be regarded with concern and, provided they arise from private sector financial transactions, are actually both beneficial and desirable.

The Right Price

The Efficient Markets Hypothesis implies that prices generated by stock markets and other asset markets are the best possible estimate of the "right" price for the assets concerned. But what does it mean to say "the price is right"? From the point of view of an investor, the value of an asset is determined by the flow of income it generates over the period for which it is held and the disposal value (if any) at the end of the period. This stream of payments can be converted into a current value by a discounting procedure (the opposite of working out a future value using compound interest): the problem is to choose the "right" risk adjusted discount rate.

---

[6] The term is an allusion to the "Thundering Herd," a nickname for the iconic Wall Street investment bank, Merrill Lynch. In October 2008, Merrill Lynch was rescued from imminent collapse through a takeover by Bank of America. BoA was, in turn, bailed out to the tune of billions of dollars by the U.S. government.

Given efficient markets, economic analysis suggests that the discount rate should be determined by the socially efficient allocation of the aggregate risk for the economy as a whole among individual consumers. This gives rise to a model of the determination of the prices of capital assets called (perhaps unsurprisingly) the capital asset pricing model, or CAPM. Economists who want to emphasize the point that asset prices are ultimately determined by the preferences of consumers sometimes make this explicit and refer to CCAPM, the Consumption-based Capital Asset Pricing Model.

The difficulties of CCAPM will be discussed in chapter 5 (Privatization). What matters for the moment is the fact that the model depends critically on the Efficient Markets Hypothesis.

If a stock price is the best possible estimate of the risk-adjusted value of future dividends and resale values, then individual investors can do no better than to buy a portfolio of stocks and other asset prices that matches their risk preferences.[7] There is no need for these investors to make their own estimates of the value of individual assets. In this sense, the price is right for them.

But there is a stronger, and more important sense in which the Efficient Markets Hypothesis implies that market asset prices are the right prices. Given any possible set of investments that companies might make in new products or processes, market participants can estimate the value of those investments by considering the likely immediate impact on the stock prices of the companies concerned, or the likely return in an initial public offering (IPO). Capital markets will fund the subset of investments with the highest market value. If there are no relevant market failures outside capital markets, the Efficient Markets Hypothesis says that these will also be the most socially valuable investments.[8]

---

[7] At least, those without inside information, according to the semi-strong Efficient Markets Hypothesis.

[8] Suppose, for example, a company is considering an investment that will be highly profitable but environmentally damaging. Stock markets will value the company on the basis of the profits, and will fund the investment, even though it may be less socially valuable than an alternative, more environmentally friendly choice. But, an advocate of the Efficient Markets Hypothesis will say, the answer is not to try and change financial markets, but to address the market failure directly by "getting prices right" in the relevant market, for example, by taxing polluters.

Asset Bubbles and Imbalances

The Efficient Markets Hypothesis implies that there can be no such thing as a bubble in the prices of assets such as stocks or houses. Such a claim, seeming as it does to fly in the face of centuries of experience, requires a fair bit of faith in the analysis underlying the Efficient Markets Hypothesis. But, in the euphoric atmosphere of the 1990s, such faith was in abundant supply.

The argument begins with the claim that if a bubble in stock prices were indeed observable speculators would sell the asset in question. If that did not end the bubble, short-sellers would enter the market, selling assets they did not hold in the expectation of being able to buy them later at a lower price. This would ensure that the price returned rapidly to the true market value. At the same time, it would make the speculators and short-sellers rich.

But as Keynes had pointed out decades earlier, this argument only stands up if bubbles are short lived, so that speculators are quickly vindicated:

> He who attempts it [speculating on the bursting of a bubble] must surely lead much more laborious days and run greater risks than he who tries to guess better than the crowd how the crowd will behave; and, given equal intelligence, he may make more disastrous mistakes. There is no clear evidence from experience that the investment policy which is socially advantageous coincides with that which is most profitable. It needs more intelligence to defeat the forces of time and our ignorance of the future than to beat the gun. (Keynes 1936, 140)

More succinctly, in words widely (though apparently apocryphally) attributed to Keynes, "The markets can stay irrational longer than you can stay solvent." Lots of investors, from small-scale individual speculators to billion-dollar fund managers like Julian Robertson of Tiger Investments bet against the stock market bubble of the 1990s and lost.

A second argument is that, even if bubbles are real, there is little or nothing policymakers can or should do to burst them. This was the conclusion reached by a number of central bankers who saw irrational exuberance in stock markets and property markets as a likely source of future trouble.[9] A study by Claudio Borio and Philip Lowe of the Reserve Bank of Australia pointed out the dangers of asset bubbles. However, in a policy environment where the only way of restraining speculation was to raise interest rates, they concluded that central banks could do little more than issue warnings.[10]

Finally, some supporters of the Efficient Markets Hypothesis argued, along lines first popularized by Austrian economist Joseph Schumpeter, that, even if bubbles lead to massively wasteful investment, they generate innovations that are beneficial in the long run. Schumpeter's striking phrase "creative destruction" was widely used in this context.

Supporters of the Efficient Markets Hypothesis also engaged in a fair amount of historical revisionism to argue that famous historical examples of bubbles, from the Dutch tulip mania to the Roaring Twenties and beyond, were actually rational responses to new market conditions, often exaggerated in subsequent retellings. The Dutch tulip mania saw the price of a contract for a single tulip bulb exceed ten times the annual income of a skilled craftsman. Economist Peter Garber argued that these contracts were never fulfilled, and were little more than "bar bets," and so, did not violate the Efficient Markets Hypothesis.

Implicit in these arguments was the conclusion that, in a well-developed modern market, with transparent dealing and with all parties subject to the scrutiny of auditors and ratings agencies, an irrational bubble could not possibly develop or be sustained. This conclusion formed the basis of financial policy in the decade leading up to the Global Financial Crisis of 2008.

The Growth of the Financial Sector

In most of the simple models from which the Efficient Markets Hypothesis was derived, the financial sector did not exist as an industry. Financial markets were assumed to set the price of assets without any cost to the

---

[9] When he was not cheering on the growth of bubbles, Alan Greenspan held this position.

[10] Although Australia experienced a strong boom in land prices, lending standards were held to much stricter levels than in the United States or other markets. It may be that the warnings of the Reserve Bank had some influence on the policy decisions of prudential regulators. (Quiggin 2010).

economy. As we have seen, the question of how those with information or forecasting skills could gain the returns they needed to justify their efforts was a significant theoretical problem for strong forms of the Efficient Markets Hypothesis.

Although no truly satisfactory analysis of the role of financial institutions in efficient markets was ever produced, advocates of the Efficient Markets Hypothesis came to accept that the cost of financial market transactions was equal to the value of the information these transactions incorporated in asset prices. It followed that, as financial transactions were liberalized and the economy became ever more sophisticated, it was economically and socially desirable that the financial sector should grow.

And grow it did. The growth of the financial sector since the mid-1970s has been staggering. The financial services industry's share of corporate profits in the United States rose from around 10 percent in the early 1980s to 40 percent in 2007, at a time when the profit share of national income was also growing strongly.

Volumes of financial activity grew at rates that defy any simple interpretation. The Bank for International Settlements has estimated the global volume of outstanding derivative contracts at around $600 trillion, about ten times the world's total output. In the normal course of events, most of these transactions net out to zero, but even a small mismatch can produce losses (or gains) of many billions.

Along with all this, the income and wealth of those working in the financial sector grew massively, as did their numbers. The salaries of financial sector executives outstripped those prevailing in other industries, at a time when executive salaries in general rose to huge multiples of the incomes of ordinary workers.[11] Such massive accumulations of wealth translate naturally into political power. Particularly in the United States, both major political parties were heavily influenced by generous donations from Wall Street firms.

---

[11] This development was accompanied by a good deal of rhetoric, laughable in retrospect, suggesting that management was becoming "lean and mean," with flat organizational structures replacing old-fashioned hierarchies. The first to blow the whistle on this nonsense was David Gordon of the New School for Social Research in his book, *Fat and Mean*, published in 1996, just before his premature death at the age of 51.

But the political power of the finance sector does not depend solely on command over economic resources. After the economic dislocation of the 1970s, the financial sector became, in perception and to some extent in reality, the most important guarantor of economic stability and prosperity. Governments sought desperately to gain and maintain the AAA ratings issued by agencies such as Moody's and Standard & Poor's. The alternative was the political disgrace of a downgrading and the ultimate threat of capital flight, as occurred when the Mitterrand government in France attempted to introduce an expansionist macroeconomic policy in the early 1980s.

Yet despite its mind-boggling growth, the financial sector came nowhere near achieving the completeness implicit in the Efficient Markets Hypothesis, which requires that financial assets encompass all the risks relevant to economic activity. On the contrary, for households, workers, and small businesses, the weakening of governmental protections against risks like unemployment and severe income fluctuations was not offset by the development of new financial assets that could provide similar protection. As Peter Gosselin has documented in *High Wire*, economic life for ordinary households has become ever more risky.

Proposals, like those of Robert Shiller, for the development of new financial assets to allow households to hedge against fluctuations in housing markets, have gone nowhere. The financial sector has been far more interested in providing people with new ways to get into debt.

Private and Public Investment

Casual observation suggests that both the private and public sectors have difficulty in managing investments. Public sector investments, from the time of the Pharaohs onward, have included plenty of boondoggles, white elephants, and outright failures. But the private sector has not done better. Waves of extreme optimism, leading to massive investment in particular sectors, have been followed by slumps in which the assets built at great expense in the boom lie unfinished or idle for years on end.

The Efficient Markets Hypothesis supports the first of these observations, but suggests that the second must be mistaken. Since public investments are not subject to the disciplines of financial markets, there is no reason to expect their allocation to be efficient. By contrast, according to the Efficient Markets Hypothesis, private investment decisions are the product of an information system that is automatically self-correcting.

The value given by the stock market to any given asset, such as a corporation, is, by hypothesis, the best possible estimate, as discussed above. If the managers of a given corporation make bad investment decisions, the value of stocks will decline to the point where the corporation is subject to takeover by better managers.

The Efficient Markets Hypothesis, which enshrines the market price of assets as the summary of all relevant information, is inconsistent with any idea that managers should pursue the long-term interests of corporations, disregarding short-term fluctuations in share prices. According to the Efficient Markets Hypothesis, the current share price is the best possible estimate of the long-term share price and therefore of the long-term value of the corporation to shareholders.

If the Efficient Markets Hypothesis is accepted, public investment decisions may be improved through the use of formal evaluation procedures like benefit-cost analysis, but the only really satisfactory solution is to turn the business over to the private sector. In the 1980s and 1990s this reasoning fitted neatly with the global push for privatization, discussed in chapter 5.

The Efficient Markets Hypothesis implies that governments can never outperform well-informed financial markets. The only exception is where mistaken government policies, or a failure to define property rights adequately, leads to distorted market outcomes. In this case, the best response is to fix the policies, not to intervene in financial markets. If governments are better informed than private market participants they should make this information public rather than using superior government information to inform public policy, and thereby substitute for private choices.

To sum up, the Efficient Markets Hypothesis implies that private enterprise will always outperform government, and that governments should confine their activities to the correction of market failures, and to whatever income redistribution is needed to offset the inequality of market outcomes.[12]

---

[12] In the view of most Efficient Markets Hypothesis proponents, not very much.

Macroeconomic Implications

There are also important implications for macroeconomic variables such as the balance of international trade. From a traditional Keynesian perspective, large imbalances in trade are a sign of trouble to come, since they will inevitably produce an unsustainable buildup of debt. Economists like Nouriel Roubini and Brad Setser were particularly vocal in warning, from the early 2000s onward, of the trouble ahead for the U.S. economy.

By contrast, the Efficient Markets Hypothesis leads to the conclusion that economic analysis should be focused on asset values rather than on income flows. Observations of current income flows are informative only about the present, whereas asset values capture all relevant information about current and future income flows. An increase in asset values implies an increase in the present value of future income and therefore in the optimal level of consumption.

Once the Efficient Markets Hypothesis is accepted, there is no need to worry about imbalances in savings and consumption. International capital movements can be seen as the aggregate of a large number of transactions between "consenting adults," buying and selling financial assets in markets which, according to the Efficient Markets Hypothesis, have already taken into account all available information about future risks. If a national government has better information, the appropriate response is not to act on it but to release the information to the markets.

In the United Kingdom, this view became known as the Lawson doctrine, after Chancellor of the Exchequer Nigel Lawson. Lawson argued in 1988 that current account deficits that result from a shift in private sector behavior should not be a public policy issue.[13]

On the traditional income-based view, by contrast, asset-based arguments are misleading and dangerous. By the time sentiment shifts in asset markets, the opportunity for an orderly adjustment will already have been lost. Advocates of the traditional view pointed to episodes

---

[13] Lawson is better known nowadays as father of celebrity chef Nigella Lawson, and as an advocate of crank pseudoscience regarding climate change.

of contagious panic in financial markets, such as those of the Asian financial crisis of 1997.

The traditional response to macroeconomic imbalances such as trade deficits was the adoption of contractionary monetary and fiscal policies aimed at reducing demand for imports and at forcing domestic producers to seek export markets as a response to lower demand at home. The resulting "stop-go" policies caused substantial suffering and economic dislocation.

Once it is realized that sustained macroeconomic imbalances ultimately reflect financial market failures, this response can be seen to be inappropriate, as can the benign neglect associated with the "consenting adults" view. The appropriate response is to intervene in financial markets to restrict the unsound lending practices that drive the growth of such imbalances.

DEATH: THE CRISIS OF 2008

As with the other doctrines discussed in this book, the death of the Efficient Markets Hypothesis was not a sudden shock arising from the Global Financial Crisis. The evidence for the strong forms of the Efficient Markets Hypothesis was never particularly convincing. Rather, it was an idea that suited both the demands of the times and the intellectual tendencies that were dominant within the economics profession.

During the 1970s and 1980s, assessment of the Efficient Markets Hypothesis was largely confined to econometric studies. The process of financial deregulation, beginning with the breakdown of the Bretton Woods system in the early 1970s was a gradual one. It was only by the mid-1980s that most restrictions on international capital flows and exchange rate movements were completely removed. Completing the process of domestic deregulation took even longer. So, it was not until the 1990s that failures of the global financial system could reasonably be regarded as evidence against the Efficient Markets Hypothesis.

That evidence was not long in coming. A number of developing countries experienced severe financial crises in the 1990s, even though their governments had done their best to follow the policy prescriptions of market liberalism, in particular by deregulating financial markets and encouraging foreign investment.

The experience of the United State itself provided plenty of evidence against the Efficient Markets Hypothesis. The government-orchestrated rescue of hedge fund LTCM provided a preview of the massive bailouts of 2008 and 2009, undermining some key assumptions of the Efficient Markets Hypothesis in the process. Even more significantly, the boom and bust in the stocks of "dotcom" companies that promised to generate vast profits from the Internet showed that all the sophistication and complexity of modern financial markets only served to make possible bigger and better bubbles.

Sadly, these lessons went unlearned. Despite repeated failures to meet the test of experience, the Efficient Markets Hypothesis remained central to finance theory and to policy practice right up to its final catastrophic collapse in the meltdown of 2008.

Econometric Testing

Even in its heyday, the Efficient Markets Hypothesis was not particularly well supported by empirical evidence. The weak form of the hypothesis was reasonably successful when subjected to the statistical tests applied by econometricians, but the strong and semistrong forms much less so.

The weak form of the hypothesis precludes the existence of predictable patterns in asset prices, unless predictability is so low that transactions costs exceed the profits that could be gained by trading on such patterns. Broadly speaking, this weak version of the Efficient Markets Hypothesis is consistent with the evidence. At least, there are no simple and reliable trading strategies that have been shown to beat the market consistently.

On the other hand, econometric studies give little support to the strong forms of the hypothesis. Most important, as economists such as Robert Shiller have shown, the volatility of asset prices is much greater than is predicted by the Efficient Markets Hypothesis. That is, where the Efficient Markets Hypothesis suggests that financial markets provide a way of managing economic risk, the evidence suggests that they are actually a major source of such risk.

The behavior of currency markets after the breakdown of the Bretton Woods agreement provides a good example. Advocates of floating exchange rates confidently expected that financial markets would bring exchange rates into line with underlying economic values, and thereby lead to greater stability. In fact, the reverse has happened. In the decade since the creation of the euro, its value has been as low as 85 U.S. cents and as high as U.S. $1.59.

Stock markets similarly display much more volatility than the Efficient Markets Hypothesis suggests is consistent with the observed variability of aggregate consumption. A recent survey by Stephen LeRoy of the University of California at Santa Barbara concluded, "No single convincing explanation has been provided for the volatility of equity prices. The conclusion that appears to follow from the equity premium and price volatility puzzles is that, for whatever reason, prices of financial assets do not behave as the theory of consumption-based asset pricing predicts."[14]

Financial Crises in "Emerging Markets"

After the turmoil of the 1970s and 1980s, developed countries enjoyed a period of sustained economic expansion in the 1990s. The United States led the way. For a while, less-developed countries, now relabeled as "emerging markets," enjoyed similarly smooth sailing. But from the mid-1990s onward, there were a string of financial crises in Mexico, Argentina, Russia, and most spectacularly, in Asia.

The financial crises of the 1980s had followed a pattern that supported an Efficient Markets Hypothesis. Governments had borrowed heavily, spent the proceeds on military adventures or prestige projects, intervened to distort market prices, and attempted to restrict international capital flows. When they got into trouble, as they inevitably did, they were forced to call on the International Monetary Fund for help.

The standard prescriptions of the International Monetary Fund, supported by the U.S. Treasury and the World Bank, were christened the "Washington Consensus" by John Williamson of the Institute for International Economics. Williamson listed ten elements of the standard

[14] LeRoy (2006).

package, notably including financial deregulation and privatization of state enterprises.

Although Williamson's initial presentation included discussion of the need for appropriate prudential regulation of financial institutions, later versions of the Washington Consensus dropped this element and incorporated more radical versions of market liberalism, to the point that Williamson himself disavowed the phrase.

The crises of the mid-1990s hit countries that had, in general, embraced the policies of the Washington Consensus. The pattern was the same in each case. Following financial deregulation, countries enjoyed strong capital inflows and booming stock markets. Some seemingly minor event produced a reversal in market sentiment and a sudden flight of capital, producing an economic crisis. Following the crisis, the International Monetary Fund (IMF) and world markets sought to impose the 1980s package of public expenditure cuts and economic contraction, which only exacerbated the problem. Finally, in retrospect, the victims were blamed for minor divergences from the free market ideal which, before the crisis, had been seen as unimportant, or even praiseworthy.

Asian economies had enjoyed decades of strong growth through policies of export-oriented industrialization, rejecting the "import replacement" policies, aimed at economic self-sufficiency, that had failed in other developing countries. From the early 1990s onward, they had been engaged in a process of financial deregulation. Only a year before the crisis hit, the World Bank had produced a glowing report praising the "Asian economic miracle" as an exemplar of market liberal reform.

The Asian financial crisis cast doubt on the idea that globalization was both inevitable and beneficent, as did the failure of Washington Consensus policies in Argentina. Even more embarrassing was the success of Malaysia, which imposed controls on the movements of foreign exchange, the cardinal sin against global financial markets. Whether because of this sin or despite it, Malaysia was less severely affected by the crisis than were neighbors who followed the advice of the IMF.

The case of Argentina was equally striking. Rejecting the failed policies of the Peron era, Argentina had adopted the most extreme version of the Washington Consensus, privatizing industry on a large scale and even establishing a currency board to guarantee a fixed exchange rate with the

U.S. dollar. Yet when the economy ran into trouble, the financial markets left the people of Argentina to fend for themselves.

Despite all this, the confidence of financial markets and policymakers in the Efficient Markets Hypothesis was unshaken. The Asian and Latin American countries that had been seen as reflecting the fruits of reform were suddenly denounced as embodiments of "crony capitalism." The conclusion drawn was that only with a fully developed, transparent, and incorruptible financial system, like that of Wall Street or the City of London, could the benefits of financial markets be fully realized.

The Long-Term Capital Management Fiasco

The debate over the Efficient Markets Hypothesis gave rise to the view that the market is just close enough to perfect efficiency that the returns available from exploiting any inefficiency are equal to the cost of the skill and effort that goes into discovering it. This idea is central to the operations of hedge funds, which seek to discover strategies by which investors willing to take a risk can earn above average returns.

This idea imploded in spectacular fashion in 1998. The crisis began at a hedge fund called Long Term Capital Management (LTCM), which employed as its expert advisers none other than Robert Merton and Myron Scholes.

The strategy employed by LTCM was to discover small deviations from efficient market pricing, on which it could make bets that were sure to win. Instead of simply betting with its investors' money, it used that money as equity for massive borrowings, which ensured that the payoff from its winning bets was multiplied many times over. Reliance on "leverage" to multiply profits has been a characteristic of many financial bubbles, a point reflected in the saying, "Genius is leverage in a rising market." But it has never before operated on the scale seen in the Great Bubble, and exemplified by LTCM.

Thanks to the use of complex derivatives, LTCM turned an equity base of less than $5 billion into derivative positions with a notional value of approximately $1.25 trillion. These derivatives, such as interest rate swaps, were developed with the supposed goal of allowing firms to manage risk on exchange rates and interest rate movements. Instead, they allowed speculation on an unparalleled scale.

LTCM looked for divergences between the margins generated by the markets and the values predicted by its computer models, then bet that the market would "correct itself" over time. These bets paid off for a number of years, making big profits for LTCM owners and investors. But, in 1997 with the Asian and Russian financial crises, all its bets failed at once.

The unregulated status of hedge funds had been justified on the basis that the investors were sophisticated and wealthy individuals, and that only their own money was at risk. But it soon turned out that the leveraged investments made by LTCM had been financed by huge loans from major Wall Street and international banks, and that a failure by LTCM ran the risk of generating a systemic collapse.

The U.S. Federal Reserve, under Chairman Alan Greenspan, orchestrated a rescue package. Major banks were pressured to contribute to the rescue. Among the Wall Street investment banks, Bear Stearns was the only one to refuse, a refusal that contributed to its demise in 2008. The crisis was staved off. The LTCM principals and investors escaped with much of the wealth gained from their earlier successful bets intact.

The LTCM episode had numerous lessons, many of which were pointed out at the time but few of which were taken to heart by policymakers.

In retrospect, the strategy pursued by LTCM can be seen as a variant on the ancient "martingale" betting strategy. As Slate writer (and mathematician and novelist) Jordan Ellenberg explained, the strategy can be illustrated by betting on a coin:

> Bet 100 bucks on heads. If you win, you walk away $100 richer. If you lose, no problem; on the next flip, bet $200 on heads, and if you win this time, take your $100 profit and quit. If you lose, you're down $300 on the day; so you double down again and bet $400. The coin can't come up tails forever! Eventually, you've got to win your $100 back. *(Ellenberg 2008)*

The problem with the martingale is that you are trading off a steadily diminishing probability of losing against a steadily increasing loss if you do. At some point, there will be a run of tails long enough to bankrupt you. In the words of writer and investor Nassim Taleb, such strategies are like "picking up pennies in front of steamrollers."

What is true of the martingale is true of more sophisticated variants, like the strategies of LTCM. This point ought to have been evident from the LTCM failure. Instead, the conclusion drawn by both financial markets and regulators was that the problem could be solved by designing ever more complicated derivatives. By the time the whole thing blew up in 2008, the complex trades that had brought LTCM to grief looked like child's play.

A second crucial point is that diversification of risks only works to a certain extent and can be undermined by attempts to exploit it. Once the limits of diversification have been reached, rearranging the set of claims involved isn't going to reduce risk any further. So, if all parties appear to be making risk-free profits, the risk must have been shifted to some low probability event with high losses for at least some participants.

There were also lessons for regulators. The first was that no system of financial regulation can survive if some firms are guaranteed and regulated but are allowed to deal on a large scale with others that are not regulated. The second is the old one of "moral hazard": if people are protected by insurance from the bad consequences of risks, they will tend to take more risk as a result.

Financial market players ignored all these lessons, but they did learn one big one, which was the opposite of the moral hazard lesson ignored by regulators, namely, the existence of the "Greenspan put." A put is a kind of option allowing you to sell a stock at an agreed price on a given date. In effect, the holder of a put has a one-way bet on the stock they own. If it goes up, they sell the stock on the market and collect the profits. If it goes down, they exercise the put option and collect the agreed price.

Precisely because they are so attractive, put options are valuable (the Black-Scholes rule shows how to value them). What was special about the Greenspan put was that it was free. The treatment of LTCM showed that, if financial markets ever got into really serious trouble, the Federal Reserve would bail them out. So, any kind of risk-taking behavior became a one-way bet, as long as sufficiently many of the big financial institutions were making the same bet.

The first exercise of the Greenspan put came in the wake of the dotcom crash, discussed in the next section. The second, and much bigger one came in October 2008, at the hands of Greenspan's successor, Ben Bernanke. This time, though, not even a trillion dollar bailout was enough to save all the big financial institutions from the consequences of their reckless speculation.

The dotcom Bubble

Stock markets in the United States and elsewhere rose strongly in the 1980s and 1990s, interrupted only briefly by the crash of October 1987 (which, in retrospect, fostered the illusion that any decline in stock prices would be quickly reversed). By 1996, the boom had reached the point where, with the Dow Jones index at 8000, Alan Greenspan warned of the dangers of "irrational exuberance" in asset markets. Greenspan never repeated the warning and soon returned to his customary role as a cheerleader for speculative markets. However, the catchphrase was adopted by economist Robert Shiller as the title of a penetrating analysis of the role of self-deception and collective over-optimism in stock market bubbles.

The bubbles had raised stock prices in general, but it was propelled to new heights by the arrival of the "dotcom" sectors. The Internet, developed as a public service by the U.S. government research agency the Defense Advanced Research Projects Agency and by the university sector worldwide, was opened to commercial use in the 1990s, just as its most popular manifestation, the Worldwide Web, was coming online.

In 1995, the Mosaic web browser, created at the publicly funded National Center for Supercomputing Applications, was converted into a commercial product named Netscape, which formed the basis of a spectacularly successful IPO. The stock was set to be offered at fourteen dollars per share. But a last-minute decision doubled the initial offering to twenty-eight dollars per share. The stock's value soared to seventy-five dollars on the first day of trading, nearly a record for a first day gain.

Never profitable on an annual basis, Netscape was acquired in 1998 by America Online (AOL) in a stock swap that valued Netscape at U.S. $4.2 billion. A couple of years later, in the biggest merger in history, AOL merged with Time Warner. The deal gave AOL a market value of more than $100 billion. In December 2009, AOL was spun off again, with an estimated market value of $3.15 billion, less than the value imputed to Netscape alone a decade previously.

The Netscape IPO and AOL takeover set the pattern for a string of ever-more dubious "dotcom" ventures, producing huge gains for investors despite the absence of significant profits, and in many cases, even revenues or products. The history of Netscape and AOL was mirrored by thousands of firms that attached the dotcom suffix to businesses selling items as mundane as dog food and garden supplies. Some were as spurious as that of the pioneering entrepreneur of the South Sea Bubble in 1713 who sold shares in "a company for carrying out an undertaking of great advantage, but nobody to know what it is." Indeed, whereas Netscape and AOL had substantial revenues, and AOL had a profitable business as an Internet service provider, the typical dotcom company never made a genuine sale, let alone a profit.

Speculation on dotcoms centered on the NASDAQ stock exchange.[15] The NASDAQ index rose from 800 in the mid-1990s, to more than 5000 at its peak in March 2000 when it collapsed suddenly, falling below 2000.[16] Hundreds of dotcom companies failed or were taken over at prices far below those of the late 1990s.

Even more than the complex global crisis now underway, the NASDAQ bubble and bust provided a sharp test of the Efficient Markets Hypothesis, a test that had failed egregiously. It was obvious, and pointed out by many observers, that the prices being paid for dotcom investments could not be justified on the basis of standard principles of valuation. Even if some turned out to be the spectacular successes promised in their business plans, it was impossible that the sector as a whole could do so. In fact, only a handful of dotcom firms ever produced sustained profits.[17]

---

[15] A competitor to the New York Stock Exchange that had been established by brokers including Bernard Madoff, who confessed in late 2008 to having operated the biggest Ponzi scheme in history.

[16] As of 7 July 2010, the index stood at 2159.

[17] The most successful, Google, was not traded on the stock market until 2004, so its gains did not offset the losses of those who invested during the dotcom boom.

Previous bubbles might have been dismissed on the basis that the markets concerned weren't fully informed and transparent, or that speculators were prevented from betting against the bubble assets and thereby bringing prices back to earth. The dotcom bubble showed that none of these defenses worked.

As regards transparency, no market in history has been subject to such intense scrutiny and obsessive coverage as the NASDAQ of the late 1990s. Stocks and the companies that issued them were assessed by investment banks, stockbrokers, and the financial press. The dubious projections on which they relied were set out in prospectuses that warned (in a pro forma fashion) that they might not be fulfilled.

Speculators did attempt to burst the bubble. Julian Robertson of Tiger Investments, speculated that grossly overvalued tech stocks would decline in the late 1990s and lost billions when the stocks rose even further in 1999. He quit managing other people's money, telling clients that he no longer understood the markets.

Although the dotcom bubble and bust was spectacular, the 2000–2001 crash was at least equally significant for the exposure of corporate fraud on a scale unparalleled (at the time) since the 1920s. The two biggest frauds, Enron and Worldcom offered a sharp contrast. The Enron frauds relied on a complex network of trading schemes, special purpose vehicles, and elaborate accounting devices. By contrast, the managers of Worldcom simply invented revenue numbers that made the company look massively profitable when it was actually losing money hand over fist.

The Crisis of 2008

The bursting of the dotcom bubble spelled, or should have spelled, the end of belief in the strong forms of the Efficient Market Hypothesis. On the other hand, by exposing weaknesses in the systems that were supposed to keep financial markets operating properly, it gave regulators and financial institutions a chance to clean up, so that future outcomes could be more like those predicted by theory.

Neither of these things happened. Advocates of the Efficient Markets Hypothesis ignored the dotcom fiasco, and went on as if nothing had happened. The accounting scandals at Enron and other companies produced the Sarbanes-Oxley Act, which sought to reform corporate governance. But the act was limited and largely ineffectual. Within a year or two, the conventional wisdom of the financial markets was that Sarbanes-Oxley was an overreaction to isolated cases of fraud, and that a new push for deregulation was needed.

Financial institutions could disregard the failures of the dotcom bubble because of the (seemingly) successful operation of the Greenspan put. Rather than let the financial sector suffer the consequences of the bursting bubble, Greenspan relaxed monetary policy and inflated a whole new bubble, this time in housing.

The housing boom in the United States was not spectacular by global standards. Its crucial characteristic was that both the boom and the subsequent bust took place in all major markets simultaneously. As with the LTCM disaster a decade earlier, the models used by financial instruments to rate the riskiness of mortgages and assets derived from those mortgages incorporated the assumption that separate housing markets in the United States were largely independent of each other. So, a diversified portfolio of U.S. mortgages was highly unlikely to suffer losses on all or most of its holdings at once.

But the very transactions justified by the models undermined the assumptions on which they were based. The demand for diversified portfolios meant that lenders lowered their standards in all markets at once. Whereas previous U.S. real estate booms had been based on local factors leading to optimism about the prospects for particular markets, the boom of the early 2000s was based on a general belief that real estate, as an asset, was bound to go up in value.

This assumption was embodied in the construction and pricing of an ever more complex range of financial derivatives. The process began with the observation that, if house prices kept on rising, the absence of a down payment was not a problem, since the borrower's equity would rise with the price of the house. That in turn meant that it would be possible to refinance a loan on more favorable terms.

So, on this assumption, it made sense to offer "negative-amortization" loans, in which, for an initial period of two or three years, the borrower did not pay down the debt at all, but added to it. After the initial "honeymoon" period, these loans were set to revert to much more stringent terms, but it was convenient for everyone to assume that, when the time came, the loan could be refinanced.

Based on these assumptions, investment banks were prepared to buy securities based on loans made by mortgage lenders such as Countrywide. The resulting loss of market share by Fannie Mae and Freddie Mac led these institutions to lower their standards.

Beginning in 2004, Fannie and Freddie entered the subprime market on a large scale, relying on their implicit guarantee to hold down borrowing costs. Increasingly competitive securitization also reduced the incentive of the original lenders to monitor the creditworthiness of borrowers; once they had packaged the mortgages into securities they were no longer exposed to the risk of default, and the demand for securities was so strong that quality was not a major problem.

The growth in demand for mortgage-backed securities reflected a range of innovations, such as the rise of bond guarantors, and the development of collateralized debt obligations (CDOs). Using these devices, a portfolio of mortgage-backed securities was transformed into a set of assets some of which were supposed to pay off even in the event of a downturn in local housing markets. The possibility of a national downturn was excluded from consideration in the models used to rate these securities.

These and other devices, combined with optimistic assumptions about default and repayment rate, made it appear that the risks associated with lending could be made to vanish. With the blessing of ratings agencies such as Moody's and Standard & Poor's, loans to people who might have neither a regular income, nor a job, nor any asset except the house itself were transformed into "super-senior" bonds given the same AAA credit rating accorded to the U.S. government itself.[18]

By late 2006, loans to borrowers with weak or nonexistent credit formed the basis of an inverted pyramid amounting to trillions of dollars of spurious assets created by banks and hedge funds around the world. Some of these institutions were explicitly backed by national governments. Many others were "too big to fail" or, more precisely, too interconnected to fail. Given the complex and fragile web of financial

---

[18] The acronym NINJA (no income, no job or assets) was used to describe these borrowers.

transactions built up since the 1970s, the breakdown of even a medium-sized player could bring the whole system to a halt.

The stage was set for a global economic meltdown. The crisis built up slowly over the course of 2007, as the growth in house prices slowed, and "subprime" borrowers faced foreclosure. By mid-2007, the problems had spread more widely, to classes of borrowers seen as less risky. CDOs and other derivatives, originally rated as AAA, were downgraded on a large scale and some went into default.

Throughout all this, the dominant view, informed by the Efficient Markets Hypothesis, was that nothing would, or could, go badly wrong. It was not until investment bank Bear Stearns was rescued from imminent bankruptcy in March 2008, that confidence started to crack. By this time, as the National Bureau of Economic Research subsequently determined, the U.S. economy had been in recession for several months. But as late as August 2008, the most common response from financial markets was that of denial.

The meltdown began with the sudden nationalization of the main U.S. mortgage agencies, Fannie Mae and Freddie Mac in early September 2008. Two months later, the investment banking industry had collapsed, with Lehman Brothers bankrupt, Merrill Lynch swallowed by Bank of America, and Goldman Sachs, and JP Morgan forced to seek the safety of government guarantees, by becoming bank holding companies. A year later, the list of casualties included banks around the world, whole countries such as Iceland, and the archetypal embodiment of corporate capitalism, General Motors.

Every bubble in history has come with a story to show why, in the words of Carmen Reinhart and Ken Rogoff, "this time it's different." But the current crisis has two features that should spell the end of the Efficient Markets Hypothesis once and for all. The first is that, in scale and scope, it is larger than any financial failure since the Great Depression. The estimated losses from financial failures amount to $4 trillion or about 10 percent of the world's annual income. Losses in output from the global recession are also likely to be in the trillions before the world economy recovers.

And, unlike the Great Depression, this crisis was entirely the product of financial markets. There was nothing like the postwar turmoil of the 1920s, the struggles over gold convertibility and reparations, or the Smoot-Hawley tariff, all of which have shared the blame for the Great Depression. Financial markets and major banks were lightly regulated by governments under systems that relied, in large measure, on risk assessments undertaken by the banks themselves, and based, in large measure on the ratings issued by agencies such as Standard & Poor's and Moody's.

All of the checks and balances in the system failed comprehensively. The ratings agencies offered AAA ratings to assets that turned out to be worthless, on the basis of models that assumed that house prices could never fall. This was not simple incompetence. The entire ratings agency model, in which issuers pay for ratings, proved to be fundamentally unsound. But, these very ratings were embedded in official systems of regulation. Thanks to the Efficient Markets Hypothesis, crucial public policy decisions were, in effect, outsourced to for-profit firms that had a strong incentive to get the answers wrong.

To these systemic failures was added the exposure of long-running fraud on a massive scale. The Ponzi scheme operated by Bernie Madoff, former head of the NASDAQ exchange and leading light of the New York financial sector, took place on a scale that matched the gargantuan growth of the financial sector itself.

The original Ponzi scheme, promoted by Charles Ponzi in 1920 on the basis of bogus investments in postal coupons, brought in an amount equal to $5 million in today's value. Madoff estimated the proceeds of his racket at $50 billion—ten thousand times Ponzi's take. And while Madoff put others in the shade, the collapse of the bubble brought to light a string of frauds involving tens or hundreds of millions of dollars.

The cases of Madoff and other frauds brings to mind J. K. Galbraith's idea of the "bezzle." The bezzle is the amount of undetected corporate fraud. As a boom continues, and everyone does well, people realize they can siphon off money and use it to make even more money. If they are threatened with detection, the original amount stolen can be returned to the till, and they are still ahead. But, in a crisis, this can't be done and, in any case, outside accountants are all over the books. So, embezzlers are caught and the bezzle shrinks. It stays small in the early stages of recovery when most decisions are being made by the cautious types who survived the crisis. But as the boom continues, hungrier and less risk-averse types come to the fore and the bezzle begins to grow again.

Under a system where the financial sector grows out of proportion to the real economy, and where, by virtue of the Efficient Markets Hypothesis, values recorded in financial markets are taken to be real, however absurd they may seem, the bezzle grew to unprecedented magnitudes.

REANIMATION: CHICAGO REVIVES THE DEAD

The ultimate zombie is one that is completely invulnerable. Neither special bullets nor hammer blows nor even decapitation can finally lay this undead being to rest. But dramatic logic requires that a zombie invulnerable to external threats must be subject to a subtle, but ultimately terminal, flaw that ends in its own destruction.

Ultimate zombies arise quite commonly in science and economics in the form of ideas that are immune from refutation. The classic examples arise from the popularized versions of Freudian psychology, centered on the Oedipus complex, named for the Greek tragic hero who unknowingly killed his father and married his mother. If a son hates his father, this is, obviously, evidence of the Oedipus complex. But, if he loves his father, this is explained as a repressed Oedipus complex. With rules like this, Freudian psychology can never be refuted.

But as a string of philosophers of science, beginning with the late Karl Popper, have shown, a theory that can't be refuted by any conceivable evidence isn't really a theory at all. All it says, in the end, is "anything can happen, and probably will."

The Global Financial Crisis, along with the earlier dotcom crisis has shown that, on any ordinary understanding of its terms, the Efficient Markets Hypothesis can't be right. Despite reaching a scale and sophistication unparalleled in history, global financial markets have shown themselves subject to the same manias, bubbles, and busts that were seen in the Dutch tulip craze of the seventeenth century.

Supporters of the Efficient Markets Hypothesis have sought a redefinition that would make it invulnerable to refutation. Their central argument is one that has already been discussed: if it is possible to diagnose the existence of a bubble, then it should be possible to make arbitrarily large profits betting against it. And if someone like Warren Buffett has in fact done this, that can be put down to luck. Only if everybody can make money betting against the market can the EMH be wrong. But, of course, it's impossible for everyone to bet against the market—the market is just the aggregate of bets.

This argument in one form or another has been put forward by all the leading defenders of the Efficient Markets Hypothesis, notably including Eugene Fama and John Cochrane of Chicago and Scott Sumner of Bentley University.

This set of observations from Scott Sumner, in a blog post aptly titled "Defending the Indefensible," at least recognizes the difficulties of the position:

> But why is Fama's theory now in such disrepute? Because in the past ten years the world economy has seen two very important bubble-like patterns, indeed arguably the only two such market cycles in the US during my lifetime with macro significance. And they were both predicted by lots of experts because they violated popular theories of fundamentals. So start with the cognitive illusion that people have that makes them see bubbles even where they don't exist. People think they have made accurate predictions because an upswing is always EVENTUALLY followed by a downturn. Then add in the fact that The Economist really did make accurate predictions in two of the most important events in modern history. Do you think it will be possible to convince them that they just got lucky? About as likely as a husband convincing an already suspicious wife that he is innocent after twice being caught in bed with two separate women. So I feel sorry for Fama. He's probably right, but I don't see how he could ever convince anyone in this environment. It would be like trying to convince someone that neoliberalism was the right policy in 1933.

Indeed. Looking at the evidence of the two gigantic bubbles of the last decade, it's hard to see how Sumner maintains his own faith, and he never really gives an explanation, except to say that it's easy to misperceive bubbles. As far as macroeconomics is concerned, the experience of the Great Depression and of the current Global Financial Crisis (which as Sumner implies, really began with the 2001 recessions) is pretty strong evidence that market liberalism is not the right policy, at least not for all occasions and not in the forms that prevailed in the 1920s or the 1990s.

The ultimate response to this invulnerable zombie must be the same as that of Popper to Freudian psychology. If the Great Depression, the dotcom boom and bust, and the current Global Financial Crisis are all consistent with the Efficient Markets Hypothesis, the hypothesis can't tell us much of interest about anything. At most, it says that even when markets are way out of line with economic reality, it is hard to exploit this fact to make a profit.

AFTER THE ZOMBIES: THE STATE AND THE MARKET

With the dogma of the Efficient Markets Hypothesis discarded, we can return to a more reasonable assessment of the role of financial markets.

Financial markets are necessary intermediaries between lenders (whose loans are ultimately derived from household savings) and borrowers, both consumers and investors. In a mixed economy, this function is typically undertaken mainly by the private sector, and this is unlikely to change in the medium term. Although we may see the establishment of some publicly owned financial institutions, this trend will be more than offset by the return to private ownership of institutions partially or wholly nationalized during the crisis.

But accepting that financial markets are necessary does not imply acquiescence in the claim of the Efficient Markets Hypothesis that the prices generated in those financial markets are the "right prices" in the sense that no alternative judgment can ever do better. On the contrary, governments can reasonably override or disregard the prices generated by financial markets in at least two important ways.

First, the experience of the last decade demonstrates beyond reasonable doubt that private financial markets can generate bubbles, and that economic policy should seek to prevent this from happening. This cannot be done by central banks using interest rates as their sole policy instrument.

Rather, a combination of macroeconomic policy and regulatory measures is required. If a real estate bubble is under way, for example, central banks must have the power and willingness to direct bank lending away from the overheated sectors without unnecessarily constraining productive investment.

Second, in evaluating public investments, governments should employ the tools of benefit-cost analysis (taking nonmonetary benefits into account) rather than relying on the judgments of financial markets, ratings agencies, and the like. This point leaves open the question of which investments should be public.

Once the Efficient Markets Hypothesis is abandoned, it seems likely that markets will do better than governments in planning investments in some cases (those where a good judgment of consumer demand is important, for example) and worse in others (those requiring long-term planning, for example). The logical implication is that a mixed economy will outperform both central planning and laissez-faire, as was indeed the experience of the twentieth century.

As regards financial markets, the core of a policy response to the failure of the Efficient Markets Hypothesis must be based on a sharp separation between the socially necessary functions of the financial system, which require public guarantees, and the hopeful ventures of speculators, which must be left to stand or fall on their own merits. In the resulting system of "narrow banking," the financial sector would become, in effect, an infrastructure service, like electricity or telecommunications. While the provision of financial services might be undertaken by either public or private enterprises, governments would accept a clear responsibility for the stability of the financial infrastructure.

Realistic Theories of Financial Markets

The theoretical analysis underlying the Efficient Markets Hypothesis shows that perfectly rational investors, operating in perfectly efficient financial markets, will produce the best possible estimate of the future value of any asset. The catastrophic failure of the Efficient Markets Hypothesis in reality suggests the need to reexamine not only the theoretical premises of individual rationality and market efficiency but also the whole concept of "best possible estimate."

The first of these tasks is well under way. For the past twenty-five years or so, economists have been seeking to replace assumptions of perfect rationality with more realistic models of how individuals make choices under uncertainty and over time. Much of this work goes under the banner of "behavioral economics" or "behavioral finance."[19]

Many of the crucial ideas of behavioral economics are derived from the work of psychologist Daniel Kahneman and his longtime collaborator, the late Amos Tversky.[20] Among other crucial ideas, Kahneman and Tversky showed that people have difficulty in handling probability judgments and, in particular, tend to overweight certain kinds of low probability events, such as the chance of winning the lottery or dying in an airplane crash.

While people are mostly risk-averse, they tend to "chase losses," taking additional risks in the hope of recouping losses to bring themselves back to an original reference point. Far from being the reliable calculating machines assumed in the standard theory, people rely on "heuristics" such as "availability," which means that they tend to overestimate the probability of events of which examples are readily available.

Another collaborator of Kahneman and Tversky, Richard Thaler, has focused on how people make decisions over time. The standard model requires people to value future flows of income using a moderate, constant discount rate, such as the rate of interest on bonds. So, if the annual rate of interest on bonds is 5 percent, a sum of $100 invested now will be worth $105 in a year's time and (because of compound interest) about $110.25 in two years' time. Turning this argument around, a sum of $105 received in a year's time, or $110.25 in two years' time, should be worth $100 today.

---

[19] In true academic fashion, there is some dispute about the ownership of this term. Some economists tie it to a specific research program, but others prefer a broader view that encompasses any work based on actual behavior rather than *a priori* rationality assumptions.

[20] In 2002, Kahneman became the first, and so far only, psychologist to be awarded the Nobel Prize in economics. Tversky, uniquely in the history of the award, received a posthumous mention.

Observing what people actually do in day-to-day decisions reveals a quite different pattern, called hyperbolic discounting. People greatly prefer to receive benefits immediately rather than, say, in a year's time. They are similarly keen to defer costs from today to tomorrow or next week, even when facing high interest costs for doing so. But if asked to choose between a benefit (or cost) in one year's time, and a larger benefit or cost in two year's time, they are fairly patient.

Unawareness

Research in behavioral economics shows that people often fail to follow the precepts of rational decision-making. The economics of asymmetric information literature explains why even when participants in financial markets are entirely rational, market outcomes may not be efficient.

There is a more fundamental challenge that economists are only now beginning to address. This is the fact that, since the number of possible contingencies that may affect economic outcomes is effectively infinite, no decision-maker, no matter how well informed and sophisticated, can possibly take them all into account.

This point has arisen in popular discussion, for example with Donald Rumsfeld's famous observation, made in relation to the Iraq War that "there are known knowns. There are things we know that we know. There are known unknowns. That is to say, there are things that we now know we don't know. But there are also unknown unknowns. There are things we do not know we don't know."[21]

Rumsfeld was much derided for this statement, but it is both valid and important. The real problem was that, having made the point, Rumsfeld did not consider that, since launching a war exposes a nation to a host of "unknown unknowns," decisions to do so should be made with extreme caution.

In the financial literature, Nassim Taleb has popularized the term *black swans* to describe such unforeseen contingencies. For Europeans, the proposition that "all swans are white" was confirmed by all

---

[21] Rumsfeld (2002).

experience. It seems unlikely that Europeans ever contemplated the possibility of black swans, until they came to Australia and found them. Fortunately, there was not a large financial system built on the whiteness of swans. However, history is full of examples of careful planning brought undone by unconsidered possibilities.

It is not hard to point out that we are regularly surprised by "unknown unknowns" and "black swans." A much harder problem is to describe a system of reasoning and decision-making that takes account of events that are, by definition, unforeseen by those reasoning and making decisions. Economists, philosophers, and decision theorists have been wrestling with this problem for a long time, and at last seem to be making some progress.

It turns out that it is possible to develop formal models of bounded rationality. Unlike the hyperrational calculators of standard economic theory, boundedly rational decision-makers are unaware of some possibilities and unable to fully articulate and communicate all the possibilities of which they are aware.

The implications are profound. One is that in environments where surprises are likely to be unfavorable, it makes sense to apply a precautionary principle to decision-making. In such environments, we should prefer simple and easily understood choices to those that are complex and poorly understood, even when the complex option appears to offer greater net benefits.

A similar point relates to contracts. In standard economic theory, contracts can be drawn up to cover every possible contingency. But in the real world, contracts are never complete and complex contracts always involve some element of ambiguity. For this reason, simple contracts with terms that are understood by both parties may be preferred to the complex arrangements indicated as optimal by standard economic theory.

Trust and Crises

Individual deviations from rationality are not the only problem for the Efficient Markets Hypothesis. In perfectly efficient markets, even a small number of hard-nosed and rational speculators would be enough to ensure the outcomes predicted by the hypothesis. Such speculators could take advantage of the irrational behavior of the majority of investors, turning them into "money pumps." As Keynes observed, though, successful speculation depends on the market getting things right, not just eventually, but before the speculators run out of money. A realistic theory of financial markets must explain how bubbles can persist long enough to deter speculators from betting on a return to market equilibrium.

We also need a deeper understanding of financial collapses like the current crisis. Although the textbooks represent financial markets as involving impersonal exchanges of precisely defined assets, the actual operation of the system relies crucially on trust and, more generally, on understanding the amount of trust that should be placed in particular kinds of promises. In the last few decades, economists have spent a lot of time studying trust, and particularly the problem of when one party to a contract should trust the other to tell the truth and keep faith.

The problem of trust has been analyzed in terms of asymmetric information (when one party knows something the other does not, and both parties know this). But the problems go deeper than this, to situations where it is impossible to calculate all the possible outcomes, and individuals must decide whether to rely on the judgment and good faith of others.

Trust breaks down in crises. All institutions, both public and private, rely to some extent on trust, and when trust breaks down it is often hard to rebuild. In the crisis of the 1970s, the failure of governments to deliver on their commitments to manage the economy and maintain full employment led to a loss of public trust, which was transferred (more or less by default) to markets and particularly financial markets. This loss of trust made it difficult, if not impossible, to implement policies that might have made a difference, such as agreements to stabilize wages. By the time such agreements were feasible, in the 1980s, the balance of economic power had already shifted to financial markets.

Even more than governments (which have, after all, the direct power of the state behind them) financial markets depend on trust. The central financial institution of modern capitalism is the fractional reserve banking system, whereby banks lend out most of the money that is deposited with them, keeping only a fraction to meet calls for withdrawals. In an unregulated system, a failure of trust in a given institution leads to a "run on the bank" as depositors scramble to get money out while they can.

Systems of deposit insurance and bank guarantees now ensure that depositors' trust in banks is backed up by their trust in the ability of governments to protect them in the event of default. But other kinds of trust in the financial system are not so easily maintained. Banks are sustainable if and only if they can accurately assess the willingness and ability of borrowers to repay their debts. In normal conditions, this is not an exceptionally difficult task. Banks can look at standard measures of ability to repay, credit histories, and so on to distinguish good risks from bad, and borrowers have strong incentives to maintain good credit histories.

In a crisis all this breaks down. Formerly reliable formulas cease to work as borrowers realize they are better off walking away from their debts (through bankruptcy or foreclosure), rather than struggling to repay them and failing anyway. At this point, trust can only be restored through personal knowledge of particular borrowers, the kind that is built up through a long business relationship. But it is precisely in a crisis that such business relationships break down. Banks fail and their assets are taken over by others with no knowledge of the customers beyond what they can glean from formal records and remaining employees. In a complex and interlinked system like that built up over recent decades, the failures can cascade until the entire system ceases to function beyond a minimal level.

Financial Regulation

The Global Financial Crisis has been, above all, a failure of models of financial regulation based on the Efficient Markets Hypothesis. The approach to financial regulation developed in response to the Great Depression was highly restrictive. Financial institutions were confined to a limited range of services, and financial innovation was limited. Financial institutions seeking to create new assets had to satisfy regulators that these assets could be fitted into the existing regulatory framework, or else wait until a new set of regulatory structures was developed.

From the 1970s onward, financial deregulation put an end to these constraints. The term *deregulation* is something of a misnomer, since no system in which the public is the ultimate guarantor can be regarded as unregulated. Rather a system of regulation focused on protecting the public and stabilizing the economy was replaced by one in which the primary concern was to facilitate innovation and to manage risk in the most "light-handed" possible fashion.

The Efficient Markets Hypothesis played a crucial role in designing these regulatory systems, which went through a variety of forms before their final embodiment in the Basel Accords issued by the Basel Committee on Banking Supervision, which is made up of senior representatives of bank supervisory authorities and central banks from the G-10 countries.

The Basel Accords attempted to assess the riskiness of banks' holdings using a combination of market prices and ratings from private agencies (such as Moody's and Standard & Poor's). According to the Efficient Markets Hypothesis, market values of classes of risky assets are the best possible estimate of their value. While the Efficient Markets Hypothesis does not have direct implications for the interpretation of agency ratings, the fact that such ratings are sought by bond issuers implies, according to the Efficient Markets Hypothesis, that the ratings contain valuable and reliable information, since they would otherwise be ignored.

Until 2007, the Basel system had never had to deal with a serious financial crisis in the developed world. It failed catastrophically at its first test. Not only did many banks fail, but the measures of capital adequacy required under the Basel system proved all but useless in assessing which banks were at risk.

Radical changes in financial sector regulation have already taken place as a result of the financial crisis. Guarantees of bank deposits have been introduced or greatly expanded in all major economies. Partial or complete nationalization of failing institutions, with the resulting assumption of risk by the public, has been widespread.

However, these policies have been introduced as emergency measures. The implicit (and sometimes explicit) premise has been that they will be ended when normal (precrisis) conditions are restored. This premise is untenable. By the time the crisis is over, the financial sector will be radically transformed and will require new and different modes of regulation.

The starting point for a stable regulatory regime must be a reversal of the burden of proof in relation to financial innovation. The prevailing rule has been to allow, and indeed encourage, financial innovations unless they can be shown to represent a threat to financial stability. Given an effective public guarantee for the liabilities of these institutions, such a rule is a guaranteed, and proven, recipe for disaster, offering huge rewards to any innovation that increases both risks (ultimately borne by the public) and returns (captured by the innovators).

What is needed is a system of "narrow banking." Narrow banking begins with a clearly defined set of institutions, such as banks and insurance companies. These institutions offer a set of well-tested financial instruments with explicit public guarantees for clients. They receive a public guarantee of solvency, with nationalization as a last resort. Financial innovations must be treated with caution and allowed only on the basis of a clear understanding of their effects on systemic risk.

It is important not to suppress the activity of those willing to take risks with their own capital. As Adam Smith observed, "The chance of gain is by every man more or less overvalued, and the chance of loss is by most men undervalued, and by scarce any man, who is in tolerable health and spirits, valued more than it is worth."[22]

Smith argues that this characteristic overoptimism is crucial in promoting investment and enterprise. Later writers such as Keynes described attitudes to risk in terms of "animal spirits," and noted, in the light of experience, the occurrence of periodic panics and depressions, in which animal spirits could not be roused. But even so, there is a clear need to allow scope for those with an optimistic view to seize their chance, while ensuring that the costs of the inevitable failures are borne by those concerned in the speculative investment and not by the community as a whole.

Stabilizing financial markets does not mean that it is necessary to prohibit risky investments, or even to prevent speculators from developing

[22] Smith, ([1776] 2005), 94.

and trading in risky new financial assets. What is crucial is that these operations should not threaten the stability of the system as a whole.

Publicly regulated (and guaranteed) banks and other financial institutions should be prohibited from engaging in speculative trade on their own account and from extending any form of credit to institutions engaged in such speculation. Governments should commit themselves not to allow any bailout if speculators get into trouble. After that speculators can safely be left to sink or swim.

In this context, it is crucial to maintain sharp boundaries between publicly guaranteed institutions and unprotected financial institutions such as hedge funds, finance companies, stockbroking firms, and mutual funds. Institutions in the latter category must not be allowed to present a threat of systemic failure that might precipitate a public sector rescue, whether direct, as in the recent crisis, or indirect, as in the bailout of LTCM in 1998. A number of measures are required to ensure this.

First, ownership links between protected and unprotected financial institutions must be absolutely prohibited, to avoid the risk that failure of an unregulated subsidiary will necessitate a rescue of the parent, or that an unregulated parent could seek to expose a bank subsidiary to excessive risk. Long before the current crisis, these dangers were illustrated by Australian experience with bank-owned finance companies, most notably the rescue, by the Reserve Bank, of the Bank of Adelaide in the 1970s.

Second, banks should not market unregulated financial products such as share investments and hedge funds.

Third, the provision of bank credit to unregulated financial enterprises should be limited to levels that ensure that even large-scale failure in this sector cannot threaten the solvency of the regulated system.

The State and the Market

The Efficient Markets Hypothesis implies that governments can never outperform well-informed financial markets in making investment decisions. The failure of the Efficient Markets Hypothesis does not imply the converse claim that governments will always do better. Rather, the evidence suggests that markets will do better than governments in planning investments in some cases (those where a good judgment of consumer demand is important, for example) and worse in others (those requiring long-term planning, for example).

This inference from capital market outcomes is consistent with the general experience of the twentieth century, and particularly the decades after World War II. In these decades, governments took a central role in the development of a wide range of infrastructure services including transport and telecommunications networks, and the provision of electricity, gas, and water. They also invested in "human capital," through the massive postwar expansion in education and public health systems. These investments were not motivated by doctrinaire socialism but by a belief that the development of the market economy would be promoted by the reliable supply of infrastructure services and of skilled and educated workers.

The growth of public expenditure on infrastructure went hand in hand with a wave of private sector innovation. Computers, originally developed in publicly funded academic and military research, became the basis of a rapidly growing information and electronics industry. The development of highway systems facilitated the growth of the car industry. Above all, private sector innovation depended on a steadily more educated workforce.

The rise of market liberalism saw a substantial, though far from complete, shift of responsibility to the private sector. Reform of electricity, telecommunications, and other infrastructure services has followed a broadly similar pattern throughout the world. Integrated monopolies have been broken up and (if in public ownership) sold off, with the aim of creating competitive markets. Those sectors, such as electricity transmission and distribution, where competition was not feasible (these sectors are called "natural monopolies" by economists), were subject to regulation that was designed to be as "light-handed" as possible.

The results have been mixed, to put it charitably. In some cases, such as that of telecommunications reform in Finland, the shift to reliance on private capital has led to new and innovative investment strategies, and the rise of dynamic firms like Nokia. In others, such as electricity transmission in the United States, failure to take account of the public good character of infrastructure has led to inadequate investment by all parties, and to a gradual deterioration in the quality of the network. In still other cases, as in the creation of supposedly competitive electricity markets in California, financial engineering and market manipulation have produced catastrophic failures.

The experience of the twentieth century suggests that a mixed economy will outperform both central planning and laissez-faire. The real question for policy debates is one of determining the appropriate mix, and the way in which the public and private sectors should interact.

The economic doctrines derived from the Efficient Markets Hypothesis seemed to contradict that suggestion. It is now clear, however, that it is the Efficient Markets Hypothesis and not the mixed economy that has failed the test of experience.

FURTHER READING

For anyone interested in the rise and fall of the Efficient Markets Hypothesis, Fox (2009), *The Myth of the Rational Market: A History of Risk, Reward, and Delusion on Wall Street,* is essential reading. Malkiel's classic *A Random Walk Down Wall Street* ([1973] 2007) provides a useful guide to the Efficient Markets Hypothesis (particularly the weak form) and its implications for personal investment strategies. Lo and MacKinlay, *A Non-Random Walk Down Wall Street* (2001) provides the most detailed contrary arguments. And the George Goodman/Adam Smith classic, *The Money Game* (1968), is still full of insights after forty years. Kay (2004) provides an excellent and sympathetic view of the strengths and weaknesses of markets, and the way in which markets can only work if they are embedded in social and cultural institutions.

The technical literature on the Efficient Markets Hypothesis is hard going, since it relies critically on the theory of stochastic processes. The random walks hypothesis was first developed by French mathematician Louis Bachelier in a Ph.D. thesis in 1900 where he also developed a theory of the Brownian motion of molecules, several years in advance of Albert Einstein. An English translation and other relevant works are presented in Bachelier et al. (2006). In the modern literature the key articles are Fama (1965, 1970) and Samuelson (1965, 1973) for the Efficient Markets Hypothesis and Black and Scholes (1973) and Merton (1973) for the Black-Scholes option pricing rule.

Data on bank profits and transactions is derived from Gudmundsson (2008).

My own book (Quiggin 1993) is still the only one covering probability weighting and prospect theory from a modern point of view, but will soon be rendered largely obsolete by Wakker (2010). The crucial journal articles on prospect theory and probability weighting are Kahneman and Tversky (1979), Quiggin (1982), and Tversky and Kahneman (1992).

The literature on bounded rationality and unawareness is still embryonic, and inaccessible to the nonspecialist reader. The best popular treatment is Taleb (2007), though the author's claims to possess unique insights, not shared by any other economist, should be taken with a large grain of salt.

Economists working on trust should consider the insights of the other social sciences, such as those presented in the work of Fukuyama (1996) and Putnam (2001).

Other references cited are Ellenberg (2008); Bank for International Settlements (2009); Borio and Lowe (2003); Garber (2001); Gordon (1996); Grant, Kline, and Quiggin (2009); Grossman and Stiglitz (1980); LeRoy (2006); Quiggin (2004); Setser and Roubini (2005); Shiller (1982, 1989); and Williamson (1990).

DYNAMIC STOCHASTIC GENERAL EQUILIBRIUM

We are now all Friedmanites.
>   —*LAWRENCE SUMMERS,* Director of the White House's National
>   Economic Council and prominent New Keynesian economist

In the life cycle of ideas, the point where everyone has accepted an idea often seems to come just before its death. So it was at the high water mark of orthodox Keynesianism in the late 1960s. So it has also turned out for the elegant theoretical framework that ultimately succeeded Keynesianism. This framework went under the grandiose title of Dynamic Stochastic General Equilibrium (DSGE to its friends). At the moment of triumph, this beautiful theory was struck down by the ugly fact of the Global Financial Crisis. It now lives on, but only in zombie form.

At the end of the nineteenth century, British Liberal politician Sir William Harcourt observed "we are all socialists now." Harcourt was referring to a radical land reform measure that had been denounced as "socialist" when it was introduced but was generally accepted by the time he was speaking (a couple of years later). Harcourt's point was applicable to the whole trend of economic and social policy, in Britain and elsewhere, from the 1867 Reform Bill that gave millions of working-class men the vote (women had to wait until after World War I) to the crisis of the 1970s. From progressive income taxes to publicly owned infrastructure services, ideas that were unthinkable in mainstream politics became, first, issues of political contention and, later, established institutions.[1]

---

[1] Both were prominent items in the 10-point program of the Communist Manifesto in 1848.

As a pithy summary of the way ideas that were once radical become acceptable, and are ultimately embodied in conventional wisdom, Harcourt's quip has never been bettered. As a result, it has been reused many times over.

One of the most notable adaptations of Harcourt was that of *Time* magazine in 1965, which noted, following the successful use of fiscal policy to stabilize the economy that "we are all Keynesians now." This statement was made by Keynes's greatest modern critic, Milton Friedman (though he later said it had been taken out of context). Even more famously, it was repeated by Richard Nixon in 1971.

But whereas Harcourt was speaking at the beginning of nearly a century of reform that did indeed take economic policy in a socialist, or at least social-democratic direction, Nixon's statement marked the end of the era of Keynesian dominance.

In fact, Nixon was citing Keynes's aversion to the gold standard (a "barbarous relic") as a justification for abandoning the pegging of the U.S. dollar to gold. The gold peg was a central feature of the Bretton Woods system of fixed exchange rates that had underpinned Keynesian economic management since World War II. The outcome of Nixon's move was not a system of stable exchange rates backed by a basket of commodities rather than gold, as Keynes had proposed, but the complete breakdown of Bretton Woods and a shift to the floating exchange rate system advocated by the greatest critic of Keynesian economics, Milton Friedman.

In the course of the 1970s, Friedman and his supporters, centered at the University of Chicago, won a series of political and intellectual victories over the Keynesians. Following the failure of attempts to stabilize the economy using Keynesian fiscal policy, governments around the world switched to Friedman's preferred remedies based on controlling the growth of the money supply.

The obsessive focus on the money supply during these years prompted a famous quip from leading Keynesian Robert Solow, who observed, "Everything reminds Milton of the money supply. Well, everything reminds me of sex, but I keep it out of my papers."

Money supply targeting did not work particularly well and was later replaced by policies based on managing interest rates, but the resurgence of the Chicago School was not reversed. Their case against government intervention, both to stabilize the macroeconomy and to address market failures in particular industries, was widely accepted.

Leading Keynesians conceded Friedman's central points: that inflation is driven by the money supply, and that macroeconomic policy can affect real variables, like the levels of employment and unemployment, only in the short run.[2]

The main Keynesian response to the intellectual and policy defeats of the 1970s was to develop a "New Keynesian" economics. The central idea was that, given small deviations from the competitive market assumptions of the basic neoclassical economics model, it would be possible to explain the recurrence of booms and recessions and to justify the modest stabilization policies pursued by central banks during the Great Moderation.

Because New Keynesians were (and still are) concentrated in economics departments on the East and West Coast of the United States (Harvard, Berkeley, and others) while their intellectual opponents are most prominent in the lakeside environments of Chicago and Minnesota, the terms *saltwater* and *freshwater* schools were coined by Robert Hall, then at Stanford, to describe the two positions.

Despite his central role in the critique of Keynesianism, Friedman was never truly a freshwater economist. Most importantly, while he opposed active use of fiscal policy, he supported the use of monetary policy to maintain medium-term economic stability.

Friedman's intellectual descendants of the freshwater school sought to push his arguments to their logical conclusion, arguing that macroeconomic policy could not be beneficial even in the limited role he proposed. They tried to show that government intervention could only add uncertainty and instability to the economic system, and that, in the absence of such intervention, economic fluctuations like booms and slumps

---

[2] In economics, "real" variables are those that can be measured in terms related to physical quantities, such as the number of tons of steel produced in a given year. They are contrasted with "nominal" variables, which are expressed in dollar terms, for example, the money value of the steel produced in a given year. When comparing nominal values over time, it is necessary to adjust for inflation.

were actually good things, reflecting economic adjustments to changes in technology and consumer tastes. The resulting models went by various names, but the most popular was the "Real Business Cycle (RBC) theory."

Despite their often heated debates, saltwater and freshwater economists agreed on one fundamental point: that macroeconomic analysis must be based on the foundations of neoclassical microeconomics.[3] Although they disagreed about economic policy, these disagreements could be contained within a very narrow compass.

With a handful of exceptions, members of both schools took it for granted that macroeconomic management should be implemented through the monetary policies of central banks, that the only important instrument of monetary policy was the setting of short-term interest rates, and that the central goal of monetary policy should be the maintenance of low and stable inflation. Granting these premises, saltwater economists argued that stability could only be achieved if central banks paid attention to output and employment as well as inflation. On the other hand, the freshwater school favored an exclusive focus on price stability.

The Global Financial Crisis did not so much confirm or refute the elaborate arguments of the competing schools as render them irrelevant. The saltwater school could claim vindication for their view that the economy is not inherently stable. However, their models had little to say about the kind of crisis we have actually observed, driven by an interaction between macroeconomic imbalances and massive financial speculation. Meanwhile, the freshwater side of the dispute rapidly reverted to arguments from the nineteenth century, which had been debunked by Keynes and Irving Fisher.

As David Gruen of the Australian Treasury observed of macroeconomics in the lead-up to the crisis, "It was as if, as the Titanic was sailing into iceberg-infested waters, those with the requisite skills and training to warn of the impending danger were instead hard at work, in

---

[3] The terms *neoclassical* and *microeconomics* are complex, and the meaning of "neoclassical" in particular is contested. For our purposes, any standard textbook with a title like *Microeconomics* provides a good starting point. The particular aspects of neoclassical microeconomics that are most relevant will become clearer as the chapter progresses.

a windowless cabin, perfecting the design of ship hulls . . . for a world without icebergs."[4]

If we are to develop a macroeconomic theory that can help us to understand economic crises and improve policy responses, economics must take a different road from the one it has followed since the 1970s. The appealing idea that macroeconomics should develop naturally from standard microeconomic foundations has turned out to be a distraction. In its place, we must accept, in the language of systems theory, that macroeconomic phenomena are emergent, arising from complex interactions of behaviors we do not fully understand, but must nevertheless respond to.

BIRTH: FROM THE PHILLIPS CURVE TO THE NAIRU, AND BEYOND

Macroeconomics began with Keynes.[5] Before Keynes wrote *The General Theory of Employment, Interest, and Money*, economic theory consisted almost entirely of what is now called microeconomics. The difference between the two is commonly put by saying that microeconomics is concerned with individual markets and macroeconomics with the economy as a whole, but that formulation implicitly assumes a view of the world that is at least partly Keynesian.

Long before Keynes, neoclassical economists had both a theory of how prices are determined in individual markets so as to match supply and demand ("partial equilibrium theory") and a theory of how all the prices in the economy are jointly determined to produce a "general equilibrium" in which there are no unsold goods or unemployed workers.

---

[4] Gruen (2009), 10–11.

[5] That is not to say that no one before Keynes paid attention to the economic issues with which macroeconomics is concerned: the business cycle, inflation, and unemployment. On the contrary, serious empirical research into the business cycle began in the early twentieth century, most notably by the National Bureau of Economic Research, established in the United States. Important theoretical contributions came from economists such as Irving Fisher. And, as discussed below, the great economists of the Austrian School, F. A. Hayek and Ludwig Mises, produced an analysis of the business cycle that remains relevant today. But neither Fisher nor the Austrians took the final steps needed to create a theory of macroeconomics.

The strongest possible version of this claim was presented as Say's Law, named, somewhat misleadingly, for the classical economist Jean-Baptiste Say. Say's Law, as developed by later economists such as James Mill, states, in essence, that recessions are impossible since "supply creates its own demand."

To spell this idea out, think of a new entrant to the labor force looking for a job, and therefore adding to the supply of labor. According to the classical view of Say's Law, this new worker plans to spend the wages he or she earns on goods and service produced by others, so that demand is increased by an exactly equal amount. Similarly, any decision to forgo consumption and save money implies a plan to invest. So, planned savings must equal planned investment and the sum of consumption and savings must always equal total income and therefore can't be changed by policy.

Say's argument allows the possibility that, if prices are slow to adjust, there might be excess supply in some markets, but implies that, if so, there must be excess demand in some other market. It is this idea that is at the core of general equilibrium theory.

The first formal "general equilibrium" theory was produced by the great French economist Leon Walras in the 1870s. Walras, like many of the pioneers of neoclassical economics, was inclined toward socialist views, but his general equilibrium theory was used by advocates of laissez-faire to promote the view that, even if subject to severe shocks, the economy would always return to full employment unless it was prevented from doing so by government mismanagement or by the actions of unions that might hold wages above the market price of labor. Walras's analysis relied on informal arguments. The first fully developed theory of general equilibrium was only developed in the 1950s, by Kenneth Arrow and Gerard Debreu.

The point of Keynes's title was that "general equilibrium" was not general enough. A fully general theory of employment must give an account of recession states where unemployment remains high, with no tendency to return to full employment.

In the simplest version of the Keynesian model, equilibrium can be consistent with sustained unemployment because, unlike in the classical account of Say, the demand associated with workers' willingness to supply labor is not effective and does not actually influence the decisions of firms. So unsold goods and unemployed labor can coexist. Such failures of coordination can develop in various ways, but in a modern economy, they arise through the operation of the monetary system.

Keynes showed how the standard classical interpretation of Say's law depended on the assumption that economic transactions could be analyzed as if they were part of a barter system, in which goods were exchanged directly for other goods. In an economy where money serves both as the medium of exchange and as a store of value, the analysis works differently.

In the classical analysis, expenditure, consisting of consumption and investment, must be equal to income for every household and for the economy as a whole, and so, by the arithmetic of accounting, savings (the difference between income and consumption) must equal investment. This equality always holds true, as you can check by looking at any good set of accounts, including the national accounts drawn up for the economy as a whole. National accounts were in fact first drawn up by Keynes's student Colin Clark,[6] shortly followed by Simon Kuznets, a leading analyst of the U.S. business cycle.[7]

But, as Keynes observed, savings initially take the form of money. If lots of people want to save, and few want to invest, total demand in the economy will fall below the level required for full employment. Actual savings will equal investment, as they must by the arithmetic of accounting, but people's plans for consumption and investment may not be realized.

A simple and homely illustration is provided by Paul Krugman's description of a babysitting cooperative in Washington, DC, where babysitting credits worked as a kind of money. When members of the group tried to build up their savings by babysitting more and going out less, the result

---

[6] I work in a building named for him.

[7] In a global economy, savings in one country, such as China, can finance investment in another, such as the United States. The arguments between Keynes and the classical economists mostly focused on the "closed economy" case where international trade was relatively unimportant.

was a collapse of demand. The problem was eventually addressed by the equivalent of monetary expansion, when the cooperative simply issued more credits to everyone, resulting in more demand for babysitting, and a restoration of the original equilibrium.

Keynes's analysis showed how monetary policy could work, thereby extending the earlier work of theorists such as Irving Fisher. However, the second part of Keynes's analysis shows that the monetary mechanism by which equilibrium should be restored may not work in the extreme recession conditions referred to as a "liquidity trap." This concept is illustrated by the experience of Japan in the 1990s and by most of the developed world in the recent crisis. Even with interest rates reduced to zero, banks were unwilling to lend, and businesses unwilling to invest.

Keynes's *General Theory* provided a justification for policies such as public works programs that had long been advocated, and to a limited extent implemented, as a response to the unemployment created by recessions and depressions.[8] More generally, Keynesian analysis gave rise to a system of macroeconomic management based primarily on the use of fiscal policy to stabilize aggregate demand.

During periods of recession, Keynesian analysis suggested that governments should increase spending and reduce taxes, so as to stimulate demand (the first approach being seen as more reliable since the recipients of tax cuts might just save the money). On the other hand, during booms, governments should run budget surpluses, both to restrain excess demand and to balance the deficits incurred during recessions.

At first, it seemed, both to Keynes's opponents and to some of his supporters, that Keynesian economics was fundamentally inconsistent with traditional neoclassical economics. But the work of John Hicks and others produced what came to be called the Keynesian-neoclassical synthesis. In Hicks's synthesis, individual markets were analyzed using the traditional approach, now christened "microeconomics," while the determination of aggregate output and employment was the domain of Keynesian macroeconomics.

---

[8] Jean-Baptiste Say himself supported such measures in the early nineteenth century.

The synthesis was not particularly satisfactory at a theoretical level, but it had the huge practical merit that it worked, or at least appeared to. In the postwar era, the mixed economy derived from the Keynesian-neoclassical synthesis provided an attractive alternative both to the failed system of laissez-faire reliance on free markets and to the alternative of comprehensive economic planning, represented by the (then still rapidly growing) Soviet Union.

Modified to include a theory of market failure, neoclassical microeconomics allowed for some (but only some!) government intervention in particular markets to combat monopolies, finance the provision of public goods, and so on. Meanwhile, the tools of Keynesian macroeconomic management could be used to maintain stable full employment without requiring centralized economic planning or controls over individual markets.

Keynes's ideas had little impact on the policies pursued during the Great Depression, although some aspects of the New Deal in the United States and of the policies introduced by social democratic governments in Scandinavia and New Zealand could be seen as Keynesian in retrospect. The crucial contrast was between the experience of World War I and its aftermath, ending in the Great Depression, and that of World War II and the successful economic reconstruction that followed it.

Particularly in Britain, the financing and economic planning of World War II was undertaken on Keynesian lines, and Keynesians were quick to draw the lessons for the postwar period. The interwar years were seen as a period of economic waste that contributed greatly to the rise of Hitler and the renewed outbreak of global war in 1939.

The commitment of national governments to maintain full employment was underpinned by the global economic and financial system at the Bretton Woods conference in New Hampshire in 1944. As World War II drew to a close, the governments of the Allied countries sought to build an economic system that would prevent the recurrence of depressions, and therefore reduce the risk of renewed war.

The Bretton Woods system was based on fixed exchange rates between different currencies, ultimately anchored by the requirement that the U.S. dollar be exchangeable for gold at a price of thirty-five dollars an ounce. The Bretton Woods agreements also established key international economic institutions, most importantly the International Monetary Fund, the World Bank and the precursors of the World Trade Organization.

The architects of postwar reconstruction hoped to prevent a renewed slump like that of 1919, and to hold unemployment rates below 5 percent. They succeeded beyond their wildest dreams.

For most developed countries, the years from the end of World War II until the early 1970s represented a period of full employment and strong economic growth unparalleled before or since. With declining inequality and the introduction of more or less comprehensive welfare states, the gains were greatest for those at the bottom of the income distribution.

In an environment of stable growth and increasing demand for their products, business leaders were happy to accept a larger role for government. The implicit social contract of the postwar era guaranteed steady work and high wages for unionized employees in return for a government commitment to keep the economy at or near full employment, ensuring steady profits for business.

By 1970, the Bretton Woods system was under serious pressure. Inflation in the United States had rendered untenable the commitment to hold the price of gold at thirty-five dollars an ounce. Previous episodes of inflation had been brought under control quite rapidly through Keynesian contractionary policies. Unfortunately, these policies were becoming less effective as inflationary expectations became embedded and as the social restraint generated by memories of the Depression broke down.

The last years of the Keynesian era saw a struggle over income distribution that virtually guaranteed an inflationary outburst. Union militancy, fueled in many countries by Marxist rhetoric, came into sharp conflict with an emerging speculative capitalism, driven by revived global financial markets. Firms raised prices to meet wage demands, spurring yet further wage demands to compensate for higher prices.

The *coup de grace* came with the oil shock of 1973, which was both a reflection of the inflationary outburst that was already underway and the cause of a further upsurge. Within a couple of years the entire edifice of postwar prosperity had collapsed and the Keynesian "Golden Age" came to a painful and chaotic end. Repeatedly, seemingly promising recoveries fizzled or collapsed into even more severe recessions.

The 1970s and 1980s were decades of high unemployment and inflation. The ugly term *stagflation* (a portmanteau word derived from "stagnation" and "inflation") was coined to describe the appearance of these two economic evils simultaneously, rather than as part of a cycle of inflationary boom and deflationary bust.

The Phillips Curve

Throughout the history of capitalism it has been observed that boom periods tended to be accompanied by inflation (an increase in the general price level), and depressions by deflation. This observation formed a central part of the Keynesian economic system. While Keynes is commonly remembered for his advocacy of budget deficits to stimulate the economy in periods of recession, he also grappled with the problem of how to avoid inflation in the postwar period.

In his famous and influential pamphlet, *How to Pay for the War*, Keynes argued that inflation was the product of an excess of demand over supply. The appropriate policy response, he suggested, was for governments to increase taxes and run budget surpluses, to bring demand into line with supply.

In 1958, New Zealand economist A. W. (Bill) Phillips undertook a statistical study that formalized the relationship between unemployment and inflation in the now-famous Phillips curve.[9] The curve related unemployment to the rate of change in money wages, showing that, at very low rates of unemployment, wages tended to grow rapidly.

Since wages account for the majority of production costs, rapid wage inflation also implies rapid price inflation. The higher the rate of unemployment, the lower the rate of wage growth. However, because workers generally resist outright cuts in wages, the curve flattens out. Increases in unemployment beyond a certain rate (typically between 5 and 10 percent) have little further deflationary effect.

---

[9] Phillips was famous (or perhaps notorious) for having designed a hydraulic analog computer that could be used to represent the Keynesian economic model. The Faculty of Economics and Politics at Cambridge University still has a working version.

Despite his reputation as an exponent of (literally) "hydraulic" Keynesianism, Phillips did not endorse a mechanical interpretation of the curve. He is said to have remarked that "if I had known what they would do with the graph I would never have drawn it." The leading American Keynesian economists of the day, Paul Samuelson and Robert Solow, were less cautious, particularly in their popular writing.

In an influential article, Samuelson and Solow estimated a Phillips curve for the United States, and drew the conclusion that society faced a trade-off between unemployment and inflation. That is, society could choose between lower inflation and higher unemployment or lower unemployment and higher inflation. Although the article qualified this point with reference to possible effects on inflationary expectations, this qualification tended to get lost in discussion of the policy implications of the Phillips curve.

The trade-off between unemployment and inflation was spelt out in successive editions of Samuelson's textbook, simply entitled *Economics*, which dominated the market from its initial publication in 1948 until the mid-1970s. Given a menu of choices involving different rates of unemployment and inflation, it seemed obvious enough that, since unemployment was the greater evil, a moderate increase in inflation could be socially beneficial.

The interpretation of the Phillips curve as a stable trade-off between unemployment and inflation led to an acceptance of higher rates of inflation as the necessary price of reducing unemployment still further below the historically low levels of the postwar boom. So, whereas previous episodes of inflation had been met with the orthodox Keynesian response of fiscal contraction aimed at reducing aggregate demand, there was no such response to the acceleration of inflation in the late 1960s. The Phillips curve idea appeared to justify expansionary fiscal policy, and therefore budget deficits, except when unemployment was very low.

As inflation rates rose above the levels that would be implied by the Phillips curve for given levels of unemployment, Keynesian economists developed the idea that this was a new form of "cost-push" (as opposed to "demand-pull") inflation, arising from the monopoly power of business and unions. The appropriate response to "cost-push" inflation was not contractionary fiscal policy but direct intervention in the setting of prices and wages.

Initially, this response took the form of wage-price freezes such as that imposed by the Nixon administration in 1972. A more sophisticated version of the same idea was that of an "incomes policy" negotiated between governments, business, and unions. Neither price controls nor incomes policy had much success in stopping the acceleration of inflation in the face of strong demand pressures. They were, however, more successful in the 1980s, when inflation rates were falling in response to contractionary policy. In these circumstances, incomes policies facilitated reductions in inflation with much less unemployment than might otherwise have been the case.

Friedman, Natural Rate, and NAIRU

The Keynesian adoption of the Phillips curve paved the way for Milton Friedman's greatest intellectual victory, based on a penetrating analysis offered in the late 1960s at a time when inflation, while already problematic, was far below the double-digit rates that would be experienced in the 1970s.

In his famous presidential address to the American Economic Association in 1968, Friedman argued that the supposed trade-off between unemployment and inflation was the product of illusion. As long as workers failed to recognize that the general rate of inflation was increasing, they would regard wage increases as real improvements in their standard of living and therefore would increase both their supply of labor and their demand for goods. But, Friedman argued, sooner or later expectations of inflation would catch up with reality. If the rate of inflation were held at, say, 5 percent for several years, workers would build a 5 percent allowance for inflation into their wage claims, and businesses would raise their own prices by 5 percent to allow for the increase in anticipated costs.

Once expectations adjusted, Friedman argued, the beneficial effects of inflation would disappear. The rate of unemployment would return to the level consistent with price stability, but inflation would remain high.

Interpreted graphically, this meant that the long-term Phillips curve was a vertical line.

Friedman's analysis gave no specific answer to the question of where unemployment would stabilize. Friedman argued that this could be determined as "the level ground out by the Walrasian system of general equilibrium equations . . . including market imperfections . . . the cost of gathering information about job vacancies and labor availabilities, the costs of mobility, and so on" (Friedman 1968, p. 8). Friedman introduced the unfortunate description of this outcome as the "natural rate of unemployment," although even on his own telling there was nothing natural about it. The same terminology was adopted by Edmund Phelps, who developed a more rigorous version of Friedman's intuitive argument, for which he was awarded the Nobel Memorial Prize in economics in 2006. Another Nobel laureate, William Vickrey, called it "the most vicious euphemism ever coined."[10]

Friedman and Phelps suggested that the beneficial effects of inflation were the product of illusion on the part of workers and employers. By implication, they suggested that their Keynesian colleagues were subject to a more sophisticated form of the same illusion.

Within a few years, Friedman's judgment was vindicated, at least in part. The interpretation of the Phillips curve as a stable trade-off was proved wrong in practice by the emergence of stagflation. Inflation rates rose steadily, reaching double digits by the early 1970s, but there was no corresponding reduction in unemployment.

The simplistic Keynesian interpretation of the Phillips curve was discredited forever. No one in the future would suggest that policymakers could exploit a stable trade-off between unemployment and inflation, except under special conditions. But this idea, dating only from the 1960s, was a late development in Keynesian thought, and its failure did not imply that Keynesian macroeconomics itself was unsound. To banish the

---

[10] Vickrey (1993), 9. These days, most economists prefer to use the acronym NAIRU, which stands for Non-Accelerating Inflation Rate of Unemployment. This acronym was coined by Keynesian economist (and yet another Nobel Prize winner) James Tobin (1980) to make the point that the unemployment rate consistent with stable inflation was neither natural nor necessarily stable.

idea that governments could and should act to stabilize the economy and preserve full employment (or even Friedman's "natural rate") the critique of Keynesianism had to be pushed further.

The New Classical School

Friedman argued that exploitation of the Phillips curve could not work for long, because expectations of inflation would eventually catch up with reality. Experience seems to support this argument, at least once inflation rates are high enough for people to take notice (anything above 5 percent seems to do the trick).

But Friedman's reasonable argument was neither logically watertight nor theoretically elegant enough for the younger generation of free-market economists, who wanted to restore the pre-Keynesian purity of classical macroeconomics, and became known as the New Classical school. Their key idea was to replace Friedman's adaptive model of expectations with what they called "rational expectations," which, in its strongest form, required all participants in an economy to have, in their minds, a complete and accurate model of that economy.[11]

The term *rational expectations* had been coined much earlier, and in a microeconomic context, by John F. Muth. Although Muth had been cautious about possible misinterpretation of the term, the macroeconomic advocates of rational expectation showed no such caution. Having adopted Muth's characterization of rational expectations as "those that agree with the predictions of the relevant economic model," and defined the relevant economic model as their own, New Classical economists happily traded on the implicit assumption that any consumer whose expectations did not match those of the model must be irrational.

One of the first and most extreme applications of the rational expectations idea was put forward in 1974 by Robert Barro.[12] Barro's adoption

---

[11] This model itself had to incorporate rational expectations, a requirement that sometimes led to simple solutions and sometimes to infinite regress.

[12] Then an up-and-coming young professor at the University of Chicago, Barro now makes regular appearances, not only in academic journals and lists of likely candidates for the Nobel Prize in economics, but also in the Op-Ed pages of the *Wall Street Journal*.

of the rational expectations approach was all the more striking because his early work, with Herschel Grossman on the macroeconomics of disequilibrium, was widely seen as the most promising way forward for Keynesian macroeconomics.

Barro drew on the work of the first great formal theorist in economics, David Ricardo.[13] Ricardo observed that, if governments borrow money, say, to finance wartime expenditures, their citizens should anticipate that taxes will eventually have to be increased to repay the debt.

If citizens were perfectly rational, Ricardo noted, they would increase their savings, by an amount equal to the additional government debt, in anticipation of the higher tax burden. So it should make no difference whether the war is financed by current taxation or by debt. Having noted this theoretical equivalence, Ricardo immediately returned to reality with the observation that "the people who paid the taxes never so estimate them, and therefore do not manage their private affairs accordingly."

Barro's big contribution, in an article published in 1974, was to focus on theory rather than reality and suggest that what he called "Ricardian equivalence" actually holds in practice.

Econometric testing strongly rejected the "Ricardian equivalence" hypothesis, that current borrowing by governments would be fully offset by household saving. Some tests suggested that borrowing might result in moderate increases in household saving, but others showed the exact opposite.

Critics pointed out numerous theoretical deficiencies, in addition to Barro's reliance on ultrarational expectations. For example, Barro assumes that households face the same interest rate as governments, which is obviously untrue.

Barro's claim was never widely accepted, even among opponents of Keynesianism. Nevertheless, the Ricardian equivalence hypothesis had a significant effect on the debate within the economics profession. Extreme assumptions about the rationality of consumer decisions, that would

---

[13] A successful speculator, financier, and member of the House of Commons in the early nineteenth century, Ricardo developed the ideas presented in Adam Smith's *Wealth of Nations* into a rigorous body of analysis.

once have been dismissed out of hand, were now treated as the starting point for analysis and debate.[14]

In this way, Barro paved the way for what became known as the rational expectations revolution in macroeconomics. Barro's Ricardian arguments for the claim that Keynesian policies could not possibly work were seen as implausible, but other versions of the same claim were soon produced, and widely accepted.

The result has been called New Classical economics, a body of economic theory which reproduces the classical conclusion that government intervention cannot improve macroeconomic performance and that, in the absence of such intervention, the economy will rapidly adjust to economic shocks, returning quickly to its natural equilibrium position.

Lucas Critique and Rational Expectations

As noted above, the central idea of rational expectations goes back to the early 1960s. Agricultural economists at the time often modeled price cycles in commodity markets as the outcome of lags in the production process. The idea was that a high price for, say, corn, would occur in some season because of, say, a drought or a temporary increase in demand. Farmers would observe the high price of corn and plant a lot of it for the next season. The result would be large crop and a low price. Farmers would therefore plant less corn for the following season and the price would go up again. Eventually, this series of reactions and counter-reactions would bring the price back to the equilibrium level where supply (the amount of corn farmers would like to produce and sell at that price) equaled demand. As represented on the supply-and-demand diagrams economists like to draw, the path of adjustment resembled a cobweb. The name "cobweb diagram" was attached to the model, and has stuck.

Economist John Muth saw a problem. In the cobweb model, farmers expect a high price this season to be maintained next season, and so

---

[14] In politics, the same phenomenon is described by the idea of the "Overton window." The Overton window is the range of positions considered as reasonable enough to be the subject of policy debate. By taking an extreme position, even if it is not widely accepted, a political party or group can shift the Overton window in their preferred direction.

produce high output. But this is a self-defeating prophecy, since the high output means that the price next season will be low. Why, Muth, asked would farmers keep on making such a simple, and costly, mistake?

If farmers based their expectations on their own experience, they would not expect high prices to be maintained. What, then, would they expect? An expectation that high prices are followed by low prices, as occurs in the cobweb model, would be similarly self-defeating.

Muth's answer, both simple and ingenious, was the idea of "rational expectations." The requirement that the price expected by farmers should equal the expected price generated by the model can be incorporated within the model itself, and this requirement closes the circle in which expectations generate prices and vice versa. Muth showed that, with this requirement, the cobweb model could not work. As long as the "shocks" that raise or lower prices in one season are not correlated with the shocks in the next season, the only "rational" expectation for farmers is that the price next season will be the "average" equilibrium price that the model generates in the absence of such shocks. If farmers expect this, they will produce, on average, the supply associated with that price, and, on average, that price will, in fact, emerge.

Muth's work on rational expectations arose from an interaction with Nobel laureate Herb Simon, who was exploring the opposite idea, that economic outcomes could be explained by the fact that people were only boundedly rational. That is, rather than considering every possible contingency and formulating an optimal plan, people make decisions on the basis of simplified views of the world and "rules of thumb."[15]

In 1960, along with Charles C. Holt and Franco Modigliani, Muth and Simon collaborated on a book on inventory management. Rather than formulating a compromise proposal, Muth and Simon each derived sharper versions of their own ideas.

---

[15] Simon's concept of bounded rationality applies even to seemingly sophisticated decision-makers who employ elaborate formal models and powerful computers. Even the most sophisticated model cannot capture more than a tiny part of the complexity of the real world. Modelers must focus on those aspects of a problem they judge to be most relevant. This judgment must be based on heuristics and rules of thumb. So, even if some people are more sophisticated than others, no one is infinitely rational. Since "bounded" just means "not infinite," everyone is boundedly rational.

Fifty years later, the debate between advocates of bounded rationality and of rational expectations is at center stage in macroeconomics. But, for more than a decade, neither of these ideas received much attention. Rational expectations was the first to come to the fore.

In the late 1970s, Robert E. Lucas took Muth's idea and applied it to the macroeconomic debate about inflationary expectations. Friedman had convinced most economists that, if high rates of inflation are maintained long enough, companies and workers will come to expect it and build this expectation into price-setting decisions and wage demands. He suggested a simple adjustment process in which expectations gradually catch up with a change in the inflation rate. That process was sufficient to kill off the idea of a stable trade-off between unemployment and inflation, and to explain how continued high inflation, initially associated with low unemployment, could turn into the "stagflation" of the 1970s.

In Friedman's "adaptive expectations" model, there was a lag between an increase in the rate of inflation and the adjustment of inflationary expectations. That lag left open the possibility that governments could manipulate the Phillips curve trade-off, at least in the short run. Lucas used the idea of rational expectations to close off that possibility. In a rational expectations model, workers and businesses make the best possible estimate of future inflation rates, and therefore cannot be fooled by government policy. Lucas's ideas were developed by Tom Sargent and Neil Wallace into the "policy ineffectiveness proposition."

Lucas developed a more general critique of economic policymaking, using the case of the Phillips curve as an example. His broad point was that there was no general reason to suppose that an empirical relationship observed under one set of policies, like the Phillips curve relationship between unemployment and inflation, would be sustained in the event of a change in policies, which would normally imply a change in expectations.

The Lucas critique works with a range of assumptions about expectations, including Friedman's adaptive expectations, but it is most naturally associated with Lucas's favored rational expectations model. Lucas argued that the only reliable empirical relationships were those derived from the "deep" microeconomic structure of models, in which economic outcomes are the aggregate of decisions by rational individuals, making decisions aimed at pursuing their own goals (in the jargon of economists, maximizing their utility).

The solution, it seemed, was obvious. The Keynesian separation between macroeconomic analysis, based on observed aggregate relationships, and microeconomic analysis, must be abandoned. Instead, macroeconomics must be built up from scratch, on the microeconomic foundations of rational choice and market equilibrium.

Real Business Cycle Theory

The microeconomics-based approach to macroeconomics appealed to large segments of the economics profession, who valued the elegance and apparent precision of microeconomics more than the messy empiricism of macroeconomics. There was, however, an obvious problem. General equilibrium models like those of Walras, Arrow, and Debreu naturally generated a stable, static equilibrium. But the reality that business conditions fluctuate over time could scarcely be denied. So, the problem was posed as one of producing a general equilibrium model in which such fluctuations could arise.

The first attempt, Real Business Cycle theory emerged in the early 1980s as a variant of New Classical economics. The Real Business Cycle literature introduced two big innovations, one theoretical and one technical.

The theoretical innovation was the introduction of "autocorrelated shocks." The standard New Classical story was that the economy moves rapidly back toward full employment equilibrium in response to any shock. Real business cycle advocates recognized the existence of fluctuations in aggregate demand and employment but argued that such fluctuations represent a socially optimal equilibrium response to exogenous shocks such as changes in productivity, the terms of trade, or workers' preference for leisure.

The persistence of recessions was explained using the idea that shocks such as fluctuations in productivity growth are "autocorrelated." That is, if productivity growth is weak in one quarter, it will probably be weak in the next. This autocorrelation drives cycles of strong and weak economic growth. These are called "Real Business Cycles" to convey the idea that they are driven by "real" economic variables rather than by monetary fluctuations.

In technical terms, Real Business Cycle models were typically estimated using a calibration procedure, developed by Finn Kydland and Edward Prescott, in which the parameters of the model were adjusted to give the best possible approximation to the observed mean and variance of relevant economic variables and the correlations between them (sometimes referred to, in the jargon, as "stylized facts"). This procedure differs from the standard approach in which the parameters of a model are estimated using statistical techniques such as regression analysis.

There is no necessary link between these two innovations, and there gradually emerged two streams within the Real Business Cycle literature. In one stream were those concerned to preserve the theoretical claim that the observed business cycle is an optimal outcome, even in the face of data that consistently suggested the opposite.[16] In the other stream were those who adopted the calibration approach to modeling but were willing to introduce nonoptimal market behavior into the model to get a better fit to the stylized facts.

The big exception that was conceded by most Real Business Cycle theorists at the outset was the Great Depression. The implied analysis that the state of scientific knowledge had suddenly gone backward by 30 percent, or that workers throughout the world had suddenly succumbed to an epidemic of laziness was the subject of some well-deserved derision from Keynesians. Initially, the Depression was simply treated as an inexplicable exception by theorists such as Robert Lucas:

> The Great Depression . . . remains a formidable barrier to a completely unbending application of the view that business cycles are all alike. . . . If the Depression continues, in some respects, to defy explanation by existing economic analysis (as I believe it does), perhaps it is gradually succumbing under the Law of Large Numbers. (Lucas 1980, 273, 284)

---

[16] This claim was supported by calculations that seemed to show that recessions weren't really all that socially costly. As will be explained in chapter 5, such calculations are mistaken, to put the point as charitably as possible.

But toward the end of the 1990s, at a time when Real Business Cycle theory had lost the battle for general acceptance, some of its more hard-line advocates tried to tackle the Depression, albeit at the cost of ignoring its most salient features.

First, Real Business Cycle advocates ignored the fact that the Depression was a global event, adopting a single-country focus on the United States. Then, they downplayed the huge downturn in output between 1929 and 1933, focusing instead on the slowness of the subsequent recovery, which they blamed, unsurprisingly, on Franklin D. Roosevelt and the New Deal. The key paper here is by Cole and Ohanian who put particular emphasis on the *National Industrial Recovery Act*. A popular presentation of the hard-line right case against FDR is Amity Shlaes's *The Forgotten Man (2007)*.

There are plenty of difficulties with the critique of the New Deal, and these have been argued at length by Eric Rauchway among others. The more critical problem is that Real Business Cycle theory can't possibly explain the Depression as most people (including most economists) understand it, that is, the crisis and collapse of the global economic system in the years after 1929. Instead, Cole and Ohanian want to change the subject. The whole exercise is rather like an account of the causes of World War II that starts at Yalta.

New Keynesian Macroeconomics

In the wake of their intellectual and political defeats in the 1970s, mainstream Keynesian economists conceded both the long-run validity of Friedman's critique of the Phillips curve and the need, as argued by Lucas, for rigorous microeconomic foundations. "New Keynesian economics" was their response to the demand, from monetarist and New Classical critics, for the provision of a microeconomic foundation for Keynesian macroeconomics.

The research task was seen as one of identifying minimal deviations from the standard microeconomic assumptions that yield Keynesian macroeconomic conclusions, such as the possibility of significant welfare benefits from macroeconomic stabilization. A classic presentation of this argument was put forward by Nobel laureate George Akerlof, in a series of joint papers with his wife Janet Yellen, who later served as chair of President Clinton's Council of Economic Advisers.

Akerlof and Yellen sought to motivate the wage and price "stickiness" that characterized new Keynesian models by arguing that, under conditions of imperfect competition, firms might gain relatively little from adjusting their prices even though the economy as a whole would benefit substantially. Greg Mankiw, who also chaired the Council of Economic Advisers (but during the George W. Bush administration) formalized part of this argument. Mankiw suggested that fixed costs for making a price change, such as the need to print new menus or price lists, inhibit price changes. The effects of price stickiness on equilibrium output might be an order of magnitude larger than the "menu cost" of price changes.

The approach was applied, with some success, to a range of problems that had previously not been modeled formally, including many of the phenomena observed in the lead-up to the Global Financial Crisis, such as asset price bubbles and financial instability generated by speculative "noise trading."

A particularly important contribution was the idea of the financial accelerator, a rigorous version of ideas first put forward by Fisher and by Keynesians such as Harrod and Hicks. Fisher had shown how declining prices could increase the real value of debt, making previously profitable enterprises insolvent, and thereby exacerbating initial shocks. The New Keynesians showed how a shock to demand would result in declining utilization, meaning that firms could meet their production requirements without any additional investment. Thus the initial shock to demand would have an amplified effect on the demand for investment goods. Ben Bernanke and Mark Gertler integrated these ideas with developments in the theory of asymmetric information to produce a model of the financial accelerator.

It would seem, then, that New Keynesian economists should have been well equipped to challenge the triumphalism that prevailed during the Great Moderation. With the explosion in financial sector activity, the development of massive international and domestic imbalances, and the near-miss of the dotcom boom and slump as evidence, New Keynesian analysis should surely have suggested that the global and U.S. economies were in a perilous state.

Yet with few exceptions, New Keynesians went along with the prevailing mood of optimism. Most strikingly, a leading New Keynesian, Ben Bernanke, became the anointed heir of the libertarian Alan Greenspan as chairman of the U.S. Federal Reserve. As we have already seen, it was Bernanke who did more than anyone else to popularize the idea of the Great Moderation.

This result occurred in part because, by the 2000s, the New Keynesian and Real Business Cycle streams of micro-based macroeconomics had begun to merge. The repeated empirical failures of standard RBC models led many users of the calibration techniques pioneered by Kydland and Prescott to incorporate nonclassical features like monopoly and information asymmetries. This "RBC-lite" stream of RBC literature converged with New Keynesianism, which also uses nonclassical tweaks to standard general equilibrium assumptions with the aim of fitting the macro data. As this convergence progressed, New Keynesian theoretical approaches lost their formerly close connection with support for interventionist macroeconomic policy and particularly for the idea that fiscal policy had a role to play.

The saltwater-freshwater distinction continued to be used to distinguish the two schools, but the lines of division were blurred. Many macroeconomists, and particularly those involved in formulating and implementing policy, shifted to an in-between position that might best be described as "brackish."

The resulting merger produced Dynamic Stochastic General Equilibrium modeling. Although there are a variety of DSGE models, they share some family features. As the "general equilibrium" part of the name indicates, they take as their starting point the general equilibrium models developed in the 1950s, by Kenneth Arrow and Gerard Debreu. Arrow and Debreu showed how an equilibrium set of prices could be derived from the interaction of households who rationally optimize their work, leisure, and consumption choices, with firms that maximize their profits in competitive markets.

The classic general equilibrium analysis of Arrow and Debreu dealt with the (admittedly unrealistic) case where there existed complete, perfectly competitive markets for every possible asset and commodity, including "state-contingent" financial assets that allow agents to insure against, or bet on, every possible state of the aggregate economy. In such a model, as in the early Real Business Cycle models, recessions are effectively impossible. Any variation in aggregate output and employment is simply an optimal response to changes in technology, preferences, or external world markets.

DSGE models modified these assumptions by allowing for the possibility that wages and prices might be slow to adjust, and of imbalances between supply and demand, thereby enabling them to reproduce obvious features of the real world, such as recessions.

But, given the requirements for rigorous microeconomic foundations, this process could only be taken a limited distance. It was intellectually challenging, but appropriate within the rules of the game, to model individuals who were not perfectly rational, and markets that were incomplete or imperfectly competitive. The equilibrium conditions derived from these modifications could be compared to those derived from the benchmark case of perfectly competitive general equilibrium.

Olivier Blanchard summarizes the standard DSGE approach using the following, literally poetic, metaphor:

> A macroeconomic article today often follows strict, haiku-like, rules:
> It starts from a general equilibrium structure, in which individuals
> maximize the expected present value of utility, firms maximize their
> value, and markets clear. Then, it introduces a twist, be it an imperfection or the closing of a particular set of markets, and works out
> the general equilibrium implications. It then performs a numerical
> simulation, based on calibration, showing that the model performs
> well. It ends with a welfare assessment. (Blanchard 2008, 27)

Not everyone was impressed. Charles Goodhart, a leading monetary economist, once said of the Dynamic Stochastic General Equilibrium approach: "It excludes everything I am interested in."[17]

---

[17] Attributed by Buiter (2009). Goodhart is famous for his eponymous Law, which states that "any observed statistical regularity will tend to collapse once pressure is placed upon it for control purposes." This observation, which spelt the death knell of the once-popular monetary targeting approach, foreshadowed the more famous Lucas critique of monetary policy.

Blanchard's description brings out the central role of microeconomic foundations in the DSGE framework and illustrates both the strengths and the weaknesses of the approach. On the one hand, as we have seen, DSGE models were able to represent a wide range of economic phenomena, such as unemployment and asset price bubbles, while remaining within the classical general equilibrium framework. On the other hand, precisely because the analysis remained within the general equilibrium framework, it did not allow for the possibility of a breakdown of classical equilibrium, which was precisely what Keynes had sought to capture in his general theory.

The requirement to stay within a step or two of the standard general equilibrium solution yielded obvious benefits of tractability. Since the properties of general equilibrium solutions have been analyzed in detail for decades, modeling "general equilibrium with a twist" is a problem of exactly the right degree of difficulty for academic economists. The problem is hard enough that solving it requires, and exhibits, the skills valued by the profession, but not so hard as to be insoluble, or soluble only by abandoning the framework of individual maximization.

DSGE macroeconomics of the kind described by Blanchard was ideally suited to the theoretical, ideological, and policy needs of the Great Moderation. On the one hand, unlike New Classical theory, it justified a significant role for monetary policy, a conclusion in line with the actual policy practice of the period. On the other hand, by remaining within the general equilibrium framework, DSGE modelers implicitly supported the central empirical inference drawn from the observed decline in the volatility of GDP, namely that major macroeconomic fluctuations were a thing of the past.

Reflecting their origins in the 1990s, most analysis using DSGE models assumed that macroeconomic management was the province of central banks using interest rate policy (typically the setting of the rate at which the central bank would lend to commercial banks) as their sole management instrument. The central bank was modeled as following either an inflation target (the announced policy of most central banks) or a "Taylor rule" (discussed below), in which the aim is to stabilize both GDP growth and inflation.

Central banks showed some interest in DSGE models, tested them out in their research departments, and invoked their findings to provide a theoretical basis for their operations. But they made little use of them in the actual operations of economic management. For practical purposes, most central banks continued to rely on older-style macroeconomic models, with less appealing theoretical characteristics, but better predictive performance. By the middle years of the decade, it finally seemed as if DSGE models might be ready to take their place as policy tools. Sadly, neither DSGE models nor their older counterparts proved to be of any real use in predicting the crisis that overwhelmed the global economy in 2008, or in guiding the debate about how to respond to that crisis.

By early 2008, just as the U.S. economy was entering the recession that became the Global Financial Crisis, the creators of the DSGE synthesis were ready to declare "Peace in Our Time," holding a conference on Convergence in Macroeconomics. The tone was set by Michael Woodford who said, "The current moment is one in which prospects are unusually bright for the sort of progress that has lasting consequences, due to the increased possibility of productive dialogue between theory and empirical work, on the one hand, and between theory and practice, on the other."[18]

Considering this event in retrospect, Paul Krugman concluded that economists, as a group, had mistaken beauty, clad in impressive-looking mathematics, for truth. The work described by Blanchard was beautiful (at least to economists) and illuminated some aspects of the truth, but beauty came first. An approach based on putting truth first would have incorporated multiple deviations from the standard general equilibrium model then attempted to work out how they fitted together. In many cases, the only way of doing this would be to incorporate *ad hoc* descriptions of aggregate relationships that fitted observed outcomes, even if it could not be related directly to individual optimization.

A critical implication of Blanchard's haiku metaphor is that the DSGE approach had failed to generate a truly progressive scientific research program.[19] A new project in the DSGE framework will typically,

---

[18] For Woodford quote, see Woodford (2009), 19.

[19] Here I'm using the term *progressive*, not in a political sense, but in the language of philosopher of science Imre Lakatos. A progressive research program is one that expands, over time, the range of phenomena it can explain and predict. The opposite, a "degenerating" research program, is one that "explains away" anomalies. The DSGE program is somewhere between the two.

as Blanchard indicates, begin with the standard general equilibrium model, disregarding the modifications made to that model in previous work examining other ways in which the real economy deviated from the modeled ideal.

By contrast, a scientifically progressive program would require a cumulative approach, in which empirically valid adjustments to the optimal general equilibrium framework were incorporated into the standard model taken as the starting point for research. Such an approach would imply the development of a model that moved steadily further and further away from the standard general equilibrium framework, and therefore became less and less amenable to the standard techniques of analysis associated with that model.

LIFE: RATIONALITY AND THE REPRESENTATIVE AGENT

While it lived, the micro-based approach to macroeconomics that culminated in DSGE profoundly influenced the way in which economists thought about economic systems. Even after the comprehensive failure of DSGE models in the Global Financial Crisis, those patterns of thought remain largely unchanged. Such is the power of zombie ideas.

Rationality Everywhere

The incorporation of rational expectations into micro-based macroeconomic models went hand in hand with the acceptance of increasingly strong forms of the Efficient Markets Hypothesis, and both fitted naturally with the rise of market liberalism. In competitive markets where participants are perfectly rational and display high levels of foresight, it is very hard to see any beneficial role for governments, and the interventionist policies to which they are prone.[20] As my colleague Paul Frijters

---

[20] The sole exception is the use of tax and income transfer policies to redistribute wealth. According to one of the most famous results in general equilibrium theory, the "second welfare theorem," any potentially socially optimal outcome can be achieved as a competitive equilibrium, given the right initial allocation of wealth.

has observed, these models take the view that "everyone is rational, except policymakers."

Even if governments are better informed than market participants, they should not, in a world of perfect rationality, act on that information. Rather, they should release the information to the public, allowing market participants to combine this public information with their own private information and secure better outcomes than would be possible from government action.

Of course, many macroeconomists, and particularly those of the New Keynesian school, explicitly rejected the ultrarational assumptions that produced such implausible conclusions as Barro's Ricardian equivalence. One of the standard moves in the construction of Blanchard's haikus was to allow the "representative individual" to deviate in some small way from perfect rationality.

A common example is the assumption of "hyperbolic" discounting, discussed in chapter 2. Liam Graham and Dennis Snower showed that the combination of staggered nominal contracts with hyperbolic discounting leads to inflation having significant long-run effects on real variables, that is, to the existence of a Phillips curve relationship that might persist into the long term.

Research in this tradition has shown that small deviations from rationality can sometimes have big effects on economic outcomes. But these deviations rarely have big implications for public policy. Rather, they point in the direction of the idea set out by Richard Thaler and Cass Sunstein in their recent book *Nudge*. Thaler and Sunstein argue that governments can sometimes exploit deviations from rationality by framing choices that will "nudge" people's decisions in a socially desirable direction.[21]

Such tweaks doubtless have their place, but major macroeconomic problems cannot be dealt with using the intellectual equivalent of optical

---

[21] George Lakoff in *Don't Think of An Elephant* makes the same argument in a political context, suggesting that the Republican Party has had more success than would be expected based on underlying support for its policies, because it has done a better job of "framing" political issues. Rather than seeking a more rational debate, Lakoff argues, Democrats should respond in kind.

illusions. The limits on rational calculation are more fundamental than this. Even sophisticated and rational decision-makers, who are perfectly capable of avoiding the inconsistencies of hyperbolic discounting, cannot consider and evaluate every possibility.

It follows that markets cannot evaluate and price every possible risk, and that, given a sufficiently large accumulation of risk, market systems of insurance will fail. The alternatives facing society are either to endure long periods of recession and depression while markets gradually rebuild failed institutions, or to call on government institutions as lenders, insurers, and employers of last resort.

The Representative Agent

One of the odder features of the DSGE modeling approach is that the interactions of hundreds of millions of firms, workers, and households, producing and consuming tens of thousands of different goods and services are commonly modeled using an economy that contains just one "representative" agent, a single good and a couple of productive inputs (labor and capital). The fact that people differ massively in their tastes, wealth, and good or bad economic fortune is assumed away on the basis that all these differences should cancel out in aggregate.

Critics of the representative agent approach have focused on the fact that, while representative agent models typically display a unique equilibrium point where aggregate demand equals aggregate supply, this uniqueness property cannot be guaranteed to hold more generally. A well-known result derived in the 1970s, and referred to as the Sonnenschein-Mantel-Debreu theorem shows that, in models with many different kinds of agents, there is no guarantee of the existence of a meaningful notion of aggregate demand.

This result, which arises from the fact that changes in prices change the relative wealth of agents with different preferences and asset holdings, means that the uniqueness of general equilibrium can't be assured in general. The Sonnenschein-Mantel-Debreu result is a big problem for theorists, but it's less clear what, if any implications, it has for macroeconomic policy.

A more immediate implication of the representative agent approach, which emerges both in macroeconomics and in discussions of the equity premium puzzle (see chapter 5) is that macroeconomics doesn't matter very much. A deep recession might reduce aggregate labor income by, say 10 percent. In a representative agent model, that translates into a 10 percent loss of labor income for every individual, which is relatively modest in comparison to the year-to-year fluctuations experienced by the average household.

In reality, however, there is no such thing as a representative agent who experiences this average loss. The 10 percent loss of labor income in a deep recession is manifested as a near-total loss of labor market income for the 10 percent of workers who lose their jobs, while those who keep their jobs are largely unaffected, except to the extent that their working hours are reduced.

Used with care, representative agent models can simplify macroeconomic analysis, allowing a focus on aggregate features of the economy, where individual differences cancel out. Unfortunately, careful attention to the limitations of simplified models has not been the norm in the era of market liberalism. The misuse of representative agent models is most obvious in the widespread acceptance of Robert Lucas's claim that recessions are not really a problem—a claim that no one who has experienced the sharp end of a recession would accept for a moment.

Fiscal and Monetary Policy

The theoretical complacency with which the DSGE school viewed the state of macroeconomic theory was matched by a similar complacency regarding macroeconomic policy. From the early 1990s to the panic of 2008, macroeconomic policy was, for all practical purposes, monetary policy, or more precisely, interest rate policy.

The standard approach involved the "Taylor rule," which was briefly discussed in chapter 1, and which was named after economist John Taylor. Taylor presented his rule as a way of describing the actual behavior of central banks, but it soon came to be used as a normative guide to policy.

The idea of the Taylor rule was to set interest rates in such a way as to keep two variables, the inflation rate and the rate of growth of gross domestic product, as close as possible to their target values. Typical targets might be an inflation rate of 2 to 3 percent, and a real GDP growth rate of 3 percent, in line with long-term growth in the labor force and labor productivity.

Within this framework, the essential functions of macroeconomic theory are relatively simple. Complex macroeconomic models can be reduced to simple relationships between one policy instrument (interest rates) and two targets (inflation and real GDP growth). Since there are two target variables, it's impossible to hit each target exactly, so the models give rise to a trade-off. Using the single representative agent who typically inhabits a DSGE model, it's possible to calculate the optimal trade-off, which can be expressed as the range of acceptable variation in inflation rates.

During the Great Moderation, all this seemed to work very well, to the extent that commentators spoke of a "Goldilocks economy," neither too hot, nor too cold but just right. Even with a tight target range for inflation, between 2 and 3 percent per year, it seemed possible to stabilize growth and avoid all but the mildest recessions. In these circumstances, the comment of Robert Lucas in 2003 that the "central problem of depression-prevention has been solved," seemed only reasonable.

DEATH: HOW DID ECONOMISTS GET IT SO WRONG?

As with the other ideas discussed in this book, the project of securing neoclassical micro-foundations for macroeconomics did not die, all at once, with the emergence of the Global Financial Crisis. The most ambitious form of the project, New Classical macroeconomics, was also the first to fail, and did so as soon as its policy prescriptions were put into effect in Britain and New Zealand. The Real Business Cycle version lasted a little longer but was unable to accommodate the empirical evidence.

By the 1990s, even the natural rate of unemployment idea, or NAIRU, was shown to be inconsistent with the evidence. Unemployment rates displayed much the same kind of persistence as had been observed with inflation in the 1970s, giving rise to a large literature on the concept of "hysteresis."

Despite these setbacks, the DSGE project was not abandoned, and a high degree of consensus was attained. The problems of New Classical economics were not seen as fundamental setbacks to the idea of basing macroeconomics on the microeconomic foundations of general equilibrium theory.

On the contrary, the need to adjust the simple (or simplistic) New Classical economics to better approximate real-world outcomes was part of the process of convergence celebrated by such leading macroeconomists as Blanchard and Woodford. The opposition between the freshwater and saltwater schools seemed to be on the verge of resolution.

By the eve of the Global Financial Crisis, the DSGE approach seemed to have conquered all rivals and to represent the future of macroeconomic theory. The crisis, and the failure of mainstream macroeconomics to offer a successful prediction, useful diagnosis, or coherent responses to this event, shattered the DSGE consensus.

The Policy Failure of New Classical Economics in the 1980s

The first government to adopt New Classical economics as the basis of macroeconomic policy was that of Margaret Thatcher in the United Kingdom. Thatcher took office after a decade of high inflation, and at a time when the framework of monetary policy was based on Friedman's "monetarist" model, in which inflation was determined, in the long run, by the rate of growth of the money supply.

The standard policy prescription was to reduce the rate of growth of the money supply, and therefore the rate of inflation, gradually over time. This prescription required governments to accept a rate of unemployment above the NAIRU (the rate at which inflation would neither accelerate nor decelerate) for a long period: as it turned out, a decade or more in many cases.

The New Classical school, championed by Thatcher's favorite macroeconomist, Patrick Minford, offered a short cut. Provided that governments announced in advance that they would reduce the growth of the money supply to a rate consistent with low inflation, and made credible commitments not to back down, businesses and workers would rationally adjust their expectations and inflation would fall quickly, without the need for a long period of high unemployment. The paradox that, according to the model, a willingness to endure economic pain would render such endurance unnecessary was pointed out by critics at the time. But a taste for paradoxical reasoning is common among economists, to the point where it is a job requirement in some circles.

The only requirement for the New Classical prescription to work was the credibility of the government's commitment. Thatcher had credible commitment in bucketloads: indeed, even more than an ideological commitment to free-market ideas, credible commitment was the defining feature of her approach to politics. Aphorisms like "the lady's not for turning" and "there is no alternative" (which produced the acronymic nickname TINA) were characteristic of Thatcher's "conviction" politics. The slogan "No U-turns" could be regarded as independent of the particular direction in which she was driving. In a real sense, Thatcher's ultimate political commitment was to commitment itself.

So, if New Classical economics was ever going to work it should have done so in Thatcher's Britain. In fact, however, unemployment rose sharply, reaching 3 million and remained high for years, just as both Keynesians and monetarists expected. New Classical economics, having failed its first big policy test, dropped out of sight, reviving only in opposition to the stimulus proposals of the Obama administration.

However, Thatcher did not pay a political price for this policy failure, either at the time (the Falklands war diverted attention from the economy) or, so far, in retrospective assessments. The only alternative to the "short sharp shock" was a long, grinding process of reducing inflation rates slowly through years of restrictive fiscal and monetary policy. While it can be argued that the resulting social and economic costs would have been significantly lower, political perceptions were very different. The mass unemployment of Thatcher's early years was either blamed directly on her predecessors or seen as the necessary price of reversing chronic decline.

New Classical ideas got another run in New Zealand, with similar results. Cuts in the growth rate of the money supply were accompanied by radical market-oriented reforms aimed at increasing the flexibility with which the economy could adjust. But, when the policies were finally abandoned fifteen years later, assessments were much less favorable. Not only had New Zealand experienced a series of severe recessions, but it fallen far behind the international pack in terms of economic growth.

The comparison with Australia, which has a similar economic structure and suffered many of the same shocks is particularly striking. The two countries had grown roughly in parallel throughout the twentieth century until their paths diverged in the 1980s. New Zealand adopted a "crash through or crash" approach to reform. Australia opted for less radical reforms and less restrictive macroeconomic policies. By 2000, when New Zealand finally abandoned radical reform, income per person was one-third less than Australia's, a gap that has been narrowed only marginally since then.

After these failures New Classical economists moderated their claims, at least in public. Extreme claims that macroeconomic policy could never be effective were dropped, and the standard public position of "freshwater" economists was close to that of Milton Friedman.

Freshwater economists were skeptical of attempts to "fine-tune" variations in the level of economic activity and supportive of low inflation as the primary goal of macroeconomic management. However, they accepted (or at least, did not seriously challenge) the idea that monetary policy could be a stabilizing factor in the economy. In particular, there was not much criticism of the monetary policy framework of the U.S. Federal Reserve, even though the Lucas critique was just as applicable to a system of monetary policy based on regular adjustments of interest rates as to attempts to stabilize the economy using fiscal policy.

New Classical economics continued to be taught to undergraduate and graduate students in freshwater schools, and to be debated in academic journal articles. As far as serious discussion of monetary policy was concerned, however, the failures of the 1980s discredited the New Classical school, seemingly forever. Whatever Real Business Cycle models might say about the optimality of economic cycles and the impossibility of macroeconomic stabilization through monetary policy, central banks were not willing to sit back and let the business cycle take its course.

Hysteresis

The experience of the 1970s showed, fairly convincingly, the strength of Friedman's argument that, since inflationary expectations would eventually catch up with the actual rate of inflation, there could be no long-run trade-off between unemployment and inflation. Thirty years later, this conclusion remains largely intact, at least for inflation rates of more than, say, 2 or 3 percent.[22]

Friedman correctly predicted that any attempt to maintain low unemployment rates by tolerating higher inflation would fail. It seemed reasonable to assume that his theory of the natural rate, or its later incarnation as the NAIRU, had been validated. Econometricians undertook a series of studies aimed at estimating the NAIRU. Given that inflation had accelerated over the course of the 1960s and early 1970s, they concluded, not surprisingly, that the NAIRU was above the current rate. It followed that an increase in unemployment would be necessary if inflation was to be brought back under control.

As monetary policy was tightened, unemployment rose sharply from the early 1970s onwards. Inflation fell from the double-digit levels reached immediately after the oil shock, but then stabilized in a range between 5 and 10 percent in most countries. Since inflation was stable, the Friedman model implied that unemployment should be at or near the NAIRU.

In fact, however, unemployment rates stayed far above any estimate of the NAIRU based on the experience of the 1950s and 1960s. And even at these high unemployment rates, the oil shock of the late 1970s saw renewed increases in inflation rates in many countries.

By the late 1980s, it was clear that the NAIRU was no more stable than the Phillips curve had been. Steady increases in the NAIRU led one cynic to observe that the estimated rate always seemed to be 2 percent higher

---

[22] Inflation targets below 2 percent create more problems. Since price or wage inflation rates are an average of many price and wage changes, maintaining inflation at rates below 2 percent requires some prices and wages to decline in nominal terms. New Zealand adopted a target range of 0–2 percent in the 1990s, but the restrictive policies required to achieve this target produced a series of recessions. The target range was later revised to 1–3 percent.

than the actual rate of unemployment. As a result, macroeconomic advice based on the NAIRU concept always advocated more contractionary policy and higher unemployment.

Economists described this phenomenon using the concept of "hysteresis," borrowed from physics. The original usage of the term refers to the fact that a piece of iron that is brought into a magnetic field retains some magnetization, even after the external magnetic field is removed.

There are several different models of hysteresis. The simplest is that unemployment caused people to lose work skills and thereby become more prone to unemployment in the future. A more complex alternative is that periods of high employment in an economy break down the informal networks of contacts that enable jobseekers to find work and employers to obtain reliable advice on the quality of job applicants. Either way the effect is that, just as long periods of inflation build up inflationary expectations, long periods of high unemployment increase the likelihood of future high unemployment.

The absence of a stable Phillips curve trade-off does not mean, as Friedman argued, that there is a unique "natural rate" of unemployment, consistent with stable inflation. On the contrary, tolerating high unemployment to bring down inflation, as suggested by Friedman's natural rate model, embeds high unemployment through hysteresis effects that can persist for decades.

There is no lack of microeconomic foundations for hysteresis effects. They are, however, difficult to model in terms of the dynamically optimizing representative agents who typically inhabit DSGE models. The existence of hysteresis effects casts doubt on the "Taylor rule" policy recommendations derived from these models, which typically place little direct weight on the goal of reducing unemployment.

The Global Financial Crisis

The obvious criterion of success or failure for a macroeconomic theoretical framework is that it should provide the basis for predicting, understanding, and responding to macroeconomic crises. If that criterion is applied to the current crisis, the DSGE approach to macroeconomics has been a near total failure.

First, during the bubble years the DSGE approach gave little or no warning of the impending crisis. Second, the DSGE approach encouraged a benign view of the developments that gave rise to the crisis such as the growth and globalization of the financial sector and the associated global imbalances. The boosterism of Alan Greenspan was an egregious example, but it was typical of the majority viewpoint.

Third, even as the crisis developed over the course of 2007 and 2008, its seriousness was persistently underestimated. This was exacerbated by the political context in which supporters of the Bush administration sought to deny the existence of a recession in an election year.

Fourth, the consensus apparent during the Great Moderation collapsed with the onset of crisis, revealing that the split between Keynesian and New Classical views had never been resolved, but merely papered over. Instead, the old divergences reemerged. Keynesians abandoned the consensus framework in favor of an Old Keynesian analysis based on the concept of the liquidity trap. In extreme cases of this kind, it was argued, monetary policy reached its limits and fiscal stimulus on a massive scale was required.

On the other side of the freshwater-saltwater divide, hard-line versions of New Classical economics, and restatements of the classical economics of the nineteenth century made a comeback in response to the crisis. This is not because economists of the New Classical school predicted the crisis (most were complacent believers in the Great Moderation) or because they have anything resembling an adequate explanation of it. Rather, it is because only a dogmatic classical perspective provides any coherent basis for opposing large-scale fiscal stimulus.

Finally, the DSGE consensus offered little or no useful guidance on the policy and theoretical issues raised by the crisis. The result is that the public policy debate has been driven mostly by academic economists from outside the DSGE school. Advocacy of policies of fiscal stimulus has come, to a large extent, from economists such as Paul Krugman, Brad DeLong, and Joseph Stiglitz who are not specialists in academic macroeconomics.[23] Rather they work in fields such as economic geography and

---

[23] To be fair, Olivier Blanchard, who is certainly a leading macroeconomist, played a significant role in cementing an international consensus in favor of a coordinated fiscal stimulus

economic development, which requires a historical understanding and are informed by Keynesian views of the economic fluctuations of the past.

On the freshwater side of the debate, the most vigorous criticism of stimulus policies has come from finance theorists like John Cochrane and Eugene Fama, mostly notable as advocates of the Efficient Markets Hypothesis. Arguments on both sides have been couched in terms familiar to economists of 1970 and earlier. Each side accuses the other of holding views that had been refuted by the 1930s.

Meanwhile, governments and international organizations, who actually had to live with the consequences of their choices, overwhelmingly favored Keynesian responses to the crisis. Governments in the United States, Europe, China, and the Asia-Pacific region expanded public expenditure to promote demand and protect jobs. The Organization for Economic Cooperation and Development, the World Bank, and the International Monetary Fund, all traditionally hawkish on the need for fiscal rectitude, strongly supported fiscal stimulus and sought to coordinate international action. As in the public debate, these responses reflected a traditional Keynesian stabilization approach rather than the influence of more sophisticated macroeconomic theories.

The failure of academic specialists in macroeconomics to influence public debate may be traced in part to problems with the micro-foundations approach underlying the DSGE framework. Micro-foundations models take general equilibrium as the starting point. Modest variations of the standard classical assumptions suggest that deviations from classical properties are also likely to be modest. In addition, DSGE models calibrated to the Great Moderation encouraged this assumption, as well as exclusive focus on monetary policy based on Taylor rules, which proved unavailing.

However, the real problem was the broader intellectual climate of market liberalism, in which thinking about macroeconomic issues was conditioned by the assumptions of the Efficient Markets Hypothesis and the apparent lessons of the Great Moderation. Concerns about market imbalances could not easily be reconciled with the implications of the

---

in major economies, but he has done so much more in his role as chief economist of the IMF than as a participant in academic analysis of the problem.

efficient financial markets hypothesis or with the triumphalism of the Great Moderation.

The End of Consensus

The underlying differences between saltwater and freshwater economists reemerged sharply in the wake of the financial crisis. Members of the saltwater school saw the massive scale of the crisis as necessitating a similarly massive policy response. This response began with the reduction of official interest rates to zero, followed by "quantitative easing" (the purchase of financial securities by central banks) and, when monetary policy was exhausted, a return to old-fashioned Keynesian fiscal stimulus on a scale sufficient to offset the collapse of private demand.

The result was that the policy options rapidly dwindled to two: do nothing and wait for the economy to recover on its own; or undertake public expenditure on a massive scale to cushion the impact of the downturn. Elaborate DSGE models offered no insight into this choice. Rather, as economist Gregory Clark acerbically observed:

> The debate about the bank bailout, and the stimulus package, has all revolved around issues that are entirely at the level of Econ 1. What is the multiplier from government spending? Does government spending crowd out private spending? How quickly can you increase government spending? If you got an A in college in Econ 1 you are an expert in this debate: fully an equal of Summers and Geithner.
>
> The bailout debate has also been conducted in terms that would be quite familiar to economists in the 1920s and 1930s. There has essentially been no advance in our knowledge in 80 years. (Clark 2009)

From the Keynesian viewpoint, the financial crisis exposed the limitations of monetary policy in the face of the conditions described by Keynes as a "liquidity trap." By late 2008, the Federal Reserve and the Bank of England had cut interest rates to zero, a step that would normally be expected to lead to an expansion of lending and investment. But there were few willing lenders. Worse, with consumer prices falling, borrowing even at zero interest was not so appealing. Borrowers would have to repay their loans with money that had increased in purchasing power as prices fell. The next step was "quantitative easing," that is, purchasing financial assets directly from banks and other financial institutions. This helped to stabilize the financial system but did little to promote new lending or to stimulate the economy.

As a result, leading members of the freshwater school were faced with a situation where the only feasible stabilization policy was massive fiscal stimulus, and where the apparent theoretical advances of the 1970s and 1980s had proved useless. In particular, the failure of Real Business Cycle theory was brought into sharp relief by the current global crisis.[24]

The difficulties faced by the freshwater school are illustrated by debates over the multiplier effects of public spending. In the consensus years, freshwater economists had generally played down the extreme claims made in the 1970s, that fiscal policy was totally ineffective, in favor of the more plausible argument that it was less effective than Keynesians claimed. If the multiplier impact of fiscal policy is small, then, in normal circumstances, it makes sense to rely on monetary policy rather than fiscal policy. But, with monetary policy already exhausted, the argument is turned around. If there is no choice but to rely on fiscal policy, then the smaller the multiplier, the larger the fiscal stimulus that is needed to offset any given shock.

Some freshwater economists, such as Martin Feldstein, accepted the need for Keynesian stimulus. Others sought refuge in silence. But a significant group reverted to an extreme classical position and the claim that Keynesianism had been not merely qualified but utterly refuted by the events of the 1970s. In the wake of the crisis, there has been a rush back to hard-line New Classical views, and even further back, to nineteenth century ideas like Say's law.

The Failure of New Keynesian Macro

The failure of the Real Business Cycle theory, and the economists who worked in this tradition, to predict or respond adequately to the Global

---

[24] The suggestion, often heard in the early months of the crisis, that it was all the fault of a minor piece of anti-redlining law (the Community Reinvestment Act) has been abandoned as the speculative excesses and outright corruption of the central institutions of Wall Street has come to light.

Financial Crisis was, in the end, unsurprising. The whole point of Real Business Cycle theory was to say that such things should not happen and that, leaving aside the special and anomalous case of the Great Depression, could not be shown to happen in reality.[25] Willem Buiter summarized this viewpoint well:

> Most mainstream macroeconomic theoretical innovations since the 1970s (the New Classical rational expectations revolution associated with such names as Robert E. Lucas Jr., Edward Prescott, Thomas Sargent, Robert Barro etc, and the New Keynesian theorizing of Michael Woodford and many others) have turned out to be self-referential, inward-looking distractions at best. Research tended to be motivated by the internal logic, intellectual sunk capital and aesthetic puzzles of established research programs rather than by a powerful desire to understand how the economy works—let alone how the economy works during times of stress and financial instability. So the economics profession was caught unprepared when the crisis struck. *(Buiter 2009)*

More surprising was the equally complete failure of New Keynesianism. DSGE models of a New Keynesian flavor were of no more use than those derived from the Real Business Cycle. Worse, the sophisticated theoretical ideas of New Keynesianism proved to be largely irrelevant, both in advising policymakers and in informing the general public.

As with most other attachments of the word *New* to left-wing or progressive terms in the 1980s and 1990s (New Democrat and New Labour, for example), New Keynesianism was a defensive adjustment to the dominance of free market ideas such as New Classical macroeconomics, and to the apparent success of a policy regime in which active fiscal policy played a minor role at most.

The New Keynesians sought a theoretical framework that would justify medium-term macroeconomic management based on manipulation

---

[25] Even before the crisis, it was necessary to ignore the fact that such things had happened in Argentina, Indonesia, Russia, and many other countries. Experience outside the OECD was dismissed as the sad result of "crony capitalism," to be contrasted with the transparent and efficient financial systems of the developed world, most perfectly embodied in Wall Street.

of interest rates by central banks, and a fiscal policy that allowed automatic stabilizers to work, against advocates of fixed monetary rules and annual balanced budgets. The central theme of new Keynesianism was the need to respond to the demand, from monetarist and New Classical critics, for the provision of a microeconomic foundation for Keynesian macroeconomics.

But now that both the intellectual foundations and the empirical claims of post-1970s market liberalism have collapsed there is no need for such a defensive stance. The big question for the crisis and its aftermath is how to develop and sustain a Keynesian system of macroeconomic management that can deliver outcomes comparable to those of the Bretton Woods era, while avoiding the excesses and imbalances that brought that system to an end in the 1970s.

New Keynesian macroeconomics has been tested by the current global financial and macroeconomic crisis and has been found wanting. This does not mean a return to the mechanical Keynesian models of the 1950s and 1960s. Rather, we need a newer Keynesianism.

REANIMATION: HOW OBAMA CAUSED
THE GLOBAL FINANCIAL CRISIS

The crucial point in a good zombie movie is the moment when zombies who seem to have been blasted into the next world by the hero's shotgun, pull themselves up from the ground and come shambling forward. In the writing of this book, that moment came for me when I read Casey Mulligan's paper (2009) "Aggregate Implications of Labor Market Distortions: The Recession of 2008–9 and Beyond."

Looking at the way in which Real Business Cycle theorists have tried to write the Great Depression out of macroeconomic history, presenting it instead as a government-induced dislocation of labor markets, it was obvious that, sooner or later, something similar would be attempted with the Global Financial Crisis. But Great Depression revisionism did not take hold until the Depression had faded out of living memory, to the point where hardly any economists who had actually experienced it were still active.

I thought a similar process of fading memory would be required for the Global Financial Crisis. As long as the subprime fiasco and the chaos of late 2008 remained vivid memories, it would be impossible to deny that this was, indeed, a crisis made in the financial markets.

I underestimated the speed and power of Zombie ideas. As early as September 2009, Casey Mulligan was willing to claim that the entire crisis could be explained in terms of labor market interventions. According to Mulligan, financial markets anticipated a variety of measures from the Obama administration, observing

> Arguably, the 2008 election was associated with an increase in the power of unions to shape public policy, and thereby the labor market. Congress has considered various legislation that would raise marginal income tax rates, and would present Americans with new health benefits that would be phased out as a function of income. (Mulligan 2009, 3)

This is truly impressive. So perspicacious are the financial markets, that even the possibility that Congress might raise taxes, or incorporate a means test in health care legislation that might be passed some time in the future (in fact, the legislation passed in March 2010 contained no such means tested benefits) was sufficient to bring down the entire global financial market. And, even though the McCain-Palin ticket was widely seen as having a good chance in mid-2008, the markets didn't wait for the election returns to come in. Rather, on Mulligan's account the financial crisis that guaranteed Obama an easy win was a self-fulfilling prophecy. Applying some superstrong version of market efficiency, market participants predicted the election outcome, applied Mulligan's neoclassical model to the predicted policies of the Obama administration, and (perfectly rationally) panicked, thereby ensuring the accuracy of their own prediction.

There is one problem with Mulligan's neat explanation. Writing in October 2008, when the crisis had already erupted, and when Obama's victory was virtually assured, Mulligan had this to say about proposals for economic stimulus, "So, if you are not employed by the financial industry (94 percent of you are not), don't worry. The current unemployment rate of 6.1 percent is not alarming, and we should reconsider whether it is worth it to spend $700 billion to bring it down to 5.9 percent."[26]

This piece, which got the endorsement of his Chicago colleague, Freakonomist Steven Levitt, doesn't even mention the possibility that a Democratic Congress might raise taxes, or that the health plan that was a central plank of candidate Obama's platform might include a means test. Yet Mulligan now claims that these hypothetical possibilities caused a massive increase in unemployment, the anticipation of which caused the crash!

AFTER THE ZOMBIES: TOWARD A REALISTIC MACROECONOMICS

If the micro-foundations approach underlying DSGE is of little use in understanding the macro-economy, where should we turn. As I observed in the Preface, the best answer has been given by George Akerlof and Bob Shiller, in their book, *Animal Spirits*: "In our view, economic theory should be derived not from the minimal deviations from the system of Adam Smith but rather from the deviations that actually do occur and can be observed.[27]

Animal Spirits was mostly written before, or in the early stages of, the Global Financial Crisis, but the crisis has made its central point more important than ever. For many years economists have worked like the anecdotal drunk who searches for his dropped keys under a lamppost because the light is better there. In the future, and particularly in macroeconomics, economists will need to look where the keys are and build tools that will improve the chances of success.

This does not mean abandoning all the work of the past thirty years and returning to old-style Keynesianism. But it does mean starting from the traditional Keynesian perspective that a general macroeconomic theory must encompass the reality of booms and slumps, and particularly that sustained periods of high unemployment cannot be treated as marginal and temporary deviations from general equilibrium. We must

---

[26] Mulligan (2008).
[27] *Akerlof and Shiller (2009), 5*

model a world where people display multiple and substantial violations of the rationality assumptions of microeconomic theory and where markets depend not only on prices, preferences, and profits but on complicated and poorly understood phenomena like trust and perceived fairness.

First, the program needs more realistic micro-foundations. As Akerlof and Shiller observe, we need to look at how people actually behave, and how this behavior contributes to the performance of the economy as a whole.

Second, we need to reconsider the concept of equilibrium. The whole point of Keynes's *General Theory* was that the market-clearing equilibrium analyzed by the classical economists, and central to DSGE models, was not the only possible stable state. An economy can settle for long periods in a low-output, high-unemployment state that may not meet the neoclassical definition of equilibrium but does match the original concept, borrowed from physics, of a state in which the system tends to remain and to which it tends to return. More importantly, perhaps, we need a theory that encompasses crises and rapid jumps between one kind of equilibrium and another. Ideally this will combine "old Keynesian" analysis of economic imbalances with a Minsky-style focus on financial instability.

Between these two levels, we need to consider the fact that the economy is not a simple machine for aggregating consumer preferences and allocating resources accordingly. The economy is embedded in a complex social structure, and there is a continuous interaction between the economic system and society as a whole. Phenomena like "trust" and "confidence" are primarily social, but they affect, and are affected by, the performance of the economic system.

Finally, now that Keynesian macroeconomic policy has reemerged as a practical tool, we need to reconsider the real and perceived failures of the past, and in particular, the emergence of stagflation in the 1970s. If the revival of Keynesian policy is to be sustained, it must provide not only an emergency response to the present crisis but a set of tools that can deliver sustained noninflationary growth.

Better Micro-foundations?

People are not, and cannot be, the infinitely foresightful, unbounded rational utility maximizers assumed in DSGE models. On the contrary, economic behavior, even that of highly sophisticated actors like the "rocket scientists" who design financial instruments for investment banks, is inevitably driven by a partial view of the world. Heuristics and unconsidered assumptions inevitably play a crucial role. For finite beings in a world of boundless possibilities, nothing else is possible.

The problem for a new macroeconomics is not so much a failure of economists to understand this point. Rather, there is an embarrassment of riches. Several decades of research in behavioral economics, decision theory, and other fields have demonstrated, to anyone willing to look, a wide variety of ways in which real economic behavior differs from the neoclassical ideal. The problem is to focus on behavioral foundations that are most relevant to the problems of macroeconomics.

An obvious place to start is with attitudes toward risk and uncertainty. Keynes himself wrote extensively on this topic and was highly skeptical of the ideas that led to the emergence of the now-dominant expected utility theory. This theory was first formalized in John von Neumann and Oskar Morgenstern's classic *Theory of Games and Economic Behavior*, published in 1944.

The starting point for expected utility was the idea that people can, and should, reason about uncertainty on the basis of their perceived probability of relevant events such as an increase in interest rates or a slump in exports.

By contrast, Keynes argued:

> By "uncertain" knowledge, let me explain, I do not mean merely to
> distinguish what is known for certain from what is only probable.
> The game of roulette is not subject, in this sense, to uncertainty. . . .
> The sense in which I am using the term is that in which the prospect
> of a European war is uncertain, or the price of copper and the rate
> of interest twenty years hence. . . . About these matters there is no
> scientific basis on which to form any calculable probability whatever.
> We simply do not know. (Keynes 1937, 213–14)

Post-Keynesian economists such as Davidson and Shackle argued that this fundamental uncertainty was central to Keynes's thought and that it had been ignored as part of Hicks's development of the Keynesian-neoclassical synthesis. But, as with so many "heterodox" schools of economic thought, the post-Keynesians were much stronger on critique than on the development of a coherent and usable alternative. Shackle in particular ended up denying that we can ever know anything about probability, even in such simple cases as the toss of a coin. Such a nihilistic view was never likely to convince many.

Davidson took the critique in more productive directions and did some valuable work on the way in which attitudes to uncertainty affect individuals' demand to hold money. Attitudes to uncertainty, characterized as "animal spirits," play a crucial role in Keynes's theory of the "liquidity trap," a situation where even at interest rates of zero, investors and households would prefer to save rather than invest.

Mainstream Keynesians, such as James Tobin, argued that liquidity preference could be seen as a reflection of risk attitudes. Tobin pioneered the now-standard approach to financial portfolio analysis, based on the idea that the investment involves trading off mean returns against measures of riskiness such as the variance, which depend on the assumption that we can always formulate sensible probabilities for events. Although Tobin himself was always critical of the irrational behavior of financial markets, his analysis was easily restated in terms of expected utility theory and absorbed into models based on the efficient financial markets hypothesis.

Over the past thirty years, however, a large body of research has shown that people do not always make choices in line with the requirements of expected utility. Various models of choice under uncertainty have been proposed as more realistic representation of behavior. Probably the most famous is the prospect theory of Kahneman and Tversky, put forward in 1979, which earned Kahneman a Nobel Memorial Prize in economics and Tversky a rare posthumous mention.[28]

What specific features of a more general and realistic model of choice under uncertainty might contribute usefully to a renewal of Keynesian macroeconomics? There are at least two obvious examples. First, there is the problem of unknown unknowns, which is also, and not coincidentally,

[28] My own academic career got its start with a paper published a couple of years later, giving a tweak to the idea of probability weighting by showing that the model worked better if low-probability extreme events (large gains and large losses) were overweighted, while events leading to intermediate outcomes were underweighted. Tversky and Kahneman incorporated this idea in a revised version of their original model, called cumulative prospect theory.

a critical problem for the Efficient Markets Hypothesis. An obvious feature of economic crises is that people are forced to consider contingencies they might previously have disregarded, such as the possibility that their employer or their bank might fail, or that currency might rapidly lose its value. When such a contingency suddenly enters the minds of many people, large macroeconomic shocks may result.

Second, as I've already mentioned, although people fail to consider some low-probability extreme contingencies, they tend (perhaps in compensation) to overweight those they do consider. In the macroeconomic context, the "normal" situation is one in which people disregard or at least do not account for the risk of a serious recession. In a crisis, the normal outlook may suddenly be replaced by a far more pessimistic outlook in which the same people place a high weight on the possibility of total economic collapse.

Unsurprisingly, such a change in "animal spirits" may represent a self-fulfilling prophecy. If a lot of people expect a recession and try to increase savings and reduce investment, these defensive actions may bring about the recession against which they are designed to guard.

Of course, awareness of this fact will do nothing to moderate the potential impact; if anything the reverse. People who are suddenly worried about a recession will not, if they are looking to their own well-being, keep spending in the hope that others will do likewise and thereby keep the economy afloat. Rather they will reason that others are likely to think as they do, and that a recession is even more probable than the objective evidence would suggest.

Keynes's idea of "animal spirits" has been revived by George Akerlof and Robert Shiller in their recent book of the same name. Akerlof and Shiller consider five deviations from the standard model of rational maximization (confidence/trust, fairness, corruption, money illusion, and stories) and argue that some combination of these can be used to explain a range of economic outcomes inconsistent with the standard model. Their discussion makes a compelling case that macroeconomics needs new, and more realistic, foundations.

If the prospects for a macroeconomic analysis based on alternatives to expected utility theory are so promising, why has so little work been done along these lines? In part, perhaps, this simply reflects the effects of specialization. Decision theorists focus on individual choices, and when they seek economic applications, this leads them naturally to look at microeconomic problems.

But there is a more fundamental problem. Individuals who satisfy the conditions of expected utility theory display a property called "dynamic consistency" which, as the name suggests, is of fundamental importance in DSGE models. Dynamically consistent economic agents never change their view of the world in any fundamental way. They respond to new information by changing their subjective probabilities for particular events, but they never change their underlying prior beliefs and preferences about the world. That means, in particular, that they can fully anticipate how they will respond to any possible future situation and would never wish to change their mind about this, or to "lock themselves in" to a course of action they might be unwilling to carry through when the time comes.

Such consistency is admirable, at least in the eyes of decision theorists, and makes it much easier to obtain well-defined solutions for DSGE models. Unfortunately, it is far from realistic. It turns out that the decisions predicted by realistic models of choice under uncertainty always display dynamic inconsistency under certain circumstances. This problem has been the subject of considerable controversy on the rare occasions when economists have sought to introduce more realistic risk preferences into macroeconomic theory.

From the neoclassical viewpoint that dominates modern macroeconomics, the absence of a coherent dynamic equilibrium concept seems like a fatal objection. But from a Keynesian perspective, and on the basis of real world experience, this is a positive, indeed necessary, feature of a sensible macroeconomic model. The fundamental macroeconomic problem is precisely that an economy that seems to be enjoying an equilibrium path of steady growth can suddenly crash, or veer off into an unsustainable boom.

Aggregate Models and Equilibrium

If there is one thing that distinguished Keynes's economic analysis from that of his predecessors, it was his rejection of the idea of a unique full employment equilibrium to which a market economy will automatically return when it experiences a shock. Keynes argued that an economy could shift from a full-employment equilibrium to a persistent slump as the result of the interaction between objective macroeconomic variables and the subjective "animal spirits" of investors and other decision-makers. It is this perspective that has been lost in the absorption of New Keynesian macro into the DSGE framework.

Reviving these fundamental Keynesian insights is not simply a matter of modifying the way we model individual behavior. Phenomena like animal spirits, social trust, and business confidence can't be reduced to individual psychology. They arise from economic and social interactions between people.

These interactions, in turn, are mediated by economic and social institutions. At some level, for example, the subprime mortgage crisis can be explained in terms of the interaction between the social and psychological factors that lead people to assume a boom will continue indefinitely, and the policies of monetary expansion and financial deregulation that generate such a boom. Nevertheless, the details of the process depend on the set of institutions in which specific categories like "subprime borrowers" emerge and in which financial institutions based on packaging loans for such borrowers can be, at least initially, highly profitable. Different institutional structures will produce different outcomes.

It's precisely for this reason that such social aspects of individual psychology are likely to be associated with multiple equilibria in the real economy. The aggregate level of trust and confidence in an economy cannot be derived by simply adding up individual values in the way in which DSGE models aggregate consumer preferences.

As long as particular assumptions are implicitly taken for granted in a given social group, such as the business community, few members of that group are likely to consider the possibility that these assumptions might fail. Evidence against those assumptions will be ignored or explained away. For example, the spectacular examples of market irrationality and business corruption exhibited during the dotcom boom and bust did almost nothing to shake the faith of business and political leaders in the efficiency and stability of financial markets.

This faith remained strong even as the evidence of fundamental problems grew through 2007 and early 2008. Then, in the space of a few months this confidence collapsed to be replaced by a panic in which even the most reputable financial institutions would not lend to each other, and instead threw themselves on the protection of the national governments they had previously dismissed as obsolete relics.

A realistic macroeconomics requires the incorporation of variables like trust and confidence in explanatory models. Fluctuations between "irrational exuberance" and equally irrational "panics" (this old term for a financial crisis is in many ways more useful than the technical language of "recessions") give rise to bubbles and busts, which in turn drive much of the macroeconomic cycle.

The insights of behavioral economics provide good reasons to expect such fluctuations. Unfortunately, they do not, at least as yet, admit the kind of rigorous derivation of aggregate values from individual preferences that is referred to in the standard demand for "micro-foundations."

Expressed in the language of systems theory, the traditional Keynesian approach treated macroeconomic behavior as an emergent property of the economic system, to be analyzed in its own terms rather than being derived from supposedly more "fundamental" microeconomic explanations.[29] In a world of boundedly rational economic decision-makers, and, for that matter, boundedly rational economists, we need to simplify. The simplifications that are appropriate for macroeconomics may not be the same as those that are appropriate in microeconomics.

It's much easier to announce a new program for macroeconomics than to actually implement it. To give some more concreteness to the general proposals presented here, it's worth thinking about some specific problems, such as bubbles and the "Minsky moments" in which they burst.

---

[29] Unfortunately, discussion of these ideas tends to get bound up in more or less mystical claims and counterclaims about reductionism and holism. But nothing of that kind is intended here. In principle, without doubt, all social phenomena are determined by interactions between individual people, whose behavior is in turned determined by their genes and the environment in which they grew up. Genes are collections of DNA molecules, which in turn are made up of atoms made up of subatomic particles behaving according to the laws of quantum physics. If we were the unboundedly rational individuals posited in the DSGE literature, we would presumably be doing quantum physical calculations whenever we made economic decisions.

Bubbles and Minsky Moments

Macroeconomists working in the micro-economic foundations framework did not ignore bubbles. Far from it. Dozens of papers were written on the possibility or otherwise of self-sustaining bubbles in asset markets. But, characteristically, the central concern was to determine whether or not bubbles could arise in markets with market participants who were perfectly rational, or nearly so. This focus on microeconomic foundations diverted attention from the real issues.

There was a smaller policy-oriented literature, concerned with the question of whether central banks should intervene to prevent the emergence of bubbles, or to burst them early, before they became too damaging. Most of this literature followed the lead of Alan Greenspan, who initially showed some sympathy for the idea of intervention but eventually became the strongest advocate of the view that central banks should not second-guess markets. Even interventionist participants in the discussion took it for granted that an antibubble policy had to be implemented within a policy framework of inflation targeting using interest rates as the sole policy instrument. With these constraints, the conclusion that nothing could or should be done was largely inevitable.

A realistic theory of bubbles would start with the observation that every bubble has a story to explain why, in the words of Carmen Reinhart and Kenneth S. Rogoff, "this time is different."[30] For particular assets and markets, sometimes it is different. Those who got in early with land in Manhattan, or shares in Microsoft or Google multiplied their money many times over. And although the days of spectacular growth came to an end, there was no bursting of the bubble ending in losses all around.

A theory of bubbles designed to inform a policy of bubble-pricking must begin with an attempt to understand how "this time it's different" stories emerge and come to be believed and how to distinguish true, or at least plausible, stories from those that involve a collective abandonment of reality. The story-telling aspect of animal spirits, discussed by Akerlof and Shiller, is important here.

---

[30] Quote in Reinhart and Rogoff (2009).

Given a better understanding of bubbles it may be possible to develop an analysis of the costs and benefits of pricking putative bubbles. Such a policy reduces the damage from spectacular busts such as the one we have just seen, but it would require a willingness on the part of central banks to explicitly override the judgments of capital markets, rather than merely "leaning against the wind" by raising interest rates. An uncontrolled bubble must eventually burst. The bursting of a bubble is a prime example of a "Minsky moment," when euphoria suddenly turns to panic.

Avoiding Stagflation

The Keynesian Golden Age ended in the stagflation of the 1970s. The causes of this breakdown are many and complex, but they must be addressed if we are to avoid repeating them. In particular, it is important to avoid relying on easy excuses, such as the 1973 oil shock and to face the fact that the emergence of stagflation reflected serious failures in the dominant version of Keynesian macro theories, and in the political and industrial strategies of the social democratic, left, and labor movements.

Stagflation was seen as a demonstration that attempts to resist the logic of the market must ultimately fail. It took several decades to relearn the Keynesian lesson that an uncontrolled financial system will fail even more disastrously.

The inflationary surge that began in the late 1960s raises some important lessons that must be learned if we are to avoid similar failures in the future. First, it is important to maintain a focus on keeping inflation rates low and stable as well as on maintaining full employment. Once inflation rates get significantly above 3 or 4 percent per year, the risk of embedding inflationary expectations, and the eventual cost of lowering those expectations, becomes greater. It is, therefore, important to maintain a commitment to low inflation and to adopt the policies necessary to contain and reduce inflation when some shock to the system produces a significant increase in the price level.

At a theoretical level, this does not involve fundamental modifications to the standard Keynesian view. The idea of a stable long-run trade-off between unemployment and inflation, represented by the Phillips curve, was a relatively late addition and quickly abandoned. But the problem of how to deal with inflation remains largely unresolved.

In policy terms, inflation can't be reduced unless macroeconomic policy constrains excess demand and liquidity. So, Keynesian policies must be used consistently throughout the cycle, to reduce excess demand in boom periods as well as stimulating demand during recessions.

This still leaves the problem of what to do if high inflation becomes established. A number of countries showed, in the 1980s and 1990s, that a cooperative approach could reduce inflation and unemployment simultaneously. In Australia, following a deep recession in the early 1980s, the newly elected Hawke Labor government reached an agreement with the trade unions referred to as "the Accord." Under the Accord, unions agreed to reduce the rate of growth of wages in return for an increase in the social wage, most notably the introduction of a national system of health insurance, called Medicare.

At about the same time, and facing similar problems, unions and employer groups in the Netherlands negotiated the Wassenaar agreement. In this case, the trade-off for wage moderation was a reduction in working hours and the adoption of a range of measures designed to promote employment growth. The Wassenaar approach survived the stresses of the early 1990s and, according to the International Labor Organization was "a ground breaking agreement, setting the tone for later social pacts in many European countries."

The cooperative approach that motivated these policies was ultimately swept away by the ever-growing power of the financial sector. But, if a Keynesian policy framework is to be successful, it must be revived. Hopefully, the memory of past disasters will promote a more cautious and cooperative approach in future.

FURTHER READING

Keynes (1936) *General Theory* is well worth reading to get a feeling for his way of thinking, which later elaborations, starting with Hicks (1937) have clarified in some ways, but obscured in others. The model was further elaborated in *How to Pay for the War* (Keynes 1940). A good presentation of the Keynesian model at the height of its success can be found in older editions of Samuelson's famous textbook, beginning with Samuelson (1948). The latest edition, Samuelson and Nordhaus (2009) represents a broadly "saltwater" view of macroeconomics, pitched at a fairly elementary level. Krugman (1998) presents the story of the babysitting co-op, originally told by Sweeney and Sweeney (1977).

For a flavor of the very different approach embodied in most general equilibrium theory, abstract and mathematically rigorous but largely unconcerned with realism, Debreu's (1959) *Theory of Value* is a good starting point. Marglin and Schor (1990) examine the postwar Golden Age, from a mostly U.S. perspective. Sassoon's (1998) history of European socialism and social democracy is particularly good on the "trente glorieuses" and the "social democratic moment" just before the crisis of the 1970s. Helleiner (1996) gives an excellent account of the Bretton Woods system and its breakdown.

The original Phillips curve was presented in Phillips (1958). The idea that the Phillips curve presented a menu of policy choices was put forward (with some qualifications) by Samuelson and Solow (1960). The term "hydraulic Keynesianism" is apparently due to Coddington (1976). The classic statements of the expectations-based critique of the Phillips curve menu are those of Friedman (1968) and Phelps (1968). The classic work on rational expectations is Muth (1961). Barro's (1974) extreme but influential application of rational expectations ideas paved the way for widespread acceptance of the arguments of Lucas (1976, 1977) and Sargent and Wallace (1976) that Keynesian economics must be abandoned in favor of models based on standard microeconomic foundations.

The Real Business Cycle literature developed in response to this policy agenda starts with Kydland and Prescott (1982) and Long and Plosser (1983). Plosser (1989) gives a summary of the program, conveying the initial optimism of the Real Business Cycle school.

Akerlof and Yellen (1985a, b) provide examples of the early New Keynesian approach. Akerlof's (2001) Nobel lecture gives an excellent summary of the New Keynesian approach, which was largely repudiated later in Akerlof and Shiller (2009). As regards the seemingly successful Dynamic Stochastic General Equilibrium convergence, Woodford (2009) is a classic example of a badly timed declaration of victory, as is Blanchard (2008), to whom is due the "haiku" characterization of modern macroeconomics. Willem Buiter's (2009) counterblast is well worth reading and is the source for the quoted statement by Goodhart.

References for the rationality assumptions are Thaler and Sunstein (2009) and Lakoff (2004). The Taylor rule was first presented in Taylor (1993). The phrase "Goldilocks economy" is attributed to Shulman (1992).

The idea that credibility was critical to an effective anti-inflation policy based on rational expectations was put forward by Fellner (1979). Buiter and Miller (1981) were among the first to point out the failure of New Classical economics and rational expectations theories in the Thatcher experiment. Hazeldine and Quiggin (2006) describe the failure of the radical reforms undertaken in New

Zealand, particularly as compared to Australia. The concept of hysteresis was applied to unemployment by Strebel (1980) and popularized by Blanchard and Summers (1986).

The volume of articles, books, and blog posts about the Global Financial Crisis is far too great to summarize. For the purposes of this book, the important references are those discussing (or denying) the failures of the dominant schools of economic thought. Krugman (2009a) is essential reading. Other important critical views are those of DeLong (2009a) (2010) and Stiglitz (2010). The most notable response is that of Cochrane (2009). Fama (2009) presents the case against fiscal stimulus as a response. Mulligan's (2008) denial of the impending crisis, endorsed at the time by Levitt (2008), makes a striking contrast with Mulligan (2009), as is noted by DeLong (2009b).

What next? Minsky (1975, 1982, 1986) is essential reading. Turning to microfoundations, as mentioned previously, the crucial journal articles on prospect theory and probability weighting are Kahneman and Tversky (1979), Quiggin (1982), and Tversky and Kahneman (1992). Books include Quiggin (1993) and Wakker (2010). A notable application to macroeconomic theory is the robust control theory of Hansen and Sargent (2001). The critique in terms of dynamic inconsistency is presented by Epstein and Schneider (2003).

Other references are Arrow and Debreu (1954), Barro and Grossman (1976), Bernanke and Gertler (1999), Clark (1932), Cole and Ohanian (2004), Davidson (1991), Graham and Snower (2007), Hall (1976), Harcourt (1881), Harrod (1936), Hayek (1933), Holt, Modigliani, Muth, and Simon (1960), Keynes (1940), Kuznets (1934), Lakoff (2004), Mankiw (1985), Minford and Peel (1981), Mises et al. (1996), Muth (1961), Rauchway (2009), Reinhart and Rogoff (2009), Ricardo (1817), Shackle (1952), Shlaes (2007), Solow (1966), Summers (2006), Tobin (1958), von Neumann and Morgenstern (1944), and Walras (1954).

TRICKLE-DOWN ECONOMICS

The money was all appropriated for the top in the hopes that it would trickle down to the needy. Mr. Hoover didn't know that money trickled *up*. Give it to the people at the bottom and the people at the top will have it before night, anyhow. But it will at least have passed through the poor fellow's hands.
   —WILL ROGERS, *quoted at democrats.com*

As long as there have been rich and poor people, or powerful and powerless people, there have been advocates to explain that it's better for everyone if things stay that way.

The hymn "All Things Bright and Beautiful," one of the favorites in the hymnbook of my youth is, for the most part, a paean to the beauties of creation. Sadly, the real message comes in the verse, "The rich man in his castle, the poor man at his gate, God made them high and lowly, and ordered their estate." The same message is contained in several of Aesop's fables, such as the one about the tail of the snake that foolishly rebelled against its natural master, the head, with dire consequences.

By contrast, many of the greatest economists, including Adam Smith, John Stuart Mill, and John Maynard Keynes have supported income redistribution through progressive taxation, and the great majority of economists do so today. Nevertheless, there has always been a plentiful supply of economists and others willing to argue that we should let the rich get richer, and wait for the benefits to trickle down to the poor.

This idea seemed to be dead in the years after 1945, when a massive reduction in inequality went hand in hand with full employment and prosperity. The outcome, unique in history, was a society that was overwhelmingly middle-class in terms of living standards. The Marxist critique of capitalism, still issued regularly by Soviet propagandists, came to seem quaint and old-fashioned.

As inequality returned in the 1980s, so did its intellectual defenders. Advocates of lower taxes on the rich argued that, sooner or later, everyone would be better off if their policies were adopted. For a while, their promises seemed on the verge of fulfillment, as most people seemed to get some share in the prosperity of the 1990s. The failure of this promise in the 2000s has been accompanied by the death of most of the theoretical ideas that supported it. But, as with the other ideas discussed in this book, trickle-down economics lingers on in zombie form.

Like most labels, "trickle-down" is a pejorative term, used mainly by critics.[1] The "trickle-down" idea has been summed up, more positively, in the aphorism "a rising tide lifts all boats" attributed to John F. Kennedy, and a favorite of Clinton advisers such as Gene Sperling and Robert Rubin.[2]

One important version of "trickle-down" economics is the "supply-side" school of economics, which came to prominence in the 1980s. The extreme claims made by some supply-siders, summed up in the so-called "Laffer curve," threw this school into disrepute. However, more moderate versions of the same claims, referred to by terms such as *dynamic efficiency* and *new tax responsiveness*, were widely accepted during the years of the Great Moderation.

This didn't happen in a vacuum. The renewed popularity of trickle-down economics coincided with a resurgence of the political right, and with financial globalization, which constrained the ability of governments to redistribute income from capital to labor.

It was also, no doubt, influenced by the fact that most economists were among the beneficiaries of this process. That was true, in part, because most economists are in the top 20 percent of the income distribution,

---

[1] Supporters of trickle-down economics return the favor, criticizing advocates of redistribution as "class warriors" who practice the "politics of envy."

[2] This phrase is also used in the context of debates over free trade and over the effects of macroeconomic expansion. While it generally implies that we should focus on expanding aggregate income without too much concern over distribution, it is less sharply focused than the "trickle-down" pejorative.

which received most of the growth in income over this period. More importantly, perhaps, the huge growth in the financial sector, and in the incomes of those who worked there, had a flow-on effect to related professions. For economists, at least, trickle-down really worked.

BIRTH: FROM SUPPLY-SIDE ECONOMICS TO DYNAMIC SCORING

Regardless of nomenclature, the near-universal prosperity of the postwar boom seemed to constitute a refutation of trickle-down economics every bit as decisive as the refutation of pre-Keynesian economics by the disappearance of mass unemployment. Throughout the developed world, the growing prosperity of the years after 1945 was accompanied by reductions in income inequality and a softening of the differences between classes.

The experience of the United States in particular was striking. Emerging as the unchallenged economic leader of the world after 1945, U.S. firms were in a position to pay manual workers at rates that propelled them into the middle class. And the middle class itself grew and prospered to an extent that seemed to portend the end of class conflict and even the end of class itself. The American middle class enjoyed living standards that outstripped, in many respects, the best that had been enjoyed by the rich in any other time and place.

All of this was achieved under policies that are, in retrospect, hard to believe were ever politically possible. Income taxes, a relative novelty at the time, were steeply progressive. Top marginal rates often exceeded 90 percent. Inheritances were similarly heavily taxed, while ordinary people benefited from a variety of new welfare measures, such as the Social Security system in the United States, which provided protection against the risks of old age, unemployment, and ill-health.

Economic historians Claudia Goldin and Robert A. Margo called the resulting period of high equality the Great Compression. It arrived with surprising suddenness as a result of the New Deal and World War II.

As shown in figure 4.1, the Great Compression ended almost as suddenly as it began. From the early 1980s onward, the gains in equality

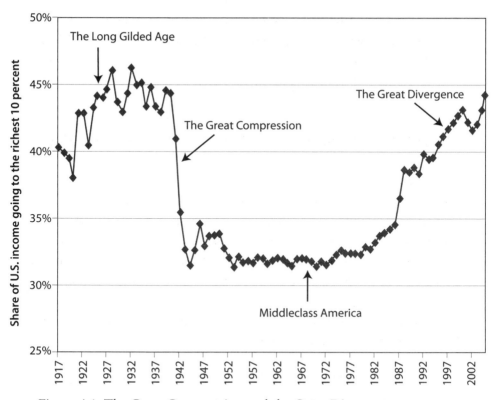

Figure 4.1. The Great Compression and the Great Divergence
Source: Paul Krugman, http://krugman.blogs.nytimes.com/2007/09/18/
introducing-this-blog/ (based on Piketty and Saez, 2003)

were reversed. This occurred partly as a result of the changes in the distribution of market incomes. Profits grew at the expense of wages, and the distribution of wages became more unequal. Changes in market income were reinforced by public policy. The steeply progressive income tax rates of the postwar era were replaced by a flatter tax system. Maximum rates were cut to 40 percent or less.

Initially, and to some extent even today, these measures were presented as providing tax relief to the "middle class." This is an elastic term but one that is typically taken to include families with incomes ranging from the median to the 90th percentile of the income distribution or sometimes even higher. Increasingly, however, tax reductions were focused on those in the top 10 percent of the income distribution, people who could not be called "middle class" even on the broadest use of the term.

The pattern set by the United States in the 1980s, was followed, to a greater or lesser degree, by other English-speaking countries as they embarked on the path of market liberalism. The most striking increases in inequality were in Britain under the Thatcher government, where the Gini coefficient rose from 0.25, a value comparable to that of Scandinavian social democracies to 0.33, which is among the highest values for developed countries.[3]

New Zealand started a few years later, but experienced even more radical reforms, cutting the top marginal rate of income tax from 66 percent in 1986 to 33 percent by 1990. Unsurprisingly, this pushed the Gini index from an initial value 0.26 to 0.33 by the mid-1990s. Canada and Australia all followed a similar path, as did Ireland in the 1990s. Most countries in the European Union resisted the trend to increased inequality through the 1980s and 1990s, but recent evidence suggests that inequality may be rising there also.

The increase in inequality did not go unnoticed. By the 1980s, economists, such as Katharine Bradbury, Gary Burtless, and Paul Krugman were pointing with alarm to the disappearance of the middle-class America in which they had grown up. This concern has grown steadily, as the growth of inequality has become ever more visible.

On the other hand, many economists and other commentators regarded the growing inequality of the market liberal years with complacency or positive approval, typically focusing on its supposed consequences such as economic dynamism. The growth of inequality attracted attention only briefly, when it was blamed on policies favored by market liberals, such as free trade and expanded immigration. A flurry of studies demonstrated that these factors were unlikely to be important. It was concluded, by default, that technological change must be the driving force.

---

[3] The Gini coefficient is a standard statistical measure of inequality. It is equal to half of the average income gap between households, divided by the mean income. So if average income is $10,000, then a Gini of 0.25 means that the expected income gap between two randomly selected individuals is 2*0.25*10,000=$5000. More at http://en.wikipedia.org/wiki/Gini_coefficient.

Supply Side

As inequality increased, so did the demand for theoretical rationalizations of policies benefitting the wealthy, and in particular for reductions in taxation. A variety of ideas of this kind were put forward under the banner of "supply-side economics."

The term *supply-side economics* dates back to the 1970s, when it was popularized by Jude Wanniski, then an associate editor of the *Wall Street Journal*, and later an economic advisor to Ronald Reagan. Wanniski, a colorful figure, did not let his lack of academic credentials deter him from taking on big names in the economics profession, including not only Keynes and his followers but also Milton Friedman.[4]

The central idea of supply-side economics followed directly from the negative conclusions of New Classical economics regarding the possibility of successful demand management. If, as the New Classical school believed, such demand-side policies were bound to be ineffectual or counterproductive, the only way to improve economic outcomes was to focus on the supply side, that is, to increase the productive capacity of the economy. Although many policies, such as improved education, might be advocated as ways to improve productivity, Wanniski focused on the kinds of policies favored by market liberals, such as reduced regulation and lower income taxes.

Wanniski started the process with his "Two Santa Claus" theory of politics. This was the idea that, in a contest between one political party (the Democrats, in the United States) favoring higher public expenditure, and another (the Republicans) favoring lower spending, the high-spending party would always win. So, the correct political strategy for conservatives was to campaign for tax cuts, without worrying too much about budget deficits. Any problems with budget deficits would

---

[4] He was later to become one of the first commentators to suggest, correctly, that Saddam Hussein's "weapons of mass destruction" had been found and destroyed by the UN weapons inspection process. This assessment proved more accurate than most of his economic predictions.

be resolved by the higher growth unleashed by improved incentives and reduced regulation.

This idea was the starting point for a famous lunch meeting between Wanniski, Donald Rumsfeld, Dick Cheney, and University of Southern California economist Arthur Laffer. These four, relatively obscure figures at the time, were to play a central, and disastrous, role in the economic and political events of the next thirty years.

Everyone knows the story of how Laffer drew a graph on a napkin, illustrating the point that tax rates of 100 percent would result in a cessation of economic activity and therefore yield zero revenue. Since a tax rate of zero will also yield zero revenue, there must exist some rate of taxation that yields a maximum level of revenue. Increases in tax beyond that point will harm economic activity so much that they reduce revenue.

Wanniski christened this graph the "Laffer curve," but as Laffer himself was happy to concede, there was nothing original about it. It can be traced back to the fourteenth-century Arabic writer Ibn Khaldun. Laffer credited his own version to the nemesis of supply-side economics, John Maynard Keynes. And while few economists had made much of the point, that was mainly because it seemed too obvious to bother spelling out.

What was novel in Laffer's presentation was what might be called the "Laffer hypothesis," namely that the United States in the early 1980s was on the descending part of the curve, where higher tax rates produced less revenue.

Unfortunately, as the old saying has it, Laffer's analysis contained a mixture of correctness and originality. The Laffer curve was correct but unoriginal. The Laffer hypothesis was original but incorrect.

More sophisticated market liberals could also see that the Laffer hypothesis represented something of an "own goal" for their side.[5] If the debate over tax policy turned on whether tax cuts produced higher revenue, and were therefore self-financing, the advocates of lower taxes were bound to lose, at least in policy circles where empirical evidence

---

[5] In soccer, an "own goal" is one accidentally kicked by a player on the defending side, and counts as a goal for the other side.

was taken seriously. Embarrassingly for their more sophisticated allies, supply-siders made, and continue to make, obviously silly arguments.

Fairly typical is the claim that, despite cutting taxes, Ronald Reagan doubled U.S. government revenue, a claim derived from the work of right-wing think tanks such as the Heritage Foundation. Leaving aside the fact that revenues did not, in fact, double under Reagan, such claims ignore the reality that tax revenues, and the cost of providing any given level of government services, rise automatically with inflation, population growth, and increases in real wages.[6] Even with cuts in tax rates, revenues are bound to rise over time as the nominal value of national income increases.

For the Laffer hypothesis to be supported, tax cuts would have to increase revenue more rapidly than would be expected as a result of normal income growth. In fact, as Richard Kogan of the Center on Budget and Policy Priorities has reported, income tax receipts grew noticeably more slowly than usual in the 1980s, after the large cuts in individual and corporate income tax rates in 1981.

To the extent that there was an economic response to the Reagan tax cuts, and to those of George W. Bush twenty years later, it seems largely to have been a Keynesian demand-side response, to be expected when governments provide households with additional net income in the context of a depressed economy. In fact, some supply-siders, happy to push any argument for tax cuts, ended up embracing the most simplistic forms of Keynesianism, much to the disgust of more consistent market liberals.

The Dynamic Trickle-down Hypothesis

Mainstream market liberals were generally disdainful of the "voodoo economics" of the Laffer hypothesis. They nonetheless accepted the central postulate of trickle-down economics, namely, that policies favorable to the wealthy will, in the long run, produce benefits for everyone, compared to the alternative of progressive taxes and redistributive social welfare policies. Rather than rely on the simplistic, and easily refuted, Laffer

---

[6] The Heritage Foundation figures add in some of the first Bush presidency's statistics.

hypothesis, market liberals claimed that the trickle-down effect would work through so-called "dynamic" effects of free-market reforms.

The appeal of this argument depended, in large measure on conflating the ordinary language meaning and connotations of "dynamic" with the technical economic meaning.[7] In technical terms, "dynamic" effects are those realized over time, as the capital stock in an economy grows. But in political discussion, it is easy to slide from this technical use into rhetoric about dynamism and sclerosis that relies on the ordinary language meaning.

The crucial distinction between the two is that while dynamic effects, in the technical sense, can raise or lower the level of national income in the long run, they do not, in standard economic models, affect the long-term rate of economic growth, which depends ultimately on productivity. Standard economic analysis suggests that the adoption of tax policies more favorable to owners of capital will increase savings and investment, and therefore raise the level of national income in the long run.

This analysis formed the basis of a number of "dynamic scoring" exercises aimed at estimating the effects of the George W. Bush tax cuts of 2001. Supporters of the Laffer hypothesis hoped that these exercises would show tax cuts paying for themselves in the long run.

Dynamic scoring analyses found some positive effects on capital accumulation, but they were too small, in terms of their effect on incomes and tax revenues, to offset the initial costs of the tax cuts. The most optimistic study, undertaken by Greg Mankiw, former chairman of President George W. Bush's Council of Economic Advisors, and Matthew Weinzierl, found that, assuming that the conditions of the standard neoclassical model were satisfied, dynamic effects would offset about 17 percent of the initial cost of a cut in taxes on labor income and about 50 percent of the cost of a cut in taxes on capital income.

However, as subsequent analysis showed, these results depended critically on technical assumptions about how the tax cut was initially financed. Mankiw and Weinzierl assumed that tax cuts are associated with expenditure cuts sufficient to maintain budget balance, and that

---

[7] "Efficiency" is another term for which the economic meaning is only tangentially related to the ordinary meaning.

these expenditure cuts do not create any additional market failures (that is, that the expenditure in question was a pure transfer).

Eric Leeper and Shu-Chun Susan Yang examined the case when, as actually happened with the Bush tax cuts, the cuts were initially financed by higher debt. In this case, it turns out that dynamic effects can actually increase the initial cost of a tax cut.

A further difficulty was that, since the increased income was the result of additional savings, it could not, in economic terms, be regarded as a pure economic benefit. The relevant measure of economic benefit, netting out costs from benefits, is the change in the present value of consumption, which is much smaller than the final change in income. Even for large tax cuts, the net dynamic benefit is rarely more than 1 percent of national income.

The same point may be made in terms of the effects on the government budget. Even if tax cuts eventually generated enough extra revenue to match the annual cost of the cuts (and of course they never do!) the budget would still be in long-term deficit because of the need to service the debt built up in the transitional period.

The implications for the trickle-down hypothesis are even worse. Under standard assumptions about the way the economy works, all the benefits of additional investment go to those whose savings finance that investment. That is, cutting taxes for the rich may lead them to save and invest more, thereby making themselves still richer, but there is no reason to expect any benefit for the rest of the community, except to the extent that the cost of the original tax cut is partially defrayed.

Finally, and most importantly of all, the neoclassical model used to derive estimates of dynamic benefits implicitly incorporates the Efficient Markets Hypothesis. The extra investment generated by more favorable tax treatment is supposed to be allocated efficiently so as to produce higher rates of long-term economic growth.

Until the financial crisis, the experience of countries that followed this logic and cut taxes on capital income appeared to bear out this view. Iceland, Ireland, and the Baltic States among others, experienced rapid economic growth as a result of high domestic investment and strong capital inflows.

But the economic crisis proved that this apparent success was built on sand. Much of the extra investment went into real estate, or into speculative ventures that collapsed when the bubble burst. Having cut taxes drastically, governments were left with inadequate financial resources to convince (now-cautious) investors that their bonds were a safe investment.

Another version of the argument was put forward by economists associated with the Republican Party, most notably Martin Feldstein (chairman of the Council of Economic Advisers and chief economic advisor to Ronald Reagan) and Lawrence Lindsey (director of the National Economic Council under George W. Bush).[8] Feldstein and Lindsey presented a set of arguments referred to as the "new tax responsiveness" theory, suggesting that tax cuts for the very rich would lead them to reduce their efforts at tax avoidance and thereby raise additional revenue. Subsequent work found that the results of Feldstein and Lindsey were overstated, and led to the commonsense conclusion that the best way to minimize tax avoidance was to tighten up on tax loopholes and tax havens. The latter effort, at least, is bearing some fruit with a series of recent OECD initiatives forcing tax havens to enter into information-sharing agreements.

LIFE: EXCUSES FOR INEQUALITY

Defenders of the trickle-down hypothesis frequently employ what blogger John Holbo calls the "the two-step of terrific triviality," which is to "say something that is ambiguous between something so strong it is absurd and so weak that it would be absurd even to mention it. When attacked, hop from foot to foot as necessary, keeping a serious expression on your face."[9]

The self-evident and weak version of the trickle-down theory starts with the observation that we all benefit, in all kinds of ways, from living

---

[8] Lindsey was forced out when he estimated that the cost of the Iraq War could reach $200 billion, as against the belief of the Bush administration that the invasion would cost no more than $50 billion. Current estimates exceed $2 trillion.

[9] See Holbo, posted at crookedtimber.org, April 11, 2007. http://crookedtimber.org/2007/04/11/when-i-hear-the-word-culture-aw-hell-with-it/.

in an advanced industrial society, with access to modern medical care, consumer goods, the Internet, and so on. Stretched widely enough, the term *capitalism* includes all advanced industrial societies, from Scandinavian social democracies to the Hong Kong version of laissez-faire. So, in this sense, the benefits of capitalism have trickled down to everyone.

The strong version of the claim is obtained by shifting the meaning of "capitalism" to mean "the free-market version of capitalism favored by market liberals." Relatively few of the benefits mentioned above can be traced directly to this form of capitalism. Many advances in medical care have come from publicly funded research and from innovations developed in the public health sector. The contributions of for-profit pharmaceutical companies, though important, have been modest by comparison. Similarly, the Internet was developed by the publicly funded university sector. Even now, the most exciting developments are nonprofit innovations like Wikipedia.

The crucial question is not whether technological progress and economic development yields benefits to everyone. Clearly it does, at least in material terms. What matters is whether market liberal policies generate more such progress than more egalitarian alternatives, so much more that everyone is better off in the end. It is this strong claim that was made repeatedly during the era of market triumphalism in the 1990s and was repeated, though with somewhat less conviction, through the 2000s.

The growth in U.S. inequality during the Great Moderation was undeniable (though that didn't stop some commentators and think tanks trying to deny it). Optimistic assessments of economic performance during the Great Moderation appeared to support the claim that rising inequality must be good for, or at least consistent with, economic growth that would ultimately benefit everybody.

Now, in the wake of the Global Financial Crisis, this claim can be seen to be unambiguously false.

Income, Inequality, and Taxation

The most obvious implication of the trickle-down hypothesis is that inequality in market incomes is not only harmless, but positively desirable, producing benefits for everyone in the long run. The general idea is that, the greater the rewards given to owners of capital and highly skilled managers, the more productive they will be. This will lead both to the provision of goods and services at lower cost and to higher demand for the services of less-skilled workers who will therefore earn higher wages.

In the abstract language of welfare economics, the central implication of the trickle-down hypothesis is that policy should be aimed at promoting efficiency rather than equity, since in the long run, equity will take care of itself. Put in terms of a more homely metaphor, we should focus on making the pie bigger, rather than sharing it out more equally.

In reality, things are not that simple. It is easy to suggest that tax and other policies should apply neutrally to all sectors of the economy, but harder to define how this should actually work. It might seem that a "flat" tax system in which all forms of income are taxed at a low, uniform rate would satisfy the efficiency criterion. But advocates of "trickle-down" have arguments to suggest that income from capital should not be taxed at all.

Going further, market liberals have claimed that, since everyone benefits from many of the services provided by government, the most efficient and equitable form of taxation is a poll tax.[10] A poll tax was in fact introduced by the Thatcher government in Britain to finance local government services but was abandoned in the face of massive protests and widespread rioting.

Once we turn from theoretical policy debate to the details of design, implementation, and enforcement, the well-off invariably do better than the theoretical design would suggest, and the poor do worse. This was true, to some extent, during the postwar Great Compression. Although the tax system appeared steeply progressive, the use of deductions, loopholes, and tax minimization schemes mean that it was, at best, only moderately progressive. Under the systems in force since the 1980s, which are only marginally progressive in their design, the actual outcome has been that many high income earners pay a smaller proportion of their income in tax than the population as a whole.

---

[10] The word *poll* means "head" but is closely associated with voting. Poll taxes are typically levied using electoral registers to define the tax base and can therefore be used to disenfranchise the poor or, as in the U.S. South in the Jim Crow era, black Americans.

The absence of substantial progressivity in the tax system is obscured by the focus, in the United States and elsewhere on the fact that high income earners pay the bulk of income tax. A good deal of the material appearing on this topic in the *Wall Street Journal* and elsewhere gives the impression that income tax is the only tax in the system. In reality, income tax is not even the sole tax imposed on income. Most countries, including the United States, levy payroll taxes which fall on labor income. Unlike the progressive income tax, which falls most heavily on high income earners, payroll taxes are regressive, falling primarily on wage employees.

In most taxation systems, capital gains are accorded concessional treatment or not taxed at all. Unsurprisingly, a large share of capital income is taken in the form of capital gains, moving the tax system closer to the "trickle-down" ideal where all taxes fall directly, or indirectly, on wage-earners.

That's not all. Taxes on income and wealth only account for about half of government revenue in most tax systems. Consumption taxes make up about half of all government revenue, and these taxes are regressive. That is, those on low incomes typically pay a higher proportion of those incomes in consumption taxes than do those on high incomes. There are a number of reasons for this. Low income earners generally don't save very much, so the ratio of consumption to income is higher for these groups. Taxes on items such as tobacco, alcohol, and gambling are levied at very high rates, and these items tend to make up a larger share of the expenditure of the poor (though absolute expenditure is higher only for tobacco).

Finally, there is tax avoidance and minimization. A vast industry of lawyers, accountants, money launderers, and other agents exists solely to ensure that no one with sufficient means should pay any more tax than the minimum they are obliged to pay under the most creative possible interpretation of the law.[11]

History shows that, no matter how favorably the well-off are treated, there will always be arguments to suggest that they should receive even

---

[11] As recent cases involving banks such as UBS have shown, there is also a substantial "wealth management" industry catering to those who do not wish to pay anything at all.

better treatment. Trickle-down theory offers no limit to the extent to which the burdens of taxation and economic risk can or should be shifted from the rich to the poor. In the end, according to the trickle-down story, that which is given to the rich will always come back to the rest of us, while that which is given to the poor is gone forever.

The Role of the Financial Sector

The financial sector is the crucial test case for trickle-down theory. During the era of market liberalism, incomes in the financial sector rose more rapidly than in any other part of the economy and played a major role in bidding up the incomes of senior managers as well as those of professionals in related fields such as law and accounting. According to the trickle-down theory, the growth in income accruing to the financial sector benefitted the U.S. population as a whole in three main ways.

First, the facilitation of takeovers, mergers, and private buyouts offered the opportunity to increase the efficiency with which capital was used, and the productivity of the economy as a whole.

Second, expanded provision of credit to households allowed higher standards of living to be enjoyed, as households could ride out fluctuations in income, bring forward the benefits of future income growth, and draw on the capital gains associated with rising prices for stocks, real estate, and other assets.

Finally, there is the classic "trickle-down" effect in which the wealth of the financial sector generates demands for luxury goods and services of all kinds, thereby benefitting workers in general, or at least those in cities with high concentrations of financial sector activity such as London and New York.

The bubble years from the early 1990s to 2007 gave some support to all of these claims. Measured U.S. productivity grew strongly in the 1990s, and moderately in the years after 2000. Household consumption also grew strongly, and inequality in consumption was much less than inequality in income or wealth. And, although income growth was weak for most households, rates of unemployment were low, at least by post-1970 standards for most of this period.

Very little of this is likely to survive the financial crisis. At its peak, the financial sector (finance, insurance, and real estate) accounted for around 18 percent of GDP and a much larger share of GDP growth. With professional and business services included, the total share of gross financial sector output in gross domestic product was greater than 30 percent. The finance and business services sector is now contracting, and it is clear that a significant part of the output measured in the bubble years was illusory.

Many investments and financial transactions made during this period have already proved disastrous, and many more seem likely to do so in coming years. In the process, the apparent gains generated through the expansion of the financial sector will be lost.

Equality of Outcome and Equality of Opportunity

The trickle-down hypothesis is closely related to the distinction between equality of outcomes, like life expectancy, and equality of opportunity. This distinction has long been a staple of debates between market liberals and social democrats. Many market liberals argue that, as long as society equalizes opportunity, for example by providing good schools for all, it's not a problem if outcomes are highly unequal. Even though some people may do badly, their children will, it's claimed, benefit from growing up in a dynamic society where everyone has a chance at the glittering prizes.

Writing in the *Wall Street Journal*, Wisconsin Republican Paul Ryan attacked President Obama's first budget saying, "In a nutshell, the president's budget seemingly seeks to replace the American political idea of equalizing opportunity with the European notion of equalizing results."[12]

A year earlier, following his victory in the Republican primary in South Carolina, John McCain said, "We can overcome any challenge as long as we keep our courage, and stand by our defense of free markets, low taxes, and small government that have made America the greatest land of opportunity in the world."[13]

[12] See Ryan (2009).
[13] Quote in McCain (2008).

As these quotations suggest, the trickle-down hypothesis relies on the claim that equality of opportunity and equality of outcome are not only distinct concepts but stand in active opposition to each other. By removing disincentives to work such as high tax rates and elaborate social welfare systems, it is claimed, an economic system that tolerates highly unequal outcomes will also provide those at the bottom of the income distribution with the incentives and opportunities to haul themselves up into the middle class and beyond.

The idea that the United States is a "land of opportunity" and "the most socially mobile society the world has ever known" (Scott Norvell, in a piece calling for patriotic consumer spending in the wake of 9/11) is central to the American national self-image. The belief that this high social mobility derives from free markets is widely shared.

As we will see, empirical studies of social mobility do not support such beliefs. But most economists are not engaged in studies of social mobility and many of them share these popular assumptions. This is true not only of self-satisfied American economists, promoting the merits of the *status quo* and calling for more of the same, but also of European critics of the welfare state, who accept the characterization of their own societies as rigid and sclerotic by comparison with the dynamic and flexible United States.

DEATH: THE RICH GET RICHER AND THE POOR GO NOWHERE

Although the trickle-down hypothesis never had much in the way of supporting evidence, empirical testing was difficult. In particular, its proponents never specified the time period over which the benefits of growth were supposed to percolate through to the poor. But, just as the crises of the 1970s marked the end of the Bretton Woods era, the Global Financial Crisis marks the end of the era of finance-driven market liberalism. To the extent that any assessment of the distributional effects of market liberal policies will ever be possible, it is possible now.

The trickle-down theory can be examined using the tools of econometrics. At least for the United States, however, no such sophisticated analysis is required. The raw data on income distribution shows that households in the bottom half of the income distribution gained nothing from the decades of market liberalism. Apologists for market liberalism have offered various arguments to suggest that the raw data gives the wrong impression, but none of these arguments stand up to scrutiny. All the evidence supports the commonsense conclusion that policies designed to benefit the rich at the expense of the poor have done precisely that.

The United States since 1970

The experience of the United States during the decades of market liberalism, from the 1970s until the Global Financial Crisis, gives little support for the trickle-down view. The gross domestic product of the United States grew solidly in this period, if not as rapidly as during the Keynesian postwar boom. More relevantly to the trickle-down hypothesis, the incomes and wealth of the richest Americans grew spectacularly. Incomes at the fifth percentile of the income distribution doubled and those for the top 0.1 percent quadrupled.

By contrast, the gains to households in the middle of the income distribution have been much more modest. As shown in figure 4.2, real median household income rose from forty-five thousand dollars to just over fifty thousand dollars between 1973 (the last year of the long postwar expansion) and 2008. The annual rate of increase was 0.4 percent.

For those at the bottom of the income distribution, there have been no gains at all. Real incomes for the lower half of the distribution have stagnated. The same picture emerges if we look at wages. Median real earnings for full-time year-round male workers have not grown since 1974. For males with high school education or less, real wages have actually declined. According to estimates made by the Economic Policy Institute, the average annual earnings of twenty-five- to twenty-nine-year-old high school graduates, expressed in 2005 values, fell from $30,900 in 1970 to $25,900 in 2000, and have stagnated since then.

One result can be seen by looking at the proportion of households living below the poverty line. The poverty rate declined steadily during the postwar Keynesian era. It has remained essentially static since 1970, falling in booms, but rising again in recessions.

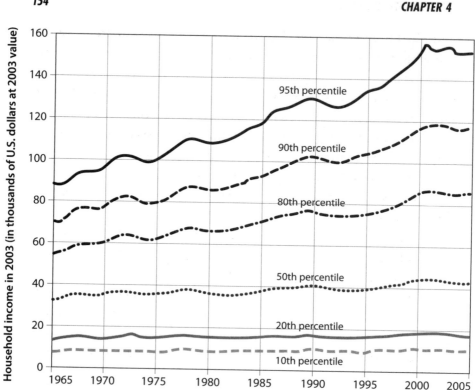

Figure 4.2. US Income Distribution, 1965–2003
Source: http://en.wikipedia.org/wiki/File:United_States_Income_Distribution
_1967-2003.svg

Unlike most developed countries, the United States has a poverty line fixed in terms of absolute consumption levels and based on an assessment of a poverty-line food budget undertaken in 1963 (Fisher 1992). The proportion of Americans below this fixed poverty line fell from 25 percent in the late 1950s to 11 percent in 1974. Since then it has fluctuated, reaching 13.2 percent in 2008, a level that is certain to rise further as a result of the financial crisis and recession now taking place. Since the poverty line has remained unchanged, this means that the real incomes accruing to the poorest 10 percent of Americans have fallen over the last thirty years.

These outcomes are reflected in measures of the numbers of Americans who lack access to the basics of life: food, shelter, and adequate medical care.

In 2008, according to U.S. Department of Agriculture statistics quoted by the Food Research Action Center, 49.1 million Americans live in households classified as "food insecure," meaning that they lacked access to enough food to fully meet basic needs at all times due to lack of financial resources. Slightly more than 17 million people (17.3 million) lived in households that were considered to have "very low food security," which means that one or more people in the household were hungry over the course of the year because of the inability to afford enough food. This number had doubled since 2000 and has almost certainly increased further as a result of the recession.

The number of people without health insurance rose steadily over the period of market liberalism, both in absolute terms and as a proportion of the population, reaching a peak of 46 million, or 15 percent of the population. Among the insured, an increasing proportion was reliant on government programs. The traditional model of employment-based private health insurance, which was developed as part of the New Deal, and covered most of the population during the Keynesian era, was eroded to the point of collapse.

More on Inequality

Homelessness is almost entirely a phenomenon of the era of market liberalism. During the decades of full employment, homelessness was confined to a tiny population of transients, mostly older males with mental health and substance abuse problems. By contrast, in 2007, 1.6 million people spent time in homeless shelters, and about 40 percent of the homeless population were families with children.[14]

The experience of the United States in the era of market liberalism was as thorough a refutation of the trickle-down hypothesis as can reasonably be imagined. The well off have become better off, and the rich have become super-rich. Despite impressive technological progress, those in

---

[14] This was actually an improvement on the situation earlier in the decade. Homelessness is one social problem where policy interventions have been sustained and at least partially successful in the United States.

the middle of the income distributions struggled to stay in place, and those at the bottom became worse off in crucial respects.

Naturally, there have been plenty of attempts to deny the evidence presented above, or to argue that things are not as bad as they seem. Some of these attempts can be dismissed out of hand. Among the most popular and the silliest is the observation that even the poor now have more access to consumer goods, such as televisions and refrigerators than they had in the past.

For example, Cox and Alm in their book *Myths of Rich and Poor* observe that, in spite of the rise in inequality, "a poor household in the 1990s was more likely than an average household in the 1970s to have a washing machine, clothes dryer, dishwasher, refrigerator, stove, color television, personal computer, or telephone."

The common feature of all the items listed in this quote is that their price has fallen dramatically relative to the general price level. This means that, even if incomes were exactly the same as in 1970, we would expect to see a big increase in consumption of these items. Unfortunately, if these items have become relatively cheaper, others must have become relatively dearer, and therefore less accessible.

It's not hard to find examples of expenditure items that have become more expensive over time. Health care has already been mentioned. Unsurprisingly, access to health care for poor households has become worse over time, as has the gap in health outcomes between the rich and the poor.[15]

College education provides another important example. The cost of college education has risen dramatically, particularly for the elite institutions that provide the pathway to the best jobs. In this case, it is the middle class who have suffered the biggest losses. Only the brightest children from poor backgrounds ever made it into elite colleges, and for this group, financial aid has remained accessible. The middle class, on the other hand, have been faced with a combination of higher fees and reduced aid.

---

[15] Emergency health care remains generally accessible and has benefitted from technical progress, which has contributed to declining mortality. But regular health care has become unaffordable for many, with the result that a wide variety of chronic conditions go untreated (Wilper et al. 2008).

As a result, between 1985 and 2000, the proportion of high-income (top 25 percent) students among freshmen at elite institutions rose steadily, from 46 to 55 percent. The proportion of middle-income students (between the 25th and 75th percentiles) fell from 41 to 33 percent.

The wider availability of goods has been offset by increased inequity in access to crucial services. There is no reason to think that the income stagnation observed in the official data is a statistical illusion. There are, however, some adjustments that should be made to measures of household income that make the picture look a little better than suggested by the statistics quoted above.

Household size has decreased. The most appropriate measure of household size for the purpose of assessing living standards is the number of "equivalent adults" derived from a formula that takes account of the fact that children cost less to feed and clothe than adults and that two or more adults living together can do so more cheaply than adults in separate households. The average household contained 1.86 equivalent adults in 1974 and 1.68 equivalent adults in 2007 (my calculations on U.S. census data). Income per equivalent adult rose at an annual rate of 0.7 percent over this period.

In earnings terms, women have done a little better than men. The median earnings for women who were full-time, year-round workers rose by about 0.9 per year over this period. Relatedly, the main factors sustaining growth in incomes for American households outside the top 20 percent has been an increase in the labor force participation of women and a decline in household savings.

Finally, until the 1990s, the consumer price index (CPI) took inadequate account of changes in product quality, so the decline in real wages was overstated somewhat. The Boskin Commission, appointed by the United States Senate in 1995 to study possible bias in the computation of the CPI, introduced a number of changes to the CPI that lowered the estimated annual rate of inflation by about one percentage point.[16] So,

---

[16] Not coincidentally, these changes reduced the cost of adjusting Social Security and other welfare payments for inflation.

while the stagnation of median incomes in the 1970s and 1980s might be overstated, that of the 1990s and 2000s is not.

The failure of the trickle-down approach has been even more severe in relation to consumer finance. The idea that increasing income inequality was unimportant when households could borrow to finance growing consumption was never defensible. The gap between income and consumption had to be filled by a massive increase in debt.

With sufficiently optimistic assumptions about social mobility (that low-income households were in that state only temporarily) and asset appreciation (that the stagnation of median incomes would be offset by capital gains on houses and other investments) these increases in debt could be made to appear manageable. Once asset prices stopped rising they were shown to be unsustainable. As we saw in chapter 1, these contradictions have been resolved for individual households by a massive increase in bankruptcy and other forms of financial breakdown.

In normal times, the renewed surge in bankruptcy would have been a major issue. In the recent crisis, however, the upward trend in bankruptcies has been overshadowed by foreclosures on home mortgages. During the boom, when overstretched householders could normally sell at a profit and repay their debts, foreclosures were rare. From 2007 onward, however, they increased dramatically, initially among low-income "subprime" borrowers but soon spreading ever more broadly. Banks foreclosed 2.3 million houses in 2008 and 2.8 million in 2009. In hard-hit areas of California, more than 5 percent of houses went into foreclosure in a single year.

The myth of trickle-down was sustained, in large part, by the availability of easy credit. Now that the days of easy credit are gone, presumably for a long time to come, reality has reasserted itself.

Econometric Studies

The relationship between inequality and economic growth has been the subject of a vast number of econometric studies, which have, as so often with econometric studies, yielded conflicting results. Early studies focused on the relationship between initial levels of inequality and subsequent levels of economic growth. These studies consistently found a negative relationship between initial levels of inequality and subsequent growth. On the other hand, increases in inequality appeared to be favorable to growth.

This apparent contradiction may be explained by the observation that the initial impact of an increase in inequality should be favorable to economic growth, but that the long-run effects are mainly harmful. In the era of market liberalism, growth in inequality was closely associated with financial deregulation and the growth of the financial sector. The short-term effects of financial deregulation have almost everywhere been favorable. The negative consequences take years or even decades to manifest themselves. So, it is unsurprising to observe a positive correlation between changes in inequality and changes in economic growth rates in the short and medium term.

It is only relatively recently that studies of this kind explicitly examined the trickle-down hypothesis. Perhaps the most directly relevant work is that of Dan Andrews and Christopher Jencks of the Kennedy School of Government at Harvard, and Andrew Leigh of the Australian National University, who ask, and attempt to answer, the question "Do rising top incomes lift all boats?" Andrews, Jencks, and Leigh found no systematic relationship between top income shares and economic growth in a panel of twelve developed nations observed for between twenty-two and eighty-five years between 1905 and 2000. After 1960, there is a small, but statistically significant relationship between changes in inequality and the rate of economic growth. However, the benefits to lower income groups flow through so slowly that, as income inequality increases, they may never catch up the ground they lose initially.

Andrews, Jencks, and Leigh simulated some results for the United States. Even assuming that the increased inequality in the United States after 1970 produced permanently higher economic growth, they found that households outside the top 10 percent of the income distribution would not have gained enough to offset their smaller share of total income over the 30 years to 2000.

The situation is much worse when the distribution of income within the bottom 90 percent is considered. Households at or below the median income level, that is, those in the bottom half of the income distribution, have lost ground relative to those above the median, even as the population as a whole has lost ground relative to the top 10 percent. There is also evidence to suggest significant adverse growth effects when inequality between the bottom and middle of the income distribution increases.

Social Mobility

The United States is characterized by highly unequal economic outcomes compared to other developed countries. The fact that these outcomes have grown more unequal during the era of market liberalism is undeniable. That hasn't stopped people denying it, especially when they are paid to do so, but at least such denials must be presented, in contrarian fashion, as showing that "everything you know about income inequality is wrong."

By contrast, the belief that this inequality is offset by high levels of social mobility is widely held in and outside the United States, and reflected in such epithets as "land of opportunity." Comfortable contrarians have shown little interest in challenging this belief.

In the late nineteenth century, the United States was indeed a land of opportunity compared to the hierarchical societies of Europe, and many believe that this is still the case. But the evidence of international comparative studies is clear. Among the developed countries, the United States has the lowest social mobility on nearly all measures, and the European social democracies the highest.

Ron Haskins and Isabel Sawhill of the Brookings Institution looked at social mobility by looking at the economic life chances of men whose fathers were in the bottom fifth of the income distribution.[17] In a world of equal opportunity, we might expect that one fifth, or 20 percent, of those men, would end up in the same group as their fathers.

In fact, Haskins and Sawhill found 42 percent of American men with fathers in the bottom fifth of the income distribution remain there as compared to: Denmark, 25 percent; Sweden, 26 percent; Finland, 28

---

[17] Since women's economic outcomes are determined, to a large extent, by marriage, the economic mobility literature focuses mainly on the outcomes of men. However, since people tend to marry within their own social class, higher mobility for men is likely to imply higher mobility for women.

percent; Norway, 28 percent; and the United Kingdom, 30 percent. Even in the Scandinavian countries, starting out poor is a disadvantage. But in the United States, starting out poor doubles the risk of ending up poor. Other studies, using different measures of mobility, reach the same conclusion.

As market liberal policies have become entrenched, social mobility has declined. As the well-off have drawn away from the rest of the community in terms of income share, they have pulled the ladder up behind them, ensuring that their children have better life chances than those born to poorer parents.

The evidence suggests that the distinction between equality of outcomes and equality of opportunity, a central theme in market liberal rhetoric, is inconsistent with empirical reality. More equal opportunities make for more equal outcomes, and *vice versa.*

It's not hard to see why this should be so. The highly unequal outcomes of market liberal policies are often supposed to be offset by an education system available to all and by laws that prevent discrimination and encourage merit-based employment and promotion.

That might work for one generation, but in the second generation the rich parents will be looking to buy a head start for their less-able children—for example, by sending them to private schools where they will be coached in examination skills and equipped with an old school tie.

One generation more, and the wealthy will be fighting to stop their tax dollars from being wasted on public education systems from which they no longer benefit. Those who remain in the public system will lobby to get their own children into good public schools and ensure that these schools attract and retain the best teachers, benefit from fundraising activity, and so on.

Education has traditionally been seen as the most promising route to upward social mobility. But as inequality has increased, wealthy parents have sought, naturally enough, to secure the best educational outcomes for their children, most obviously through private schooling, expansion of which has been a central demand of market liberals.

As a result, both the importance of ability as a determinant of educational attainment and the importance of educational attainment as a source of social mobility have declined over time. A British study found that "low ability children with high economic status" (or, in more colloquial terms, the "dumb rich") experienced the largest increases in educational attainment. As their parents have become richer, the life chances of these children have improved relative to those of more able children from poor families.

The inequities are even more evident in higher education. Thanks to scholarship programs, a handful of able students from poor backgrounds make it into Ivy League colleges like Harvard and Yale every year. But, as we have seen they are far outweighed by students from families in the top quarter of the income distribution whose have the financial resources to afford hefty fees and the cultural capital required to navigate the complex admissions process.

Those with old money, but less than stellar intellectual resources, have their highly effective affirmative action program—the (formal or informal) legacy admission system by which the children of alumni gain preferential admission. In 1998, William G. Bowen, a former Princeton University president, and Derek Bok, a former Harvard University president, found "the overall admission rate for legacies was almost twice that for all other candidates."[18]

If inequality of outcomes is entrenched for a long period, it inexorably erodes equality of opportunity. Parents want the best for their children. In a highly unequal society, wealthy parents will always find a way to guarantee their children a substantial head start.

While education is critical, high levels of inequality naturally perpetuate themselves through other, more subtle channels like health status. Barbara Ehrenreich's *Nickel and Dimed* discusses the plight of the uninsured working poor in the United States. While the problem is worse in the United States than elsewhere because of highly unequal access to health care, high levels of inequality produce unequal health outcomes even in countries with universal public systems. Children growing up with the poor health that is systematically associated with poverty can never be said to have a truly equal opportunity.

---

[18] Bowen and Bok (1998).

There are other factors at work. A widely dispersed income distribution means that a much bigger change in income is needed to move the same distance in the income distribution, say from the bottom quintile to the middle, or from the middle to the top. So, unequal outcomes represent a direct obstacle to social mobility.

Once you think about the many and various advantages of growing up rich rather than poor, it's not at all surprising that widening the gap between the rich and the poor should also make it harder for the poor to become rich, and, for that matter, *vice versa*. The evidence that, under market liberalism, social mobility is low and declining should not surprise anyone. On the other hand, it is disappointing, if not surprising, that the myth of equal opportunity continues to be believed so many decades after it has ceased to have a basis in fact.

The Unhealthiness of Hierarchies

Some of the most compelling evidence against the trickle-down hypotheses has come from studies of social outcomes such as health status, crime, and social cohesion. Not surprisingly, the poor do worse on most such measures than the rich. More strikingly, though, a highly unequal society produces bad social outcomes even for those in higher income groups, who are better off, in purely monetary terns, than those with a similar relative position in more equal societies. Only for the very well-off do the direct benefits of higher income outweigh the adverse effects of living in an unequal society.

It is commonly thought that, while it is better to be at the top of the hierarchy than at the bottom, there are some offsetting disadvantages, particularly in relation to health. While the poor suffer from lack of access to good medical care and other problems, the rich are supposed to suffer from "diseases of affluence" like heart disease, compounded by the stresses of life at the top. "Executive stress" has become a cliché. To some extent, there is thought to be a trade-off between health and wealth.

In place of this somewhat comforting picture, Michael Marmot's book *Status Syndrome* has some disturbing news. People at the top of status hierarchies live longer and have better health than those at the bottom.

This is true for a broad range of illnesses and causes of death. The effect isn't confined to the extremes of the distribution. At any point in a status hierarchy, people have, on average, better health than those a little below them and worse health than those a little above them.[19]

Marmot's work began with a study of British civil servants. The study population is interesting for two reasons. First, it excludes extremes of wealth and poverty. The civil service is not a road to riches, but even the lowest-ranking civil servants are not poor, on most understandings of the term. Second, the public service provides a clear-cut status hierarchy with very fine gradations.

Marmot found, not surprisingly, that senior public servants, at the top of the status hierarchy, were healthier than those at the bottom. More surprisingly, he found that, throughout the hierarchy, relatively small differences in pay and status were associated with significant differences in life expectancy and other measures of health.

The same finding has been replicated across all sorts of different status hierarchies. As you move from the slums of southeast Washington, DC, to the leafy suburbs of Montgomery County, twenty miles away, life expectancy rises a year for every mile travelled. Among actors, Academy-award winners live, on average, four years longer than their Oscarless costars.

Along the way, Marmot demolishes the myth of executive stress. Despite their busy lives, Type A personalities, and so on, senior managers are considerably less likely to die of heart attacks than the workers they order around. This is not a new finding, but the myth is sufficiently tenacious that Marmot needs to spend some time knocking it down yet again.

Marmot, along with others who have studied the problem, concludes that the crucial benefit of high-status positions is autonomy, that is, the amount of control people have over their own lives. Marmot's analysis is not focused exclusively on autonomy. For example, he has a good discussion of social isolation and its relationship to social status. Nevertheless, his main point concerns autonomy, and this is by far the most interesting and novel feature of the book.

---

[19] An interesting status marker is that Marmot is entitled to call himself Sir Michael Marmot, having been knighted in 2000. Presumably his life expectancy was thereby increased.

There is a complex web of relationships between health status and autonomy, both self-perceived and measured by objective job characteristics. Low levels of autonomy are associated not only with poorer access to health care but with more of all the risk factors that contribute to poor health, from homicide to poor diet.

The importance of autonomy is not, on reflection, all that surprising. Autonomy, or something like it, is at the root of many of the concerns commonly seen as part of notions like freedom, security, and democratic participation. When we talk about a free society, for example, we usually have in mind a place in which people are free to pursue a wide range of projects. The distinction between negative and positive liberty, popularized by Isaiah Berlin, goes part of the way toward capturing this point, but a focus on autonomy does better.

The points are clearest in relation to employment. Early on, Marmot debunks the Marxian notion of exploitation (capitalists taking surplus value from workers) and says that what matters in Marx is alienation. It's the fact that the boss is a boss, and not the fact that capitalists are extracting profit, that makes the employment relationship so troublesome. The more bossy the boss, the worse is the job. This is why developments like managerialism, which celebrates the bossiness of bosses, have been met with such hostility.

So part of autonomy is not being bossed around. But like Berlin's concept of "negative liberty," this is only part of the story. Most of the time it's better to be an employee with a boss than to sell your labor piecemeal on a market that fluctuates for reasons that are totally outside your control, understanding, or prediction. This is where a concept of autonomy does better than liberty, negative or positive. To have autonomy, you must be operating in an environment that is reasonably predictable and amenable to your control.

The environment consists largely of other people. So one way of increasing your autonomy is by reducing that of other people, for example, by moving up an existing hierarchy at their expense. Similarly, when employers talk about increased flexibility in the workplace, they generally mean an increase in their control over when, where, and how their employees do their job. Workers typically experience this as a loss of flexibility in their personal lives. In short, within a given social structure, autonomy is largely a zero-sum good.

But some social structures give more people more autonomy than others. This is reflected both in average life expectancy and in the steepness or otherwise of social gradients in health, that is, the extent to which changes in various measures of social status are reflected in changes in health outcomes. In general, higher levels of inequality on various dimensions are associated with lower average life expectancy and steeper status gradients.

In *The Spirit Level*, Richard Wilkinson and Kate Pickett build on Marmot's work and other statistical evidence to produce a comprehensive case for the proposition that inequalities in income and status have far-reaching and damaging effects on a wide range of measures of social well-being, effects that are felt even by those who are relatively high in the income distributions.

Wilkinson and Pickett report two main types of statistical evidence. Following Marmot, they examine social gradients. Here there are two main results. First, in all countries, there is a strong relationship between social outcomes and social rank, much greater than can be explained by income differences alone. Second, greater inequality within a country is associated with a steeper social gradient.

Wilkinson and Pickett also report cross-section studies in which a number of countries, or other jurisdictions such as U.S. states, are compared. The standard statistical approach here is regression analysis, in which differences in social outcomes such as life expectancy are statistically related to inequality levels, in a way that controls for other sources of variation, such as mean income levels. Among the outcome variables considered are measures of life expectancy and health status, crime and measures of "social capital," such as trust.

For a wide variety of social outcome measures, Wilkinson and Pickett find that more equal societies do better. The relationship is statistically significant and undiminished by the inclusion of relevant control variables.[20]

---

[20] As work by Leigh and Jencks (2007) has shown, other econometric adjustments, such as the looking at within-country changes rather than comparing countries at a single point in time, weaken the findings. The interpretation of the results of Wilkinson and Pickett remains

The United States is the obvious outlier in almost all studies of this kind. It is the wealthiest country in the world and the most unequal of the rich countries. The United States does poorly on a wide range of measures of social well-being, from life expectancy to serious crime, and even on such objective measures as average height.

These poor performances cannot be explained by the continuing black-white divide or by poor outcomes for immigrants. All but the very richest groups of Americans do worse on most measures of social well-being than people with a comparable position in the income distribution in more equal countries. These bad outcomes occur even though the average income of the non-Americans in these groups is much lower than that of the corresponding Americans.

REANIMATION: MOBILITY WITHOUT MOVEMENT

A good zombie movie needs a sequel, and so, it is almost inevitable that some zombies will survive to carry on the tradition. The best candidate for zombie immortality is probably the trickle-down hypothesis. As we've seen it can be traced back, under that name, at least to the early twentieth century, and in other forms, back to ancient times.

With such a long pedigree, trickle-down economics is unlikely to be killed. Still, given the overwhelming evidence that social mobility in the United States is low by the standards of developed countries and decreasing steadily, the task of reanimating this zombie idea looks like a difficult one. But Thomas Sowell of the Hoover Institute is up to the job.

In his latest book, *Intellectuals and Society*, Sowell excoriates liberals for their misunderstanding of economics and sweeps aside concerns about declining social mobility with the assertion that "neighborhoods may remain the home of poor people for generations, no matter how many people from the neighborhoods move out to a better life as they move up from one income bracket to another." He immediately contradicts himself with the observation that Harlem was formerly a middle-class Jewish

---

controversial, but the correlation between inequality and poor social outcomes is not seriously disputed.

community. Sowell also appears unaware of the recent (re)gentrification process in which blacks have again become a minority group in greater Harlem.[21]

This insouciant attitude to evidence is unsurprising. In earlier writing on the topic, Sowell made the observation that "if mobility is defined as being free to move, then we can all have the same mobility, even if some end up moving faster than others and some of the others do not move at all."

In fact, on Sowell's account, the United States would remain the world's most socially mobile society even if everyone ended up in the exact same social position as their parents.

As Sowell astutely observes, "A car capable of going 100 miles an hour can sit in a garage all year long without moving. But that does not mean that it has no mobility." If the poor don't succeed, he says, it's because they are not willing to make the necessary efforts and sacrifices.

Translating to the real world question, if we observe one set of children born into a wealthy family, with parents willing and able to provide high-quality schooling and "legacy" admission to the Ivy League universities they attended, and another whose parents struggled to put food on the table, we should not be concerned that members of the first group almost invariably do better. After all, some people from very disadvantaged backgrounds achieve success, and there was no law preventing the rest from doing so.

Clearly, an idea so appealing to people who can afford to reward its promulgators is unlikely to be killed by mere evidence of its falsehood. Perhaps if the political left is willing to return to class politics (something the right-wing advocates of trickle-down have never abandoned) it might at least find a way to drive this zombie idea out of the assumed background of political debate.

AFTER THE ZOMBIES: ECONOMICS, INEQUALITY, AND EQUITY

The longer-run implications of the Global Financial Crisis have yet to be fully comprehended. Even when economic activity recovers, consumer

---

[21] See http://www.nytimes.com/2010/01/06/nyregion/06harlem.html.

credit will be more restricted than in past decades. There will be no escape from the implications of decades of stagnant wages for workers at the median and below. The traditional avenues of upward social mobility, both through higher education and through promotion within large organizations are being closed off. The labor market has developed a dual structure. With good jobs increasingly depending on an education at a good university, the chances of climbing the ladder diminish all the time.

Meanwhile, for those who have done well out of the era of market liberalism, the widening gap between rich and poor makes the possibility of downward social mobility ever more threatening. A decade ago, Barbara Ehrenreich referred to the insecurity of the professional middle classes about the prospects for their children as the "fear of falling." The barriers erected to guard against that fear are getting steeper all the time.

These tendencies are most developed in the United States, but they are evident in all the English-speaking countries. At least until the Global Financial Crisis, the same tendencies seemed to be emerging even in the more egalitarian societies of Europe and Japan.

Politically, the failure of the trickle-down theory may produce a resurgence of the class-based politics pronounced dead in the era of market liberalism. The contrast between the enforced austerity of any recovery period, and the massive, and massively unjustified, excesses of the financial elite during the boom period, will produce a political environment where phrases like "malefactors of great wealth" no longer seem quaint and old fashioned.[22]

There does not yet exist a political movement ready and willing, let alone able, to mobilize popular support for a program of income redistribution. Rather, revulsion against the willingness of politicians to bail out the banking system has been reflected most clearly in the confused and angry demagoguery of the Tea Party movement, which has been manipulated to serve the very interests that have generated the feelings of injustice that drive it.

On the other hand, measures to protect individuals and families against the risks and inequities of market liberalism are gaining more acceptance.

---

[22] Just after writing this, I googled "malefactors of great wealth" and found it as the title of a piece in *Time* magazine's "Swampland" by Joe Klein (2009), who is usually in tune with the political zeitgeist.

The prescription drug benefit introduced under the George W. Bush administration provides one example. Although laden with pork-barrel benefits for pharmaceutical companies, the benefit package was a response to a real social need.

Another positive development has been the continued extension of unemployment benefits in response to the depth and duration of the current recession. A system in which unemployment benefits expire after six months has proved unable to cope with increasingly inequitable labor market outcomes.

The most critical test for developments in the United States will be the success or failure of the health reform legislation passed by Congress in March 2010. At the time of writing, this remains unclear. However, other reforms of this kind, controversial at the time, have come to be generally accepted.

In other developed countries, there has also been a renewed concern with reducing inequality and providing social protections. The "New Labour" government in Britain, has gradually shifted from the position described in its early years as "Thatcherism with a face," to the point where it raised taxes on the highest income earners to fund continued expansion of public services. The result was to slow, though not to reverse, the rapid growth in inequality evident under the previous Conservative government.

A turning point in Australian political debate was the 2004 concession by conservative Australian prime minister John Howard that "there is a desire on the part of the community for an investment in infrastructure and human resources and I think there has been a shift in attitude in the community on this, even among the most ardent economic rationalists."[23]

It remains to be seen whether the failures of the financial sector and the business elite that produced the Global Financial Crisis will translate into sustained political support for a more equitable distribution of income. Rather than consider questions of political strategy, however, I will focus on the way in which the failure of the trickle-down hypothesis

---

[23] Howard (2004), 1. "Economic rationalists" is a term commonly used in Australia to describe the group referred to in this book as "market liberals." Howard was one of the leading Australian advocates of economic rationalism in the 1980s and 1990s.

should change the questions economists ask and the way in which they should seek to answer them.

Economics, Inequality, and Equity

The failure of the trickle-down hypothesis provides economists with plenty of challenging research tasks.

A crucial problem is to understand why and how inequality increased so much under market liberalism, and why it increased so much more in the English-speaking countries. The idea, which remained the default assumption during the era of market liberalism, that growing inequality was a natural market response to unspecified changes in the structure of the economy no longer appears tenable.[24] The huge increases in remuneration in the financial sector and for senior managers more generally has not produced a more efficient and productive economy, with benefits for all. More generally, the Global Financial Crisis has undermined the view that incomes accruing to different groups in the community are an accurate reflection of their marginal contribution.[25]

The policies and institutional changes that took place under market liberalism have almost all pushed in the direction of greater inequality. Corporations have been deregulated while the full power of the state has been turned against unions. Tax schedules have been flattened. The main income sources of the wealthy, including capital gains, inheritance, and dividends have been given progressively more favorable treatment. Corporations have competed with each other to pay ever larger amounts to their CEOs. And, at the very top, there is indeed a trickle-down effect. Stratospheric CEO salaries encourage huge increases for other top executives and substantial increases in payment for senior professionals, even as wages stagnate or fall for ordinary workers.

---

[24] The term *technology* is commonly used to describe these changes, but this is just a catch-all residual term. There has been little if any evidence linking the growth in inequality to any particular technological innovation.

[25] An analysis by the New Economics Foundation concluded that for each pound paid to British bankers, society incurred a net loss of ten pounds. The opposite was true for hospital cleaners and childcare workers, who were paid much less than their social value.

But it remains unclear which features of market liberalism contributed most substantially to the growth of inequality, and how those policies interacted with each other and with other social developments. Understanding these processes will require economists and other social scientists to look beyond purely monetary aspects of inequality. We need to examine the interactions between economic, political, social, and psychological processes, all of which have contributed to the growth of inequality and economic instability.

The importance of the links between inequalities in income, health, education, and political power is evident from the work of Marmot and others. But the links between economic variables like income inequality and personal and social outcomes realized over generations are inherently complex. It seems clear enough that inequality is bad for us, but much harder to say how and why.

All of this analysis is merely a preliminary to the big question: How can the growth in inequality be reversed and the more egalitarian society of the Great Compression be restored? Some steps, such as restoring progressivity to the tax system, seem obvious.

Even these obvious steps must confront the political realities of a system in which political power has shifted overwhelmingly to the wealthy. A study by the Center for Responsive Politics showed that about two-thirds of U.S. senators were millionaires in 2008. There are similar trends in other countries.

Improving the taxation system is a comparatively easy response. The decline in union membership has almost certainly played a substantial role in promoting inequality in market incomes, not to mention the removal of checks to the power and prerogatives of managers. But, how, if at all, can this decline be reversed? This is one of many questions we need to look at with fresh eyes.

FURTHER READING

Sources for "A rising tide lifts all boats" are Bai (2007), Kennedy (1963), Sperling (2005), and Wikipedia (2010).

The phrase "the Great Compression" is due to Goldin and Margo (1992) and has been popularized by Krugman (2009b), much of whose work may be seen as a defense of the egalitarian, broadly middle-class society of the Great Compression against critics, formerly mostly on the left, but now almost exclusively on the political right. Manzi (2010) makes the case for inequality as a source of economic dynamism. Gordon and Dew-Becker (2008) provide a summary of the evidence on U.S. inequality, and some international comparisons.

Data for inequality measures is derived from CIA (2009), Easton (1999), European Anti-Poverty Network (2009), and United Nations (2010). Data on bankruptcy is from American Bankruptcy Institute (2010) and on foreclosures from RealtyTrac (2010). Fisher (1992) describes the development of poverty measures in the United States. Data on the size of the financial sector is derived from the Bureau of Economic Analysis (2010) and on British budget deficits from House of Commons (1994). Other data on the United States is derived from the U.S. Census (www.census.gov).

Wanniski's (1978), *The Way the World Works: How Economists Fail and Succeed*, named as one of the one hundred most influential books of the twentieth century by *National Review* magazine, presents the "Two Santa Claus" theory, along with other arguments for low taxes. The case for supply-side economics is put by Canto, Jones, and Laffer (1982). The new tax responsiveness literature is best represented by Lindsey (1987) and Feldstein (1995). The evidence against is put forward by Goolsbee (1999).

Thatcher's poll tax proposal, based on the work of Douglas Mason and the Adam Smith Institute, is critically assessed by Bramley (1987).

Data on income distribution is from Piketty and Saez (2003, 2006). The *State of Working America* reports prepared by the Economic Policy Institute provide a wide range of useful information. I've drawn on the 2006/07 Report (Mishel, Bernstein and Allegretto 2006).

Comparisons of U.S., British, and EU social mobility include Goodin, Headey, Muffels, and Dirven (1999) and Headey and Muffels (1999). All studies confirm that mobility in the United States and Britain is low. Haskins and Sawhill (2009) find that more American men with fathers in the bottom income quintile remain there as compared to all European countries studied. Blanden, Goodman, Gregg, and Machin (2004) find declining social mobility in Britain. Gottschalk (1997) summarizes studies from 1994 and earlier, finds that static or declining mobility in the United States. Bezruchka (2001) discussed inequality and health. Galindo-Rueda and Vignoles (2005) examine the declining relative importance of ability in predicting educational attainment. Data on access to U.S. colleges is from Astin and Oseugera (2004).

Other references cited include Andrews, Jencks, and Leigh (2009), Berlin (1958), Berman (1998, 2002), Boskin (1998), Bowen and Bok (1998), Bradbury (1986), Burtless (1990), Center for Responsive Politics (2009), Cox and Alm (2000), Ehrenreich (1990, 2001), Food Research and Action Center (2009), Heritage Foundation (2001), Krugman (1996), Leigh and Jencks (2007), Marmot (2005), McCain (2008), Norvell (2001), Ryan (2009), Sowell (2005, 2010), and Wilkinson and Pickett (2009).

CHAPTER 5

PRIVATIZATION

> We hope the fund is maintaining its push for a more flexible exchange
> rate, far-reaching reforms in the banking sector, and more privatization.
> —*TIMOTHY ASH, of the Royal Bank of Scotland speaking about the
> IMF rescue package for Ukraine, just after the RBS had been
> nationalized as a result of failed speculation and catastrophic
> mismanagement*

Zombies are often presented as incapable of speech but sometimes groan
out a few words by which they can be recognized. For the zombies in the
movies, the most common such word is "Brains." For economic zombies,
the equivalent is surely "privatization."

To understand the life, death, and undead persistence of the idea of
privatization, it is important to look at what went before. The "mixed
economy" in which public provision of a wide range of services and economic infrastructure, such as telecommunications and electricity networks, coexisted with a largely capitalist market economy was one of
the most striking features of the political and economic settlement that
emerged in Western economies after 1945.

Public ownership was not new. Governments in many countries had
played a role in providing infrastructure, social welfare systems, and services such as health and education. Before World War II, the establishment of public enterprises was seen, by supporters and critics alike, as a
step toward full-scale socialism, defined in traditional terms as the elimi-
nation of private ownership of the means of production.

The experience of the Depression and World War II produced a fundamental shift in thinking about the roles of governments and markets,

described by Sheri Berman as "the social democratic moment." Rejecting both nineteenth-century classical liberalism and the mechanistic determinism of orthodox Marxism, social democrats saw themselves, in the words of Australian historian Bede Nairn as "civilizing capitalism."

From the Swedish *Folkhemmet* (people's home) to the British reforms based on the Beveridge Report to Roosevelt's New Deal and Four Freedoms, social democrats put forward a vision of a society in which markets and business enterprise played a central role, but one subordinate to the needs of a just society. In addition to Keynesian macroeconomic management and the social policies of the welfare state, this vision required governments to make investments in the physical and economic infrastructure needed to ensure prosperity.

The growth of government intervention was supported by a series of new developments in microeconomics, collectively called the theory of market failure. In the 1920s, A. C. Pigou developed the idea of externalities as a way of incorporating obvious negative features of industrial society, such as air pollution, into economic analysis. Pigou's analysis is still in use today. It forms the basis for policy proposals such as the idea of a carbon tax to limit emissions of carbon dioxide and other greenhouse gases.

In the 1930s, Joan Robinson and Edward Chamberlin independently developed the idea of monopolistic competition, extending earlier work on industry structures such as monopoly (dominance of a market by a single seller) and duopoly (two sellers). The rise of game theory in the 1940s and 1950s, due to John von Neumann and Oskar Morgenstern, along with the crucial equilibrium concept developed by John Nash, provided a rigorous basis for analyzing markets that did not fit the standard competitive framework.

Modern theories of information and uncertainty, also derived from the work of von Neumann and Morgenstern, suggested a range of ways in which market transactions might lead to suboptimal social outcomes. The classic instance was Akerlof's discussion of the "lemons" problem. This is the idea that the sharp decline in value of new cars, occurring as soon as they are driven out of the showroom, reflects the fact that cars resold soon after purchases are likely to be those regarded by the initial buyers as "lemons." In the absence of an easy way to detect such lemons, owners of good cars will be unwilling to sell at the low price available for slightly used cars, producing a self-sustaining equilibrium in which the only near-new cars on the market are lemons. Such "asymmetric information" problems are particularly severe in the context of insurance markets where they go by the name "adverse selection."

All of these possibilities were grouped under the heading of "market failure." The view that governments should act to correct market failures where they occurred was used to justify a wide range of government action. An important implication was support for the provision of goods and services by governments and government-owned enterprises. Government provision of health services, for example, could be justified by the limitations of insurance markets. Public ownership of infrastructure utilities was justified as a response to problems of monopoly and oligopoly.

Paradoxically, the crowning theoretical achievement of neoclassical economic theory, the demonstration by Arrow and Debreu of the existence and optimality of a competitive general equilibrium, also provided the theoretical basis for the theory of market failure. Arrow and Debreu showed that *if* competitive markets existed for every possible commodity, in every possible time and place, and under every possible contingency, the resulting allocation of competitive resources could not be improved on for everyone. But that's a very big *if*.

The complete set of contingent markets required for the Arrow-Debreu proof does not exist, and cannot possibly exist. A large literature in the economics of finance explores the idea that if financial markets are sufficiently well-developed, the instruments traded in these markets can encompass all relevant possibilities. Under these conditions, the real world will be close enough to that of the Arrow-Debreu model that conclusions about the optimality of competitive equilibrium remain valid. This idea does not have a standard name, but I will call it the "Completely Efficient Financial Markets Hypothesis."

The completely efficient financial markets hypothesis makes sense only if these markets are efficient, in the sense of the strong form of the Efficient Markets Hypothesis discussed in chapter 2. In view of the evidence against the strong Efficient Markets Hypothesis, this is problematic, but the Completely Efficient Financial Markets Hypothesis is even stronger than the strong form of the Efficient Markets Hypothesis.

The Completely Efficient Financial Markets Hypothesis requires more than the existence of markets for bonds, corporate stocks, and associated derivatives. In addition, it requires that households should be able to insure themselves, at reasonable cost, against risks such as unemployment, business failure, ill-health, or a decline in the value of their home. With the exception of health insurance, which exists mainly as a result of public mandates, and publicly provided "unemployment insurance," which is not really insurance, none of the required markets exist.[1]

The term *market failure* can be interpreted as referring to the absence of many of the markets needed to satisfy the complete financial markets hypothesis and thereby guarantee the optimality of competitive market equilibrium. Arrow, in particular, made this point. His work showed that general equilibrium theory gave only the most qualified support to market liberalism.

For much of the twentieth century, the general movement of economic policy in capitalist societies was toward an expanded role for the state, including an expansion of the scope and extent of public ownership of industry. In the light of movements toward a greater role for markets in communist countries, it was anticipated that capitalist and communist economic systems would converge in a "mixed economy."

The term *mixed economy* was popularized by British economist Andrew Shonfield to describe the economic system of the postwar era. This system was not a compromise between comprehensive state socialism and free market capitalism, as is often supposed. Rather, in seeking a market system actively managed by governments, the mixed economy transcended this dichotomy. It was, and remains, unlike the vaporous offerings of Tony Blair and Bill Clinton in the 1990s, a genuine "Third Way."

During the era of the mixed economy, the boundaries between the public and private sector were regularly readjusted, and not always in

---

[1] Robert Shiller has long argued that new financial instruments could reduce the riskiness of investments in home ownership, but his efforts to promote the development of such instruments have had only limited success.

the same direction. While the predominant trend was for the role of the state to expand through the nationalization of existing private enterprises or the establishment of new public enterprises, it was quite common for publicly owned enterprises to be returned to the private sector.[2]

By 1970, the success of the welfare state and the mixed economy seemed undeniable. Hopes turned to the prospect of a further transformation, not fully defined, in which the remaining inequalities and injustices of capitalism would be greatly reduced, if not eliminated.

The most promising proposals centered on notions of industrial democracy. In Sweden, the largest union body, the LO (Landsorganisationen I Sverige, or Swedish Trade Union Confederation), put forward a proposal, developed by economist Rudolf Meidner to require all companies above a certain size to issue new stock to workers, so that within twenty years the workers would control 52 percent of the companies they worked in. Similar ideas were developed in other countries.

It seemed that the transformation of capitalism into a society without vast differences in wealth or power was inevitable. But it was not to be.

BIRTH: WE ARE ALL MARKET LIBERALS NOW

In the event, the real challenge to the mixed economy came from market liberals, who dominated the policy debate from the mid-1970s onward. Milton Friedman's success in macroeconomic debates attracted new attention to the market liberal position he presented in works such as *Free to Choose* where he (along with his wife and coauthor Rose) argued that even core areas of state activity such as education could be left to private provision, funded through voucher schemes.

Meanwhile, the economic performance of public enterprises deteriorated sharply in the 1970s. In an inflationary environment, public enterprises found it hard to resist demands for increased wages, but equally hard to pass on the resulting costs in the form of higher prices. Weak

[2] The term commonly used at the time was *denationalization*. Although the term *privatization* is commonly attributed to Peter Drucker, Germà Bel concludes that it was first used with reference to the program adopted by the German Nazi Party in the 1930s.

economic growth and rising unemployment pushed government budgets into deficit.

A common short-term response was to cut investment spending, including that of public enterprises. Although this response made little economic sense, it was enshrined in policy by rules limiting aggregate public borrowing, whether this was used to finance current expenditure or income generating investment. The most famous policy target of this kind was the Public Sector Borrowing Requirement adopted in Britain under the Thatcher government.

Over time, these problems were mostly overcome, and public enterprises returned to profitability. But, in the general atmosphere of disillusionment with government that was common in the 1970s, there was a receptive audience for claims that public enterprises were inherently inefficient and represented a fiscal burden on governments.

The strength of public sector unions, at a time when unions in the private sector were being pushed onto the defensive by mass unemployment, also contributed to the push for privatization. Governments keen to weaken the power of unions, but unwilling to confront their own employees, could resolve the problem by handing public enterprises over to private owners, keen to break unions and eliminate overstaffing and above-market pay and conditions (at the shop-floor level, if not for senior management).

Criticism of the mixed economy gained theoretical bite with the rise of public choice theory, which sought to model democratic political institutions as "markets for votes." The typical conclusion, unsurprisingly given the theoretical starting point, was that real markets were to be preferred to political markets. A variety of arguments was used to show that most market failures were unimportant or self-correcting.

Conversely, the rise of the "public choice" theory of politics popularized the idea of "government failure." It was argued that, because of the systematic distortion of the policy process by interest groups, the costs of government intervention were greater than the costs of the market imperfections that government policies were supposed to remedy.

The rise of "property rights" theory in the late 1970s produced a theoretical critique of public ownership. It was argued that, since private corporations were responsible to their shareholders, their managers would always have stronger incentives to seek efficiency than would bureaucrats or managers of public enterprise. Although it contradicted decades of research showing that ordinary shareholders are virtually powerless, property rights theory met the political needs of the time and was widely embraced.

Theory turned to practice with the election of the Thatcher government in the United Kingdom in 1979. Following the failure of Keynesian macroeconomic management in the 1970s, the relatively disappointing performance of the British economy since 1945 (or earlier), and the full-blown crises of the late 1970s, the stage was set for a reaction against the mixed economy and public ownership.

Whereas previous Conservative governments had denationalized some of the acquisitions of their immediate Labour predecessors, the Thatcher government began selling off enterprises, such as British Telecom, which had been in the public sector since their establishment. Starting with popular proposals such as the sale of council houses to the tenants who occupied them, Thatcher began a program under which publicly owned enterprises in telecommunications, electricity, water, and transport were sold, usually through public floats. The idea of privatization, conceived as the systematic removal of the state from the production and provision of goods and services, was born.

Thatcher's example was soon emulated by governments of all political persuasions in the English-speaking world. Her radical measures were much admired, and imitated, in Australia and New Zealand, which still tended to follow the British lead with respect to economic policy. In both countries, the crucial steps were taken by governments associated with the labor movement.[3] In Australia, the Hawke and Keating governments, in office from 1983 to 1996 moved slowly and cautiously, but eventually privatized the national airline, Qantas, and the publicly owned Commonwealth Bank, outraging many of their traditional supporters.

---

[3] For obscure historical reasons, the Australian party uses the American spelling, Labor, while its New Zealand cousin uses the British spelling, Labour.

In New Zealand, caution was thrown to the winds. Labour finance minister Roger Douglas rapidly gained a reputation as "more Thatcherite than Thatcher." Among a series of radical free-market reforms, large-scale privatization began with the sale (by public float) of the Bank of New Zealand and continued apace thereafter with the sale of assets such as Air New Zealand.

New Zealanders had tired of the reforms by 1990. They replaced Labour with the conservative National Party, which promised a more moderate approach. In office, however, the Bolger National government continued to push radical free-market measures, notably including the sale of New Zealand Rail (1993) and corporatization of the health system with a view to eventual privatization. The Labour Party split in opposition. The radical free-market group left to form the Association of Consumers and Taxpayers (later the ACT Party). The era of radical reform finally ended when Labour regained government under Helen Clark in 1999.

The privatizations of the 1980s reversed the century-long trend toward greater state involvement in the capitalist economy. The collapse of Soviet communism seemed to confirm that free-market reforms represented more than a swing of the political pendulum and constituted, in the words of the great triumphalist text of the age, *The End of History*. It was inevitable, given the collapse of centrally planned economies, that large numbers of state-owned enterprises would be converted, one way or another, to private ownership. The ideology of privatization encouraged the adoption of a radical "shock treatment" approach based on wholesale privatization.

In this context, it was inevitable that privatization should become part of the standard Washington Consensus package of reforms advocated for less-developed countries by the World Bank, the IMF, and U.S. Treasury. By the 1990s, the privatization trend had spread to EU countries that had often been dismissive of such "Anglo-Saxon" notions.

The large-scale privatization of publicly owned enterprises in the 1980s and 1990s played a big role in promoting the triumphalist claims of market liberals. Commentators and think tanks rushed to conflate the real, but manageable, financial difficulties of long-established public infrastructure services in countries like Britain, New Zealand, and Australia with the collapse of communism in Eastern Europe and the stagnation of North Korea.

Public ownership of infrastructure was seen as a relic of the past, doomed to vanish as governments rushed to sell off assets. Having claimed victory in the infrastructure sector, market liberals turned their attention to the core of the welfare state with proposals for privatization of health services, prisons, and the school system. In the United States, the most ambitious assault on the institutions of the New Deal era was the proposal, pushed hard by the George W. Bush administration, to privatize Social Security.

Few would have predicted that, a decade or so later, governments would be debating, and in some cases undertaking, the nationalization of such iconic capitalist enterprises as Citigroup, Bank of America, and General Motors. Although these rescue operations mostly involve only temporary public ownership, they make the rhetoric of the 1990s look absurd. Further, they raise the question of whether some or all of the privatizations of past decades should be reversed permanently.

But despite these failures and reversals, systematic privatization of public enterprises remains part of the standard package of policy reforms recommended by bodies like the IMF. There has been little serious effort to reconsider the theoretical rationale for these policies or to ask who gains and loses from their implementation.

LIFE: A POLICY IN SEARCH OF A RATIONALE

A Policy in Search of a Rationale

From its earliest days, privatization was described as a "policy in search of a rationale." Actually the problem was not so much the absence of a rationale as the presence of too many. As with the war in Iraq, different players in the policy process supported privatization for different reasons, and expected different outcomes.

Sometimes it was a simple matter of class politics. Privatization is bad for unions, which tend to be stronger and more effective in the public sector. It is usually good for the incumbent senior managers of privatized firms, who move from being rather modestly paid public sector employees, constrained by bureaucratic rules and accountability, to doing much the same job but with greatly increased pay and privileges, and far fewer constraints. Then there are the profits gained where the asset is underpriced and can be quickly resold at a much higher market value. For politicians eager to bash unions, or beholden to the financial sector, this was a great deal. Hostility to unions was strong on the political right, particularly after the upsurge in strikes and militancy in the 1970s.

But more and more, privatization was driven by the power of the financial sector, which benefits both directly and indirectly from privatization. The direct benefits include the massive fees and bonuses derived from managing privatizations, not to mention the returns from advising the bidders.

The indirect benefits include the enhanced economic and political power of the financial sector in an economy where all major investment decisions are driven by the demands of financial markets. In the era of market liberalism, this power extended over all major political parties. As U.S. senator Dick Durbin said, "The banks are still the most powerful lobby on Capitol Hill. And they frankly own the place."[4] He could equally well have been talking about the City of London and its dominance of British politics. The situation in other developed countries is similar.

In Australia, for example, it has become routine for retired politicians, of all political persuasions, to be offered cushy jobs in the financial sector, provided, of course, that they have followed the right kinds of policies when in office. This has become a career path, creating a self-perpetuating cycle. Typically in this path a young person serves for a while as a staffer or adviser, followed by a decade or so in elective politics, and then a move to the business sector. Public office is no longer a goal in itself but a stepping stone to bigger and more profitable goals. The incentives to promote the interests of the financial sector while in office are obvious.

[4] For Durbin quote, see Doster (2009).

Governments mostly thought about privatization as a way of fixing problems of public finance. Government ministers short of money to pursue pet projects, to finance tax cuts, or simply to deal with growing budget deficits saw the sale of valuable assets as an easy and politically costless source of cash. The question of what would be done when there were no more assets to sell was left for another day.

In other cases, faced with the need to spend money modernizing infrastructure, but unwilling to take the necessary steps to pay for it, by raising taxes and charges or by adding to public debt, governments used privatization as a way of shifting the problem to the private sector. The privatization of the water supply industry by the British government, in response to pressure from the European Union to improve environmental health and safety is one well-known case.

Economists, at least when they were thinking clearly and speaking honestly, were as one in rejecting the most popular political reasons for privatization: as a source of cash for governments or a way of financing desired public investments without incurring public debt.

On the first point, it is a basic principle of economics that the value of a capital asset is determined by the flow of earnings or services it generates. The cash gained from selling public assets comes with the cost of forgoing the earnings it would have generated in continued public ownership. In a world where both governments and markets were perfectly efficient the cost would be exactly equal to the benefit and privatization would not change anything. As we'll see below, things are more complicated in reality. That doesn't make the idea of selling assets as a source of free cash any less silly.

A more sophisticated version of the same error is to suppose that governments facing debt constraints that restrict investment in desirable projects can get around those constraints by bringing in private investors. Once again, the problem is that the returns (such as proceeds from toll roads) needed to attract private investors represent money that could have been used to service public debt. The more private money is used to finance public infrastructure, the smaller the amount governments can invest without running into the same problems that would have arisen if they had taken on the debt themselves. As the exasperated secretaries of Australian state treasuries once put it, privatization and public-private partnerships create no new "pot of money" to spend on public infrastructure.

Privatization will yield net fiscal benefits to governments only if the price for which the asset is sold exceeds its value in continued public ownership. This value depends on the flow of future earnings that the asset can be expected to generate. The question of how to determine this value remains controversial. As discussed below, it turns on complex arguments about risk and the "equity premium puzzle."

Economists mostly focus on the potential benefits of privatization in promoting competition. Although hard-line market liberals gave unconditional support to privatization, the majority of economists, including market liberals, favored breaking up public enterprises and stripping them of monopoly privileges before privatization. However, since such measures inevitably reduced sale prices, and the opportunities for incumbent managers to enrich themselves, they were rejected in many cases. Going beyond such structural changes, economists emphasized the importance of governance as opposed to ownership.

The dominant view was that, given appropriate regulation and pro-competitive policies, it should not matter whether enterprises were publicly or privately owned. So, assuming private firms were more efficiently run, this view suggested that privatization should always be the preferred policy, provided that opportunities for competition were not compromised in the process.

A variety of rationales for privatization were put forward by a variety of political actors. The competing rationales for privatization share one common thread, namely, the belief that there is always a net social benefit to be realized from converting a publicly owned enterprise into a private firm. Some advocates of privatization, notably including the financial sector, hope to appropriate the gains for themselves. Others, including many politicians, hope that this benefit will take the form of an improvement in the net worth of the public sector. Still others, including economists, hope that it will mean lower prices for consumers. But this disagreement over who should benefit masks a shared assumption that there are net benefits to be fought over.

The claim that privatization always yields net social benefits was not always made explicit, but it was implicitly taken as common ground in most of the discussion of economic reform during the era of market liberalism. It is important, then, to understand what this claim entails.

Markets, Governments, and Efficiency

When all the spurious arguments for privatization are stripped away, the central tenet of the ideology of privatization is simple. It is the claim that an economy in which all major decisions on investment, employment, and production are left to private firms will outperform a mixed economy where governments play a significant role in such decisions. Provided private firms are free to compete on a "level playing field," this means they will always have a higher value than they would have under public ownership.

If the Efficient Markets Hypothesis represents the negative side of the market liberal case, implying that no alternative institution can outperform markets, the case for privatization represents the positive side, implying that more private ownership will always improve economic outcomes. In its strongest form, the ideology of privatization asserts that private firms can outperform governments in the production of goods and services of all kinds, including those that have long been funded and provided by the public sector, such as education. This assertion includes both a short-run component, based on the claim that private enterprises will operate more efficiently than their publicly owned counterparts, and a long-run component, based on claims that privatization will improve investment decisions.

The short-run claim is that, because of the incentives associated with private ownership, private enterprises are always more efficient than comparable public firms. Broadly speaking, this claim is true to the extent that profitability is a good guide to efficiency, which in turn depends largely on the absence of significant market failures. Private firms are controlled by their managers who may or may not be accountable to outside shareholders. In general, both managers and shareholders benefit significantly from increased profitability, though the relationship is more direct for shareholders.

By contrast, public enterprises are accountable to governments and therefore indirectly to any group to which governments respond. In the presence of market failure, such accountability is likely to be beneficial, since government enterprises are under more pressure to promote better social outcomes, even at the expense of profitability. On the other hand, where market failure is unimportant, requirements for accountability are likely to impede efficient decision-making. As public choice theorists pointed out in the 1970s, accountability requirements may be used by special interest groups to demand favorable treatment, such as above-market wages for unionized workers or better service for politically influential customers.

The long-run case for privatization is based on the idea that the allocation of investment will be better undertaken by private firms than by government business enterprises. Private investments will be guided by the evaluation of risk and returns undertaken by investment banks and stock markets, with the assistance of ratings agencies, and the availability of sophisticated markets for complex derivatives. This, it is claimed, will be far superior to anything that could be obtained by seemingly more rational approaches, using engineering calculations of the need for investment in various kinds of infrastructure, and implementing the resulting investment plans on a coordinated basis. The Global Financial Crisis has shown that, for most of the past decade, market estimates of the relative riskiness and return of alternative investments have been entirely unrelated to reality.

DEATH: PUZZLES AND FAILURES

The turning of the tide against privatization predated the Global Financial Crisis. Internationally, a number of major privatizations have been reversed. The British government was forced to renationalize its rail network after the failure of the privately owned operator. In Australia, dissatisfaction with the privatized telecommunications monopoly has led the government to announce that it will get back into the telecommunications business by constructing a publicly owned national broadband network. New Zealand, where market liberalism was implemented in a radical form in the 1980s and 1990s, renationalized its national airline in 2001 and its railways a couple of years later. Even relabeled as "choice," Social Security privatization proved so politically unsalable that it was abandoned early in George W. Bush's second term.

Even more significant was the collapse, under scrutiny, of nearly all the main theoretical and political rationales for privatization. Some, such as the idea that selling assets provided instant cash for governments were recognized as nonsensical early on, but like the bigger zombie ideas discussed in this book, keep on coming back. Other rationales such as the hope that privatization would produce competitive markets in industries thought to be natural monopolies have held up longer but have ultimately proved unfounded.

The crucial issue, however, is the claim that privatization always yields net social benefits and therefore that, other things being equal, the price for which a public asset can be sold will exceed its value in continued public ownership. This claim has never had much empirical support. Rather it has been taken on faith as a consequence of the Efficient Markets Hypothesis. With that hypothesis discredited, it is possible to consider how the public might lose from privatization. To understand the issues it is necessary to take a brief look at one of the enduring puzzles of economics. This is the high rate of return demanded by investors in equity (company stock and its derivatives) relative to the much lower rate of interest on government bonds.

The Equity Premium Puzzle

The equity premium puzzle is one of those problems that is easy to state in summary form but hard to explain in the detail necessary to understand it, and impossible to resolve (at least within the "rules of the game" as played by economists in recent decades). The existence of a large equity premium has profound implications for economic analysis of issues ranging from climate change to macroeconomic policy, but it is most directly relevant in relation to privatization, and so I will discuss it here.

The facts are simple and well known. Over very long periods, and in many different countries, investments in equity have yielded much higher returns, in the long run, than investments in bonds. The annual rate of interest on U.S. government bonds, adjusted for inflation, has averaged between 1 and 2 percent since the late nineteenth century. Over the same period, returns on stocks (dividends and capital gains) have averaged around 8 percent.

The difference between the two rates of return, about six percentage points, is called the equity premium. The existence of the equity premium is not, in itself, a puzzle. Stocks are riskier than bonds. Investors expect a higher rate of return to compensate for this risk. The problem is that the premium is much higher than would be expected on the basis of the standard economic model, referred to as the consumption based capital asset pricing model (CCAPM).

CCAPM starts with the observation that if financial markets are both complete and efficient, they will pool and spread all the individual risks faced by households and firms, in much the same way as a life insurance company pools the mortality risks of its group of clients.[5] Once this process of pooling and spreading is completed, the riskiness of the "average" investment portfolio should be equal to the riskiness of the economy as a whole, as measured by aggregate consumption. So, the risk premium for equity should be determined by the riskiness of aggregate consumption, which is determined by the cycle of boom and recession.

The problem is that when we look at economic fluctuations in this aggregated way, they don't appear to be very important. A deep recession might produce negative growth of 3 percent, compared to expected growth of 3 percent in a normal year. A powerful boom might produce growth of 6 percent. But variations of 3 percent one way or the other should not, on standard views about people's risk attitudes, justify a significant risk premium.[6] In the classic paper where they first pointed out the puzzle, Rajnish Mehra and Edward Prescott suggested that, if the standard CCAPM model applied, the equity risk premium should be no more than half a percentage point as opposed to the observed value of

---

[5] The technical term is *idiosyncratic risk*.

[6] The logical implication, that recessions don't really cause any economic damage, was derived by Robert E. Lucas.

six percentage points. Either the model is in need of refinement, or the assumption of complete and efficient financial markets is badly wrong.

Unfortunately, in presenting the anomalously large risk premium as a "puzzle," Mehra and Prescott encouraged subsequent writers in the literature to search for clever explanations, rather than to consider the economic implications of the puzzle. Under the implied rules of the puzzle-solving game, two kinds of explanation were allowed. The first kind were clever refinements of the completely efficient financial markets model. In these refinements, usually based on alternative assumptions about risk and time preferences, completely efficient financial markets generated larger equity risk premiums than the standard model. The second kind of explanation, reminiscent of Blanchard's macroeconomic haikus (see chapter 3), involved introducing a market imperfection into the standard completely efficient financial markets model, then showing that a large equity risk premium would result.

Although many solutions along these lines have been proposed, none has been generally accepted. The problem is the same as in the micro-based literature. Financial markets are incomplete and inefficient in many different ways, most of which have the effect of making investments in the stock market riskier than they would be in the ideal world assumed in the CCAPM.

The equity premium is the outcome of complex interactions between investors who cannot insulate themselves from the personal and business risks generated by the economy. Investors cannot easily form expectations about the value of stocks. Worse still, they must deal with banks who are sometimes willing to lend to them and sometimes not. It is unsurprising that investors are unwilling to buy equity in the absence of an assurance of high long-run returns.

What matters is not solving the "puzzle" but understanding its implications. These are wide-ranging. First, contrary to the claims of Robert Lucas, the macroeconomic variability associated with recessions is very expensive. Conversely, policies of economic reform that promise long-term gains at the expense of short-term pain are much less attractive if their benefits are risky. Much of the reform agenda of market liberalism was of this kind.

Turning to the valuation of investments, the magnitude of equity premium means that equity risk robs the stock market of most of its value. Indeed, if it weren't for the equity risk premium, the claim made in the late 1990s, by Glassman and Hassett that the Dow Jones index was bound to rise to 36000, would have been justified. The fact that the magnitude of the risk premium grows with the duration of the investment means that that corporate executives face (often irresistible) pressure to make short-sighted, myopic decisions that will provide an immediate boost to profits.

Finally, there are implications for public policy and these bear directly on the debate over privatization. In view of the high cost of equity capital, there is a strong case for public investment in long-term projects and corporations, provided that publicly owned firms can achieve levels of operating efficiency comparable to those of private sector competitors.

Privatization and the Equity Premium

In the case of privatization, the implications of the equity premium arise from the fact that governments can finance investments entirely by issuing bonds. The guarantee of repayment is based on governments' capacity to raise revenue from taxes. Private corporations must rely on a mixture of equity and debt, with the result that their weighted average cost of capital is around 6 percent, compared to around 2 percent for governments. That is, investors place a value of one hundred dollars on both a government bond returning a safe two dollars each year and a typical investment in company bonds and stocks generating an average of six dollars a year.

This creates a problem for privatization, which can be illustrated by an example. Suppose a government business enterprise is generating earnings of $60 million each year. At an interest rate of 2 percent, that's enough to service the interest on $3 billion in public debt (2 percent of $3 billion is $60 million). Now suppose that the government decides on privatization. Equity investors will want a return of 6 percent. If potential buyers don't see any opportunity to increase profits, they will only be willing to pay $1 billion (since 6 percent of $1 billion is $60 million). So, if the government uses the sales proceeds to repay $1 billion in debt, saving $20 million a year in interest, it will need to find another $40 million a year to replace the lost earnings of the enterprise they have sold.

On the other hand, if private buyers expect that they can increase annual profits to, say $300 million, they will be willing to pay $5 billion for the enterprise. If the government uses the proceeds to repay debt, the interest saving will be $100 million a year, yielding a net fiscal benefit of $40 million a year.

If increases in profitability arise from improvements in operating efficiency or from improvements in the value of goods and services provided to consumers, the net fiscal benefit is also a net benefit to society as a whole. On the other hand, if private owners increase profits by cutting wages or reducing the quality of customer services, then there is no such net gain. Losses (and, more rarely, gains) to workers and consumers need to be taken into account in any assessment of privatization.

In view of the popularity of privatization with policymakers, and the frequency with which it has been recommended, it is striking that assessments of this kind have rarely been undertaken. The International Monetary Fund, which noted in 2000 that there had been few studies of the question, apparently did not feel that the lack of any empirical evidence should qualify their recommendations in favor of privatization.

The IMF points to the difficulty of choosing a "counterfactual," that is, of saying what would have happened in the absence of privatization. However, this problem can be overcome by one of two ways. It can be analyzed by taking a conservative projection of future earnings under continued public ownership. Or we can look at cases where a proposal for privatization was put forward, with an estimated sale price, but the enterprise was not sold, and remained in public ownership.

Most evidence on privatization comes from developing countries and is decidedly mixed. There are favorable cases, such as that of the steel industry in Brazil where privatization turned loss-making and declining public enterprises into profitable and growing private corporations. On the other side of the ledger, there are cases like that of Russia where privatization was the occasion for wholesale looting, allowing self-described democratic "reformers" to enrich themselves massively. Most cases fall between these two extremes, but the view that privatization is always, or even mostly, beneficial is not supported by the evidence.

Examining a number of actual privatizations in Australia, I found that the government made net fiscal gains in only two cases.[7] In both cases, the sale took place in a bubble atmosphere, with the result that the buyers subsequently resold at a loss. Looking at cases where privatization was proposed, but did not go ahead, the returns to government under continued public ownership clearly exceeded the benefits they would have obtained from selling the assets. On balance, there was a net fiscal loss from privatization in most cases. This was not offset by benefits to workers (who were mostly worse off) or consumers (who experienced gains on some measures and losses on others). This implies that there was also a net social loss.

Budgetary Effects

The claim that selling off income-earning assets provides governments with extra money that can be spent on public services is based on a confusion between income and capital. It is the same reasoning that led householders to finance consumption by borrowing against the equity in their homes. In the short run, it can produce apparent benefits, but in the longer term using asset sales to finance current expenditure is a road to financial ruin.

The sale of assets to fund current expenditure and tax cuts was pioneered by the Thatcher government in Britain. By the late 1980s, Thatcher's chancellor of the exchequer Nigel Lawson was proudly announcing that the government had replaced the deficits it inherited with surpluses, and celebrated with tax cuts all round. By the mid-1990s, with the economy having been through a serious slump and no more assets left to sell, the budget deficit hit new records, exceeding 6 percent of GDP.

---

[7] As discussed below, these were the privatization of the Victorian electricity industry in the early 1990s and the second stage of the privatization of Telstra, the former telecommunications monopoly, and also the dominant Internet service provider. In the Victorian case, the deregulation of the U.S. electricity industry had produced a group of cashed-up buyers, competing for a limited pool of assets. The Telstra sale took place during the dotcom boom.

In most cases, the income foregone from privatization exceeded the interest saved, resulting in a net fiscal loss. An extreme example was the Thatcher government's 1985 sale, by public float, of half of the public holding in British Telecom (BT). Net proceeds from the sale of the first 50 percent of BT were about 3.65 billion pounds.

In 1984–85, BT had a gross operating surplus of about 3 billion pounds and interest liabilities of 0.5 billion pounds, implying a net post-tax profit of around 2 billion pounds, or 1 billion pounds for the 50 per share holding that was sold. The real bond rate at the time was around 5 percent. So, the income flow from BT could have serviced public debt of 20 billion pounds. Thus, the British public incurred a loss of more then 15 billion pounds on this transaction.

The loss was partly due to deliberate underpricing. This was reflected in the fact that the stock price nearly doubled on the first day of trading. However, even if the offering had been priced at market value, the loss (that is, the difference between the sale proceeds and the debt that could be serviced by BT earnings) would have been around 10 billion pounds.

Only on rare occasions has the sale of public assets in sectors like tele-communications and electricity been profitable for governments. During the "dotcom" mania, stock prices were wildly inflated, to the point where sales of some public assets, particularly those related to the Internet and mobile telephony, were profitable. Similarly, during the deregulation of the early 1990s, U.S. electric utilities pursued international expansion ag-gressively, paying high prices for assets that subsequently proved unjusti-fied in commercial terms. For example, a number of Victorian electricity distribution and generation enterprises were bought by U.S. utilities and subsequently resold at markedly reduced prices. It is only in exceptional circumstances like this that the privatization of profitable government infrastructure enterprises, run on a commercial basis, is likely to improve the fiscal position of governments.

Despite the evidence that privatization mostly makes governments worse off, it continues to be promoted as a solution to short-term financial difficulties. In my home state of Queensland, Australia, the state govern-ment has used a budgetary crisis to justify privatization. The publication of a statement by more than twenty of Australia's leading economists (including some prominent supporters of privatization) pointing out that their rationale was entirely spurious has done nothing to deter them from pushing this bogus argument.

Some Notable Failures

Privatization has been a central component of market liberalism for more than thirty years. In that time, there have been sufficiently many failures to give us a reasonable idea of when privatization is likely to work and when it is not. The following list of examples is selected to illustrate particularly problematic areas of privatization, as opposed to those where privatized firms fail as a result of bad luck or the failure of individual managers.

The privatization of railway systems has proved consistently problematic. In the United Kingdom, the last major privatization under the Conservative government of 1979–97 was that of the rail system, which was divided into two parts. A single company Railtrack owned and managed the rail network itself. A number of different companies, each responsible for a different region, ran the train services. A series of failures forced the Blair government to renationalize Railtrack in 2002. Dissatisfaction with the private train operators remains intense, and the biggest rail contract, the East Coast main line was renationalized in November 2009. The partially privatized London Underground was renationalized in 2008. New Zealand similarly renationalized its rail network in 2003, and train operations in 2008.

Privatization has been at best a mixed success in the telecommunications industry. In most cases, former public monopolies have remained dominant. The expected benefits of competition have been slow to emerge. Capital expenditure by privatized companies has focused on maintaining market dominance rather than on improving customer service. In Australia, the Rudd Labor government, elected in 2007, announced plans for a new National Broadband Network which will, at least initially, be publicly owned.

Consistently poor outcomes have been observed where privatization has been extended to the core areas of the welfare state such as education, health, retirement income, and criminal justice.

Education at the school and university level has traditionally been provided by a mixture of public and nonprofit private institutions. For-profit education has played a peripheral role, most notably in the provision of short, vocationally oriented courses, such as those of trade schools.

There was a major push toward privatization of the school system in the United States in the 1990s. The push was led by the Edison Schools corporation, which rapidly became a stock market darling, running hundreds of schools in dozens of states. But Edison was unable to deliver on its promises. The company was delisted in 2003 and is now largely out of the school management business. Paradoxically, school privatization has been more successful in Sweden, where a voucher system was introduced in the 1990s. However, even with an effectively level playing field, only 10 percent of students attend private schools and most of these are nonprofit institutions.

In the 1990s, New Zealand attempted to commercialize its public hospital system, turning hospitals into "Crown Health Enterprises." The results were disastrous, including huge blowouts in debt and a drastic decline in the quality of service to patients. Following the election of the Clark Labour government in 1999, the reforms were abandoned, and the Crown Health Enterprises were folded back into District Health Boards, run by elected members.

The United States, where the private sector plays a larger role in health services than in any other developed country, spends substantially more on health but achieves notably poor outcomes. The reforms introduced by the Obama administration, and the introduction of a pharmaceutical benefit scheme under the Bush administration, have been a response to these problems. However, the exclusion of a "public option" from Obama's health reform package has reduced its potential to improve the efficiency of the system.

Perhaps the most pernicious form of privatization has been the creation of private police, prisons, and mercenary military forces. There is no evidence that privatization of the use of state power yields cost savings. Privatization of this kind, however, yields significant political benefits to the governments that undertake it. First, it allows them to avoid political responsibility for improper, and even criminal, use of force.

Immigration detention centers are one noteworthy example. Even worse are the activities of companies like Blackwater, whose operatives can kill with impunity, subject neither to military nor to civil justice.

Not all privatizations have failed. For example, while infrastructure systems as a whole have strong natural monopoly characteristics, it is often possible to separate competitive or potentially competitive components of the system, in which case privatization may be feasible. In the case of electricity supply, for example, electricity generation is more competitive than transmission and distribution. The retail functions (billing, arranging connections, and so on) are even more competitive. Privatization is more likely to be beneficial where competition is sustainable.

The most successful privatizations have been those of firms that never really belonged in the public sector, and particularly firms that have been rescued from imminent death for social or political reasons. Rolls-Royce in Britain and General Motors in the United States are notable examples. Where a competitive market can be sustained, and there is no special requirement for close regulation, privatization has usually been successful.

The issue is further complicated by the fact that privatization tends to work best when it is undertaken by governments that are competent, efficient, and accountable, but this is precisely the case when the potential benefits are smallest. Incompetent and corrupt governments do a bad job of running public enterprises but, as in Russia, often do an even worse job of selling them.

Markets, Competition, and Regulation

The ideology of privatization has some implications regarding regulation that appear, at least superficially, paradoxical. Privatization and deregulation are commonly seen as going hand in hand.[8] Yet, in practice, privatization has been accompanied by the creation of a vast range of new regulatory bodies and expansion of the powers of many existing regulators. Britain, the birthplace of the modern privatization movement,

---

[8] They are items 8 and 9 in the list of 10 policy prescriptions in John Williamson's original description of the "Washington consensus."

has seen the creation of a string of regulatory institutions such as OFTEL (Telecoms), OFWAT (Water), OFGEM (Gas and Electricity Markets), OFSTED (Education), and OPRA (Occupational Pensions Regulatory Authority) among many others. As well as these specific regulators, industry as a whole is subject to the Office of Fair Trading and the Competition Commission.

None of these bodies existed in any form in 1970 and all have gained greatly enhanced powers in the era of privatization. Membership of the European Union adds a whole new layer of regulation.

The apparent paradox reflects the fact that public ownership was introduced as a response to market failures. Privatization did not resolve these market failures. In particular, even in cases where public infrastructure enterprises were broken up prior to sale, substantial natural monopoly elements remained. The hopes of privatization advocates that regulation would be needed only temporarily, until robust competition emerged, have gone largely unfulfilled.

There are some benefits associated with the new model of regulation. Under traditional models of public ownership, infrastructure service providers were responsible for management of all aspects of their industry, including environmental protection, pricing, and service provision. This did not always work well. Environmental concerns, in particular, were often given scant attention by engineering-dominated organizations. Pricing was driven primarily by requirements for cost recovery rather than by the need to use resources efficiently. In some cases, the creation of separate regulatory bodies has yielded improved outcomes. Privatization is not, however, a necessary step in this progress.

The continued heavy reliance on regulation, and the conspicuous failure of "light-handed" regulatory models such as those applied to electricity markets in the United States and telecommunications in New Zealand substantially undermines the view that public enterprises represent a barrier to the emergence of competitive markets capable of generating socially optimal outcomes. Public ownership is not the only answer to market failure, but in the absence of strong regulation, privatization is not an answer at all.

REANIMATION: DEAD FOR GOOD?

Some zombies can be killed once and for all. It seems that the Global Financial Crisis may finally have buried the idea of comprehensive privatization. Throughout the world, the need for governments to act as the ultimate guarantors of economic and financial stability has been evident.

Even fringe right-wing groups, such as the Tea Party movement in the United States, which have opposed both the bailout of the banking system undertaken by the G. W. Bush administration and the stimulus package put forward by Obama, have focused their ire on the alleged misuse of public money involved. Enthusiasm for a genuinely minimal government appears lacking even here, as is evidenced by the famous statement of one such protestor "keep your government hands off my Medicare." While most on the right have tried to avoid such obvious self-contradiction, they have, as Paul Krugman has noted, abandoned serious attempts to scrap or privatize the key elements of the welfare state such as Medicare and Social Security.

What is true in the United States is true internationally. The British Conservative Party, once the standard bearer for privatization under Margaret Thatcher, has announced plans to allow public sector workers to set up cooperatives to run services such as primary schools and job centers. While some have expressed concern that this might be a backdoor route to privatization, the central point is that the idea itself can no longer be defended in public, even by the party that did most to popularize it.

Elsewhere in Europe, the Global Financial Crisis has hit hard at the countries and governments that embraced the ideology of comprehensive privatization most enthusiastically. Iceland, which hosted a triumphal meeting of the ultra–free market Mont Pelerin Society only a few years ago, is now working its way through national bankruptcy. Ireland is not much better off. The Baltic States are basket cases. Even in cases such as that of Greece, which seem, at first sight, to involve a simple excess of spending over tax revenue, it turns out that a variety of quasi-privatization measures helped to disguise the problem until it was too late to fix.

With the national exemplars of comprehensive privatization in disarray, and its advocates in full retreat, it seems unlikely that this zombie idea will return from the grave any time soon. That does not mean that we will see no more privatization of government enterprises.

Sensible proponents of the mixed economy have never argued that privatization should be opposed in all cases. As circumstances change, government involvement in some areas of the economy becomes more desirable, in others less so. In cases of the second kind, the appropriate response may well be to privatize existing government enterprises. And, unfortunately, whether or not any particular privatization is justified, politicians will always be tempted to rely on superficially appealing, but spurious arguments of the kind discussed here.

The crucial condition for the stability of a mixed economy is that shifts between the private and public sector should, broadly speaking, balance out. Privatizations may take place, but they are balanced by extensions of government activity through the establishment of new public enterprises or public services, the expansion of existing ones, or where private ownership has clearly failed, the nationalization or renationalization of private firms.

AFTER THE ZOMBIES: THE MIXED ECONOMY

The death of the case for comprehensive privatization does not imply acceptance of the opposite extreme position in favor of comprehensive public ownership, or that privatization is never justified. There are large areas of the economy, such as agriculture and retail trade, where public enterprises have rarely operated at a profit. No fiscal benefit can arise from public ownership of a loss-making enterprise. Relatively modest reductions in profitability arising from the constraints associated with public ownership are sufficient to offset the benefits of a lower cost of capital.

In particular, arguments about the cost of equity capital are irrelevant for small unincorporated businesses, where there is no reliance on external equity. Such small businesses typically face a high cost of external capital, relying primarily on bank loans. However, the higher cost of capital for small businesses, relative to both government enterprises and large private corporations, is offset by the efficiency advantages of combining ownership and control.

The idea that we must choose between pure laissez-faire capitalism and comprehensive socialization is part of what might be called the Great Forgetting of the lessons of the mixed economy. The mixed economy was not, and is not, a simple compromise between incompatible extremes. Rather it has given rise to an effective and productive interaction between the private and public sectors. The balance of that interaction will change over time, sometimes requiring privatization of public enterprises and sometimes extension of the public sector through nationalization or the creation of new government business enterprises.

This is not a surprising conclusion, being little more than a restatement of the conventional wisdom that prevailed for much of the period after World War II. Nevertheless, it is inconsistent with the market liberal ideas that have been dominant since the economic crisis of the 1970s. In the market liberal framework, the superiority of the private sector and the persistence of large-scale public sector provision of goods and services is assumed to be the result of unjustified political resistance to market-oriented reform.

The Mixed Economy

Determining the right balance between the public and private sectors in a mixed economy does not require any radical innovations in economic thinking. The main task remaining for economists is to understand more fully the capital market failures that make the cost of equity capital so high. There are a number of factors involved, and the implications for the cost of equity capital depend on the interactions between them.

First, as was discussed in chapter 2, equity markets are subject to irrational bubbles and busts. The result is that equity investments fluctuate more than does the true economic value of the corporate profits from which returns to equity are derived. Since equity is riskier than it should be under the assumptions of CCAPM, investors will demand higher average rates of return.

Second, many important risks, such as the risk of becoming unemployed, cannot be traded away. This "background risk" leads investors to be more averse to equity investments that yield low or negative returns in a downturn, when the risk of unemployment is high. Finally, equity markets have shown themselves to be uneven playing fields where large and politically powerful firms like Goldman Sachs are guaranteed high returns while ordinary investors lose out.

To the extent that these failures can be overcome, the equity premium will decline and the case for private provision of goods and services will be strengthened.[9] In the meantime, economists need to abandon the search for a clever solution to the equity premium "puzzle" and focus more on the implications of the messy reality.

The existing theory of natural monopoly and market failure provides an indication of the areas where public ownership is likely to prove beneficial, as does the observation that, across many different countries, the areas of the economy that have been allocated to the private and public sectors have been broadly similar. The boundaries have shifted from time to time, but broadly speaking, public provision has been most common in capital-intensive natural monopoly industries, and in the provision of human services such as health and education.

The case for public ownership is strongest in industries where market failure problems are severe. In the case of infrastructure industries, several market failures are important. First, because of the equity premium and the associated problem of short-termism, private providers of infrastructure may not invest enough, or in a way that maximizes long-run benefits. Second, infrastructure facilities often generate positive externalities that are not reflected in the returns to the owners of those facilities. For example, good quality transport facilities will raise the value of land in the areas it serves. Finally, there are problems associated with the natural monopoly characteristics of many infrastructure services.

---

[9] The rise of the "information economy" is a two-edged sword here. On the one hand, more information should improve the functioning of financial markets. On the other hand, information is an archetypal "public good," suited to free public provision, so the areas of the economy where private markets yield the best outcomes are likely to contract in relative importance.

As regards human services such as health and education, the gap between the reality of providing these services and the theoretical requirements for market optimality is so great that economists have struggled to apply economic analysis to these activities. The biggest problems relate to information, uncertainty, and financing.

The value of health and education services is derived in large measure from the knowledge of the providers (doctors, nurses, teachers and others) and their skill in applying that knowledge to benefit patients and students. By contrast, the standard economic analysis of markets begins with the presumption that both parties are equally well informed about the nature of the good or service involved. The asymmetry of information is intimately linked to the fact that the benefits of health and education services are hard to predict in advance, or even to verify in retrospect. This in turn creates severe problems for financing through market mechanisms such as health insurance and student loans. One way or another, substantial government involvement in the financing of health and education is unavoidable. Once governments are paying some or all of the bill, the most cost-effective solution is often direct public provision.

Conversely, the case for private provision is strongest where the efficient scale of operations is small enough to allow a number of firms to compete and where markets function well, rewarding firms that innovate to anticipate and meet consumer demand, and eliminating those that produce inefficiently or provide poor service. In particular, in sectors of the economy dominated by small and medium enterprises, where large corporations cannot compete successfully, it is unlikely that government business enterprises will do much better. My home state of Queensland, Australia, provides historical support for this claim, having experimented, unsuccessfully, with state-owned butcher shops, hotels, and cattle stations early in the twentieth century.

There will always be a range of intermediate cases where no solution is obviously superior. Depending on historical contingencies or particular circumstances, different societies may choose between public provision (typically by a commercialized government business enterprise), private provision subject to regulation, or perhaps some intermediate between the two, such as a public-private partnership.

Unlike most of the ideas discussed, the death of the ideology of privatization has already been reflected in "facts on the ground." Most of the emergency nationalizations undertaken during the Global Financial Crisis will ultimately be reversed. But the idea that public ownership is always a policy option, and sometimes a necessary choice, cannot be banished from public debate. The mixed economy is back, and it's here to stay.

FURTHER READING

The Ash quotation is from Krasnolutska and Martens (2008).

In addition to Berman (1998, 2002), Sassoon (1998) and Judt (2005) give excellent overviews of European social democracy.

Pigou's (1920) classic work on welfare economics set out the externality framework, which was later criticized, but not displaced, by the property rights theory of Coase (1960). Shackle (1983) gives a fascinating, if idiosyncratic, account of the atmosphere in which Robinson's (1932) work on imperfect competition was produced.

The term *market failure* was introduced by Bator (1958). The first use of "government failure" as a complementary category was McKean (1965). Shonfield (1984) defended the mixed economy against its critics. Giddens (1999) provided the intellectual basis of the claim by Blair to represent a "Third Way," this time between Thatcherism and the older social democratic tradition represented by Shonfield. Silverman's (1998) interview with Rudolf Meidner describes the intellectual atmosphere in which the plan was developed and the rise and fall of the Swedish model.

The "markets for votes" model of politics was first developed by Downs (1957), but the foundational work was that of Buchanan and Tullock (1965). Mueller (1989) provides a fairly accessible summary. In one of my own earliest papers, (Quiggin 1987), I pointed out numerous problems with the public choice approach. The property rights approach begins with Coase (1960) and remains influential in work such as that of de Soto's (2003) *The Mystery of Capital.*

Cockett (1995) gives an excellent account of the way in which market liberal ideas were turned into policy proposals by think tanks like the Institute of Economic Affairs. *A Restatement of Economic Liberalism* (Brittan 1988) gives the view from the inside. A triumphalist account of the victory of market liberalism is *Commanding Heights* by Yergin and Stanislaw (2002). Glyn (2007) describes the same developments from the viewpoint of a somewhat, but not entirely, disillusioned socialist. Easton (1997) gives an excellent account of the New Zealand reforms, coining the phrase "market Leninist" to describe the reform approach of Douglas and others. Fukuyama's (1992) *The End of History* gives an excellent insight into the mental atmosphere of the 1990s, as does Thomas Friedman's (1999) vulgarization, *The Lexus and the Olive Tree*.

The phrase "policy in search of a rationale" is due to Kay and Thompson (1986) who are critical of the tendency of the Thatcher government, and many of its successors, to privatize government enterprises with their monopoly position intact, thereby enhancing the sale price but forgoing the benefits of competition. The term *Washington Consensus* was coined by Williamson (1990), though he later repudiated its more extreme interpretations. Durbin's description of bank power was given in an interview with WJJG Radio 1530 AM in April 2009 and later reported by Doster (2009).

The discussion of privatization and the equity premium is largely based on my own work on this topic over the past fifteen years, often in collaboration with Simon Grant. Some key papers are Quiggin (1995) and Grant and Quiggin (2002, 2003, 2004, 2005, 2006). The IMF study is by Davis et al. (2000).

Other references are Akerlof (1970); Arrow and Debreu (1954); Baumol (1982); Baumol, Panzar, and Willig (1982); Bel (2006); Chamberlin (1933); Drucker (1969); Friedman and Friedman (1979), Krugman (2009c), Merah and Prescott (1985), Mill (2008, Book V); Nairn (1989); Nash (1951); Shiller (2003a, 2003b, 2008); and von Neumann and Morgenstern (1944).

ECONOMICS FOR THE TWENTY-FIRST CENTURY

The zombies of horror movies are famously hard to stop. Being already dead, they can absorb all kinds of damage and keep lumbering on toward their targets. The zombie ideas discussed in this book are similarly resilient. Throughout the crisis, the economics profession carried on, for the most part, as if nothing had changed. And now that the immediate crisis has passed, market liberals are trying to pretend that it never happened.

As Richard Posner, a rare example of a market liberal who has changed his views and embraced Keynesianism, observed in a recent interview:

> Market correctives work very slowly in dealing with academic markets. Professors have tenure. They have lots of graduate students in the pipeline who need to get their Ph.D.s. They have techniques that they know and are comfortable with. It takes a great deal to drive them out of their accustomed way of doing business. (quoted in Cassidy 2010, 28)

An approach to economics that has been dominant for more than three decades will not go away simply because its predictions are inconsistent with the facts. It is necessary to provide an alternative to the zombie economics of market liberalism. Before considering the future, however, it is worth reexamining the past.

RETHINKING THE EXPERIENCE OF THE TWENTIETH CENTURY

The failure of market liberalism calls for a rethinking of the experience of the twentieth century and, in particular, the crisis of the 1970s.

Considered as a whole, the performance of developed economies in the era of market liberalism looks considerably less impressive than that of the postwar period of Keynesian social democracy.

Yet that Golden Age ended in the chaos and failure of the 1970s. Until the current crisis, that failure was taken as conclusive. Whatever its merits, Keynesian economic management had proved unsustainable in the end, while the methods of market liberalism seemed to promise the continuing stability of the Great Moderation.

That view can no longer be sustained. The Great Moderation has ended in a failure at least as bad as that which ended the postwar boom. If there is a recovery, it will be due to the very measures that market liberalism was supposed to have rendered obsolete. How then, should we think about the Keynesian era and its failure?

One possible interpretation, a pessimistic one, is that business cycles are so deeply embedded in the logic of market economics, and perhaps of all modern economies, that they cannot be tamed. Success breeds hubris, and hubris leads us to ignore the lessons of the past: that resources are always constrained, that budgets must ultimately balance, that wages and other incomes cannot, for long, exceed the value of production, and so on. In the 1960s and 1970s, this hubris manifested itself in unsustainable budget deficits and the wage-price spiral. In the 1990s and 2000s, it was seen in the speculative frenzy unleashed by the self-styled Masters of the Universe in the financial sector.

But this is not the only possible interpretation. Perhaps the failures of the 1970s were the result of mistakes that could have been avoided with a better understanding of the economy and stronger social institutions. If so, the current crisis may mark a return to successful policies that take account of the errors of the past.

A NEW APPROACH TO RISK AND UNCERTAINTY

In one way or another, the zombie ideas described in this book center on the notion that a liberal market system in which risk is managed through financial markets will outperform one in which governments intervene to stabilize aggregate outcomes and mitigate individual risks. The Great Moderation idea was that market liberal policies had reduced aggregate risk more effectively than had Keynesian macroeconomic management. This idea found theoretical support in Dynamic Stochastic General Equilibrium macroeconomics.

The Efficient Markets Hypothesis presented the same claim as applied to individual enterprises. According to the Efficient Markets Hypothesis, financial markets do the best possible job in valuing the returns and risks associated with financial assets of all kinds. This claim finds its political expression in the ideology of privatization. Trickle-down economics suggests that the risks associated with life in a highly unequal society are more than offset by the resulting opportunities.

In the light of the Global Financial Crisis, none of these claims stand up to scrutiny. Risk can no longer be ignored or wished out of existence through financial market conjuring tricks.

Social democrats and social liberals have long emphasized the idea that we have the capacity to share and manage risks more effectively as a society than as individuals. The set of policies traditionally associated with social democracy may be regarded as responses to a range of risks facing individuals, from health risks to uncertain life chances.

Risk and inequality are closely linked. On the one hand, the greater the risks faced by individuals in the course of their lives, including the risk associated with differences in initial opportunities, the more unequal society is likely to be. On the other hand, as the financial crisis has shown, radical inequality in outcomes, such as that associated with massive rewards to financial traders, encourages risky behavior. Inequality particularly encourages a search for opportunities to capture the benefits of risky actions while shifting the costs onto others, or onto society as a whole.

A social democratic response to the crisis must begin by reasserting the crucial role of the state in risk management. If individuals are to have security of employment, income, and wealth, governments must act to establish and enforce the necessary legal and economic framework. The fact that government is the ultimate risk manager justifies and necessitates action to mitigate inequalities in both opportunities and outcomes.

Grotesque inequalities characterize unrestrained capitalism and were increasingly resurgent in the era of market liberalism.

The interpretation of the welfare state in terms of risk and uncertainty may be illustrated by considering some of its core functions. For some of these functions, such as various forms of social insurance, the risk management function has always been emphasized. However, concern with risk has traditionally been a subsidiary theme.

For instance, the public provision of retirement income and of services like health or education have been justified with reference to notions of redistribution, public goods, and the provision of basic needs. However, these interventions may equally be supported in terms of risk management.

A risk-based analysis may be extended to encompass more general programs of income redistribution. In a risk-based view, redistribution may be seen as providing insurance against a particular kind of risk, namely the risk of being born poor, socially dislocated, and without access to human and social capital.

Collective risk management through the welfare state helps to stabilize the aggregate economy. When incomes decline as a result of a recession, the design of a progressive tax system means that government tax revenues decline more than proportionally. This helps to cushion the impact on private demand and offsets the downward multiplier effects of an initial shock to the economy. Similarly, when unemployment rises, this produces an automatic increase in spending on unemployment benefits, which is commonly amplified by expansion of benefits and the creation of new employment programs.

The mechanisms by which the welfare state softens the impact of demand shocks are called "automatic stabilizers," and given robust welfare state institutions, the name is appropriate. But there is nothing automatic or guaranteed about those institutions. A balanced budget requirement such as exists in most U.S. states, will force governments to cut expenditure precisely when it is most needed, producing, in Paul Krugman's phrase "50 Herbert Hoovers."[1]

---

[1] See Krugman (2009b).

Similarly, if a government is so indebted that it can't borrow money, or print money without the risk of inflation, an economic crisis will force retrenchment. That's why it's important to stress the "hard" side shared by social democratic risk management and Keynesian demand management. Abandoning short-term budget balance doesn't mean that bills don't have to be paid. Help when we face unemployment or health risks, or for those who are unlucky in their life chances, must be paid for by tax contributions made by those who are, at least for the moment, healthy and well-off. Budget deficits to soften the impact of recessions must be matched by surpluses in good times. The "golden rule" is to balance the budget over the course of the cycle.

No one can predict the future path of the economy with any accuracy. But at the aggregate level, we can expect more instability, with more frequent and sharper shocks, than during the false calm of the Great Moderation. And the end of the Great Moderation has not reversed the *Great Risk Shift* or, except partially and temporarily, the growth in inequality produced by the decades of market liberalism.

A positive response should combine better social provision to help people deal with risk at the individual and family level with a return to active use of fiscal as well as monetary policy to stabilize the aggregate economy. The two should be designed to work together. Social risk management policies should act as automatic stabilizers in the Keynesian sense, and fiscal policies should be focused on helping those most directly affected by recession.

WHAT IS NEEDED IN ECONOMICS

Some suggestions about the way forward have been offered in this book. They can be summed up by three simple propositions. In the twenty-first century, economics should focus:

★ More on realism, less on rigor
★ More on equity, less on efficiency
★ More on humility, less on hubris

The prevailing emphasis on mathematical and logical rigor has given economics an internal consistency that is missing in other social sciences. But there is little value in being consistently wrong. Economics must move on from the infinitely rational, farsighted, and asocial beings whose decisions have been the central topic of analysis in recent decades. It will still be necessary to abstract from the messy complexity of human decision processes and focus on critical factors in decision-making. But the factors that are relevant in microeconomic analysis of goods markets may not be the same as those that matter in labor markets or in analysis of macroeconomic aggregates.

Three decades in which market liberals have pushed policies based on ideas of efficiency and claims about the efficiency of financial markets have not produced much in the way of improved economic performance, but they have led to drastic increases in inequality, particularly in the English-speaking world. Economists need to return their attention to policies that will generate a more equitable distribution of income.

Finally, with the collapse of yet another economic "New Era," it is time for the economics profession to display some humility. More than two centuries after Adam Smith, economists have to admit the force of Socrates' observation that "the wisest man is he who knows that he knows nothing." While knowledge in the sense of absolute certainty may be unattainable, economists can contribute to a better understanding of the strengths and weaknesses of markets, firms, and other forms of economic organization, and the possibilities for policy action to yield improved economic and social outcomes.

Every crisis is an opportunity. The Global Financial Crisis gives the economics profession the chance to bury the zombie ideas that led the world into crisis, and to produce a more realistic, humble, and above all socially useful body of thought.

REFERENCES

Akerlof, George (1970), "The Market for 'Lemons': Qualitative Uncertainty and the Market Mechanism," *Quarterly Journal of Economics*, 84(3), 488–500.

——— (2001), "Behavioral Macroeconomics and Macroeconomic Behavior," Sveriges Riksbank Prize in Economic Sciences in Memory of Alfred Nobel 2001 Prize Lecture, Aula Magna, Stockholm University.

Akerlof, George, and Robert Shiller (2009), *Animal Spirits: How Human Psychology Drives the Economy, and Why it Matters for Global Capitalism*, Princeton: Princeton University Press.

Akerlof, George, and Janet Yellen (1985a), "A Near-Rational Model of the Business Cycle, with Wage and Price Inertia," *Quarterly Journal of Economics*, 100(4), 823–38.

——— (1985b), "Can Small Deviations From Rationality Make Significant Differences to Economic Equilibria?" *American Economic Review*, 75, 708–20.

American Bankruptcy Institute (2010), "U.S. Bankruptcy Statistics," http://www.abiworld.org/Content/NavigationMenu/NewsRoom/BankruptcyStatistics/Bankruptcy_Filings_1.htm, accessed 28 January 2010.

Andrews, Dan, Christopher Jencks, and Andrew Leigh (2009), "Do Rising Top Incomes Lift All Boats?" Harvard University Working Paper, Cambridge, MA: Harvard University Press.

Arrow, Kenneth, and Gerard Debreu (1954), "Existence of an Equilibrium for a Competitive Economy," *Econometrica*, 22(3), 265–90.

Astin, Alexander, and Leticia Oseguera (2004), "The Declining 'Equity' of American Higher Education," *Review of Higher Education*, 27(3), 321–41.

Bachelier, Louis, Paul Samuelson, M. Davis, and A. Etheridge (2006), *Louis Bachelier's Theory of Speculation: The Origins of Modern Finance*, Princeton: Princeton University Press.

Bai, Matt (2007), "The Poverty Platform," *The New York Times*, 10 June.

Baker, Gerard (2007), "Welcome to 'the Great Moderation,'" *The Times*, 19 January.

——— (2009), "Bringing Down the Curtain on the Folly of My Faith in the Great Moderation," *The Times*, 13 January.

Bank for International Settlements (BIS) (2009), "Semiannual Over-The-Counter (OTC) Derivatives Markets Statistics," http://www.bis.org/statistics/derstats.htm, accessed 15 May 2010.

Barr, Nicholas (2001), *The Welfare State as Piggy Bank: Information, Risk, Uncertainty, and the Role of the State,* Oxford: Oxford University Press.

Barro, Robert (1974), "Are Government Bonds Net Wealth?" *Journal of Political Economy,* 82(6), 1095–117.

Barro, Robert, and Herschel Grossman (1976), *Money, Employment and Inflation,* New York: Cambridge University Press.

Bator, Francis (1958), "The Anatomy of Market Failure," *Quarterly Journal of Economics,* 72(3), 351–79.

Baumol, William (1982), "Contestable Markets: An Uprising in the Theory of Industry Structure," *American Economic Review,* 72(1), 1–15.

Baumol, William, John Panzar, and Robert Willig (1982), *Contestable Markets and the Theory of Industry Structure,* New York: Harcourt Brace Jovanovich.

Beck, Ulrich (1992), *Risk Society: Towards a New Modernity, trans. M. Ritter,* London: Sage.

Bel, Germà (2006), "Retrospectives: The Coining of "Privatization" and Germany's National Socialist Party," *Journal of Economic Perspectives,* 20(3), 187–94.

Bell, Stephen, and John Quiggin (2006), "Asset Price Instability and Policy Responses: The Legacy of Liberalization," *Journal of Economic Issues,* 40(3), 629–49.

Berlin, Isaiah (1959), *Two Concepts of Liberty: An Inaugural Lecture, University of Oxford 1958,* Oxford: Clarendon Press.

Berman, Sheri (1998), *The Social Democratic Moment: Ideas and Politics in the Making of Interwar Europe,* Cambridge, MA: Harvard University Press.

——— (2002), "The Roots and Rationale of Social Democracy," *Social Philosophy and Policy,* 20(1), 113–44.

Bernanke, Ben (2004a), "The Great Moderation," presentation to the Eastern Economic Association, Washington, DC, 20 February.

——— (2004b), *Essays on the Great Depression,* Princeton: Princeton University Press.

Bernanke, Ben, and Mark Gertler (1999), "Monetary Policy and Asset Price Volatility," *Federal Reserve Bank of Kansas City, Economic Review,* 84(4), 17–51.

Bezruchka, Stephen (2001), "Societal Hierarchy and the Health Olympics," *Canadian Medical Association Journal,* 164(12), 1701–3.

Black, Fischer, and Myron Scholes (1973), "The Pricing of Options and Corporate Liabilities," *The Journal of Political Economy,* 81(3), 637–54.

Blanchard, Olivier J. (2008), "The State of Macro," NBER Working Paper No. 14259, Cambridge, MA: National Bureau of Economic Research.

Blanchard, Olivier, and John Simon (2001), "The Long and Large Decline in U.S. Output Volatility," *Brookings Papers on Economic Activity,* 32(2001–1), 135–74.

Blanchard, Olivier, and Larry Summers (1986), "Hysteresis and the European Unemployment Problem," *NBER Macroeconomics Annual,* 1, 15–78.

Blanden, Jo, Alissa Goodman, Paul Gregg, and Stephen Machin (2004), "Changes in Intergenerational Mobility in Britain," pp. 122–46, in *Generational Income Mobility in North America and Europe*, ed. M. Corak, Cambridge: Cambridge University Press.

Borio, Claudio, and Philip Lowe (2003), "Monetary Policy: A Subtle Paradigm Shift?" *World Economics*, 4(2), 103–19.

Boskin, Michael, Ellen Dulberger, Robert Gordon, Zvi Griliches, and Dale Jorgensen (1998), "Consumer Prices, the Consumer Price Index and the Cost of Living," *Journal of Economic Perspectives*, 12(1), 3–26.

Bowen, William, and Derek Bok (1998), *The Shape of the River: Long-Term Consequences of Considering Race in College and University Admissions*, Princeton: Princeton University Press.

Bradbury, Katharine (1986), "The Shrinking Middle Class," *New England Economic Review*, (Sep), 41–55.

Bramley, Glen (1987), "Horizontal Disparities and Equalization: A Critique of 'Paying for Local Government,'" *Local Government Studies*, 13(1), 69–89.

Brittan, Samuel (1988), *A Restatement of Economic Liberalism*, London: Palgrave Macmillan.

Buchanan, James, and Gordon Tullock (1965), *The Calculus of Consent: Logical Foundations of Constitutional Democracy*, Ann Arbor: University of Michigan Press.

Buiter, Willem (2009), "The Unfortunate Uselessness of Most 'State of the Art' Academic Monetary Economics, http://blogs.ft.com/maverecon/2009/03/the-unfortunate-uselessness-of-most-state-of-the-art-academic-monetary-economics/, accessed 10 May 2010.

Buiter, Willem, and Marcus Miller (1981), "The Thatcher Experiment: The First Two Years," *Brookings Papers on Economic Activity*, 1981(2), 315–79.

Bureau of Economic Analysis (2010), "National Economic Accounts," http://www.bea.gov/national/index.htm, accessed 28 January 2010.

Burtless, Gary (1990), *A Future of Lousy Jobs? The Changing Structure of U.S. Wages*, Washington, DC: Brookings Institution Press.

Canto, Victor, Douglas Jones, and Arthur Laffer (1982), *Foundations of Supply Side Economics: Theory and Evidence (Economic Theory, Econometrics, and Mathematical Economics)*, New York: Academic Press.

Cassidy, John (2010), "After the Blowup (Letter From Chicago)," *New Yorker*, January 11, p. 28.

Central Intelligence Agency (CIA) (2009), "World Factbook," https://www.cia.gov/library/publications/the-world-factbook/index.html, accessed 28 January 2009.

Chamberlin, Edmund (1933), *The Theory of Monopolistic Competition*, Cambridge, MA: Harvard University Press.

Clark, Colin (1932), *The National Income 1924–1931*, London: Macmillan.

Clark, Gregory (2009), "Dismal scientists: How the crash is reshaping economics," *Atlantic Monthly*, Feb. 16, at http://www.theatlantic.com/business/

archive/2009/02/dismal-scientists-how-the-crash-is-reshaping-economics/614/.

Coase, Ronald (1960), "The Problem of Social Cost," *Journal of Law and Economics*, 3(1), 1–44.

Cochrane, John (2009), "How Did Paul Krugman Get it So Wrong?" http://modeledbehavior.com/2009/09/11/john-cochrane-responds-to-paul-krugman-full-text/.

Cockett, Richard (1995), *Thinking the Unthinkable: Think-Tanks and the Economic Counter-Revolution, 1931–1983*, London: HarperCollins.

Coddington, Alan (1976), "Keynesian Economics: The Search for First Principles," *Journal of Economic Literature*, 14(4), 1258–73.

Coibion, Olivier, and Yuri Gorodnichenko (2008), "Monetary Policy, Trend Inflation, and the Great Moderation: An Alternative Interpretation," NBER Working Paper No. 14621, Cambridge, MA: National Bureau of Economic Research.

—— (2010), "Does the Great Recession Really Mean the End of the Great Moderation?" http://www.voxeu.org/index.php?q=node/4496, accessed 2 March 2010.

Cole, Harold, and Lee Ohanian (2004), "New Deal Policies and the Persistence of the Great Depression: A General Equilibrium Analysis," *Journal of Political Economy*, 112(4), 779–816.

Commonwealth of Australia (1945), "Full Employment in Australia," Canberra: Commonwealth Government Printer.

Cox, Michael, and Richard Alm (2000), *Myths of Rich and Poor: Why We're Better Off than We Think*, New York: Basic Books.

Davidson, Paul (1991), "Is Probability Theory Relevant for Uncertainty? A Post-Keynesian Perspective," *Journal of Economic Perspectives*, 5(1), 129–43.

Davis, Jeffrey, Rolando Ossowski, Thomas Richardson, and Steven Barnett (2000), *Fiscal and Macroeconomic Impact of Privatization*, Washington, DC: International Monetary Fund.

Debreu, Gerard (1959), *Theory of Value*, New York: Wiley.

DeLong, Bradford (2009a), "Which Economists Got it So Wrong?" http://delong.typepad.com/sdj/2009/09/which-economists-got-it-so-wrong.html, accessed 16 May 2010.

—— (2009b), "Why Does the New York Times Publish Casey Mulligan?" http://delong.typepad.com/sdj/2009/08/why-does-the-new-york-times-publish-casey-mulligan.html, accessed 15 May 2010.

—— (2010), "How Scared of the Future Should Macroeconomists Be?" http://delong.typepad.com/sdj/2010/01/how-scared-of-the-future-should-macroeconomists-be.html, accessed 2 March 2010.

de Soto, Hernando (2003), *The Mystery of Capital: Why Capitalism Triumphs in the West and Fails Everywhere Else*, New York: Basic Books.

Doster, Adam (2009), "Durbin on Congress: The Banks 'Own The Place,'" http://progressillinois.com/2009/4/29/durbin-banks-own-the-place.

Downs, Anthony (1957), *An Economic Theory of Democracy*, New York: Harper & Row.

Drucker, Peter (1969), *The Age of Discontinuity*, New York: Harper & Row.

Dynan, Karen, Douglas Elmendorf, and Daniel Sichel (2006), "Financial Innovation and the Great Moderation: What Do Household Data Say?" Paper presented at Financial Innovations and the Real Economy, Federal Reserve Bank of San Francisco, http://www.frbsf.org/economics/conferences/0611/2_Sichel.pdf.

Easton, Brian (1997), *The Commercialisation of New Zealand*, Auckland: Auckland University Press.

——— (1999), "What Has Happened in New Zealand to Income Distribution and Poverty Levels?", pp. 55–66, in *Social Policy for the Twenty-first Century: Justice and Responsibility*, ed. Sheila Shaver and Peter Saunders, Proceedings of the National Social Policy Conference, Sydney, 21–23 July, vol. 2, Sydney: Social Policy Research Centre.

Ehrenreich, Barbara (1990) *Fear of Falling: The Inner Life of the Middle Class*, New York: Harper Perennial.

——— (2001), *Nicked and Dimed: On (Not) Getting By in America*, New York: Metropolitan Books.

Ellenberger, Jordan (2008), "We're Down $700 Billion. Let's Go Double or Nothing!" posted Aug. 2, *Slate.com*, at http://slate.com/id.2201428.

Epstein, Larry, and Martin Schneider (2003), "Recursive Multiple-Priors," *Journal of Economic Theory*, 113(1), 1–31.

European Anti-Poverty Network (Eapn) (2009), "Poverty and Inequality in the European Union," http://www.poverty.org.uk/summary/eapn.shtml.

Fama, Eugene (1965), "The Behavior of Stock-Market Prices," *The Journal of Business*, 38(1), 34–105.

——— (2009), "Bailouts and Stimulus Plans," Jan., posted at http://www.dimensional.com/famafrench/2009/01/bailouts-and-stimulus-plans.html.

——— (1970), "Efficient Capital Markets: A Review of Theory and Empirical Work," *Journal of Finance*, 25(2), 383–417.

Feldstein, Martin (1995), "The Effect of Marginal Tax Rates on Taxable Income: A Panel Study of the 1986 Tax Reform Act," *Journal of Political Economy*, 103(3), 551–72.

Fellner, William, Edmund S. Phelps, and Robert J. Gordon (1979), "The Credibility Effect and Rational Expectations: Implications of the Gramlich Study," *Brookings Papers on Economic Activity*, 1979(1), 167–89.

Fisher, Gordon (1992), "The Development and History of the Poverty Thresholds," *Social Security Bulletin*, 55(4), 3–14.

Fisher, Irving (1933), "The Debt-Deflation Theory of Great Depressions," *Econometrica*, 1(4), 337–57.

Food Research and Action Center (Frac) (2009), "Hunger and Food Insecurity in the United States," http://www.frac.org/html/hunger_in_the_us/hunger_index.html, accessed 30 January 2010.

Fox, J. (2009), *The Myth of the Rational Market: A History of Risk, Reward, and Delusion on Wall Street,* New York: HarperBusiness.

Friedman, Milton (1968), "The Role of Monetary Policy," *American Economic Review,* 68(1), 1–17.

Friedman, Milton, and Rose Friedman (1980), *Free to Choose,* New York: Harcourt Brace Jovanovich.

Friedman, Milton, and Walter W. Heller (1969), *Monetary versus Fiscal Policy,* New York: W. W. Norton.

Friedman, Thomas (1999), *The Lexus and the Olive Tree: Understanding Globalization,* New York: Farrar Strauss Giroux.

Fukuyama, Francis (1992), *The End of History and the Last Man,* New York: Free Press.

——— (1996), *Trust: The Social Virtues and the Creation of Prosperity,* New York: Free Press.

Galbraith, John Kenneth (1969), *The Great Crash, 1929,* New York: Penguin.

Galindo-Rueda, Fernando, and Anna Vignoles (2005), "The Declining Relative Importance of Ability in Predicting Educational Attainment," *Journal of Human Resources,* 40(2), 335–53.

Garber, Peter (2001), *Famous First Bubbles: The Fundamentals of Early Manias,* Cambridge, MA: MIT Press.

Giddens, Anthony (1999), *The Third Way: The Renewal of Social Democracy,* London: Blackwell.

——— (2002), *Runaway World: How Globalization Is Reshaping Our Lives (1999 Reith Lecture),* London: Routledge.

Glassman, James, and Kevin Hassett (1999), *Dow 36000,* New York: Times Books.

Glyn, Andrew (2007), *Capitalism Unleashed: Finance, Globalization, and Welfare,* New York: Oxford University Press.

Goldin, Claudia, and Robert Margo (1992), "The Great Compression: The Wage Structure in the United States at Mid-Century," *Quarterly Journal of Economics,* 107(1), 1–34.

Goodin, Robert, Bruce Headey, Ruud Muffels and Henk-Jan Dirven (1999), *The Real Worlds of Welfare Capitalism,* Cambridge: Cambridge University Press.

Goolsbee, Austin (1999), "Evidence on the High-income Laffer Curve from Six Decades of Tax Reform (with comments from R. E. Hall and L. F. Katz)," *Brookings Papers on Economic Activity,* 2, 1–64.

Gordon, David (1996), *Fat and Mean: The Corporate Squeeze of Working Americans and the Myth of Managerial "Downsizing,"* New York: Martin Kessler Books and Free Press.

Gordon, Robert, and Ian Dew-Becker (2008), "Controversies about the Rise of American Inequality: A Survey," NBER Working Paper No. 13982, Cambridge, MA.

Gosselin, Peter (2009), *High Wire: The Precarious Financial Lives of American Families,* New York: Basic Books.

Gottschalk, Peter (1997), "Inequality, Income Growth, and Mobility: The Basic Facts," *Journal of Economic Perspectives*, 11(2), 21–40.

Graham, Liam, and Dennis Snower (2008), "Hyperbolic Discounting and the Phillips Curve," *Journal of Money, Credit and Banking*, 40(2–3), 427–48.

Grant, Simon, Jeffrey Kline, and John Quiggin (2009), "A Matter of Interpretation: Bargaining over Ambiguous Contracts," Paper presented at the 5th Pan-Pacific Conference on Game Theory, Nov. 20, at http://epublications.bond.edu.au/business_pubs/69/.

Grant, Simon, and John Quiggin (2002), "The Risk Premium for Equity: Implications for the Proposed Diversification of the Social Security Fund," *American Economic Review*, 92(4), 1104–15.

——— (2003), "Public Investment and the Risk Premium for Equity," *Economica*, 70(277), 1–18.

——— (2004), "Noise Trader Risk and the Welfare Effects of Privatization," *Economics Bulletin*, 5(9), 1–8.

——— (2005), "What Does the Equity Premium Mean?" *Economists' Voice*, 2(4), Article 2.

——— (2006), "The Risk Premium for Equity: Implications for Resource Allocation, Welfare, and Policy," *Australian Economic Papers*, 45(3), 253–68.

Grossman, Sanford, and Joseph Stiglitz (1980), "On the Impossibility of Informationally Efficient Markets," *American Economic Review*, 70(3), 393–408.

Gruen, David (2009), "Reflections on the Global Financial Crisis," Paper presented at address to the Sydney Institute, Sydney, 16 June.

Gudmundsson, Már (2008), "How Might the Current Financial Crisis Shape Financial Sector Regulation and Structure?" Keynote address by Mr. Már Gudmundsson, Deputy Head of the Monetary and Economic Department of the BIS, at the Financial Technology Congress 2008, Boston, 23 September, http://www.bis.org/speeches/sp081119.htm.

Hacker, Jacob (2006), *Great Risk Shift: The Assault on American Jobs, Families, Health Care, and Retirement, and How You Can Fight Back*, New York: Oxford University Press.

Hall, R. (1976), "Notes on the Current State of Empirical Macroeconomics," mimeo, Stanford University.

Hansen, Lars, and Thomas Sargent (2001), "Robust Control and Model Uncertainty," *American Economic Review*, 91(2), 60–66.

Harcourt, William (1887), "Speech to the House of Commons on the Labourers' Allotments Bill (11 August)," quoted at http://en.wikiquote.org/wiki/William_Harcourt, accessed July 12, 2010.

Harrod, Roy Forbes (1936), *The Trade Cycle: An Essay*, (Reprints of Economic Classics), New York: A.M. Kelley.

Haskins, Ron, and Isabel Sawhill (2009), *Creating an Opportunity Society*, Washington, DC: Brookings Institution Press.

Hayek, Friedrich A. (1966) *Monetary Theory and the Trade Cycle*, New York: Augustus M. Kelley.

Hazeldine, Tim, and John Quiggin (2006), "No More Free Beer Tomorrow? Economic Policy and Outcomes in Australia and New Zealand Since 1984," *Australian Journal of Political Science*, 41(2), 145–59.

Headey, Bruce, and Ruud Muffels (1999), "Up and Down: The Rich, the Poor, and Income Mobility," *Institute of Public Affairs Review: Quarterly Review of Politics and Public Affairs* (December 1999), 3–6.

Helleiner, Eric (1996), *States and the Reemergence of Global Finance: From Bretton Woods to the 1990s*, Ithaca: Cornell University Press.

Heller, Walter (1966) *New Dimensions of Political Economy*, New York: W. W. Norton.

Heritage Foundation (2001), "The Real Reagan Economic Record: Responsible and Successful Fiscal Policy," Heritage Foundation Backgrounder 1414 by P. Sperry, update of Peter J. Ferrara, "What Really Happened in the 1980s?" pp. 3–23, in *Issues '94: The Candidate's Briefing Book*, Washington, D.C.: Heritage Foundation, 1994.

Hicks, J. R. (1937), "Mr. Keynes and the 'Classics': A Suggested Interpretation," *Econometrica*, 5(2), 147–59.

Himmelstein, David, Deborah Thorne, Elizabeth Warren, and Steffie Woolhandler (2009), "Medical Bankruptcy in the United States, 2007: Results of a National Study," *American Journal of Medicine*, 122(8), 741–46.

Holt, Charles, Franco Modigliani, John Muth, and Herbert Simon (1960), *Planning Production, Inventories, and Work Force* (Prentice-Hall International Series on Management), Englewood Cliffs, NJ: Prentice-Hall.

House of Commons (1994), "Paper No. 12, Financial Statement and Budget Report 1995–96," HMSO, http://www.archive.official-documents.co.uk/document/hmt/budget94/budget94.htm, accessed 12 February 2010.

Howard, John (2004), Interview with *Australian Financial Review*, September 22, 1.

Judt, Tony (2005), *Postwar: A History of Europe since 1945*, New York: Penguin.

Kahneman, Daniel, and Amos Tversky (1979), "Prospect Theory: An Analysis of Decision under Risk," *Econometrica*, 47(2), 263–91.

Kay, John (2004), *The Truth About Markets: Why Some Nations Are Rich But Most Remain Poor*, New York: Penguin.

Kay, J., and David Thompson (1986), "Privatization: A Policy in Search of a Rationale," *Economic Journal*, 96(381), 18–32.

Kennedy, John F. (1963), "Remarks in Heber Springs, Arkansas, at the Dedication of Greers Ferry Dam," 3 October, http://www.presidency.ucsb.edu/ws/index.php?pid=9455, accessed 12 February 2010.

Keynes, John Maynard (1936; 2008), *The General Theory of Employment, Interest, and Money*, New Delhi, India: Atlantic Publishers, Google Book edition.

——— (1937), "The General Theory of Employment," *Quarterly Journal of Economics*, 51(2), 209–23.

——— (1940), *How to Pay for the War: A Radical Plan for the Chancellor of the Exchequer,* Toronto: Macmillan Canada.

Kindleberger, Charles (2000), *Manias, Panics, and Crashes: A History of Financial Crises,* New York: Wiley.

Klein, Joe (2009), "Malefactors of Great Wealth," http://swampland.blogs.time .com/2009/01/29/malefactors-of-great-wealth/, accessed 15 June 2009.

Kogan, Richard (2003), "Will the Tax Cuts Ultimately Pay for Themselves?" Center on Budget and Policy Priorities, http://www.cbpp.org/cms/?fa=view&id =119, accessed 20 September 2009.

Krasnolutska, Daryna, and John Martens (2008), "Ukraine Gets $16.5 Billion Loan from IMF; Hungary Next in Line," http://www.bloomberg.com.au/ apps/news?pid=20601110&sid=ai.iCUxotV0k, 26 October, accessed 20 September 2009.

Krugman, Paul (1996), "The Spiral of Inequality," *Mother Jones* (November/ December), http://motherjones.com/politics/1996/11/spiral-inequality.

——— (1998), "Baby-sitting the Economy," *Slate,* http://www.slate.com/id/ 1937/, accessed 2 February 2010.

——— (2009a), "Why Americans Hate Single-Payer Insurance," http://krugman .blogs.nytimes.com/2009/07/28/why-americans-hate-single-payer-insurance/, accessed July 12, 2010.

——— (2009b), *The Conscience of a Liberal,* New York: W.W. Norton.

——— (2009c), "How Did Economists Get It So Wrong?" *New York Times,* 2 September.

Kuznets, S. (1934), "The National Economic Accounts of the United States: Review, Appraisal, and Recommendations," http://library.bea.gov/u?/SOD,88, accessed 15 January 2010.

Kydland, F. E., and E. C. Prescott (1982), "Time to Build and Aggregate Fluctuations," *Econometrica,* 50(6), 1345–70.

Lakoff, George (2004), *Don't Think of an Elephant! Know Your Values and Frame the Debate—The Essential Guide for Progressives,* New York: Chelsea Green.

Leeper, Eric, and Shu-Chun Yang (2008), "Dynamic Scoring: Alternative Financing Schemes," *Journal of Public Economics,* 92(1–2), 159–82.

Leigh, Andrew, and Christopher Jencks (2007), "Inequality and Mortality: Long-run Evidence from a Panel of Countries," *Journal of Health Economics,* 26(1), 1–24.

LeRoy, Stephen (2006), "Excess Volatility Tests," in *The New Palgrave Dictionary of Economics,* ed., S. Durlauf and L. Blume, London: Palgrave Macmillan, online at http://www.dictionaryofeconomics.com/article?id=pde2008 _E000294&q=leroy&topicid=&result_number=4.

Levitt, Steven (2008), "My Colleague Casey Mulligan in the Times: There is No Reason to Panic," http://freakonomics.blogs.nytimes.com/2008/10/10/my -colleague-casey-mulligan-in-the-times-there-is-no-reason-to-panic/, accessed 15 May 2010.

Lindsey, Lawrence (1987), "Individual Taxpayer Response to Tax Cuts: 1982–1984, with Implications for the Revenue Maximizing Tax Rate," *Journal of Public Economics*, 33(2), 173–206.

Lo, Andrew W., and A. Craig MacKinlay (2001), *A Non-Random Walk Down Wall Street*, Princeton: Princeton University Press.

Long, John, and Charles Plosser (1983), "Real Business Cycles," *Journal of Political Economy*, 91(1), 39–69.

Lucas, Robert (1976), "Econometric Policy Evaluation: A Critique," pp. 19–46, in *The Phillips Curve and Labor Markets*, ed. K. Brunner and A. Meltzer, New York: Elsevier.

——— (1977), "Understanding Business Cycles," pp. 7–29, in *Stabilization of the Domestic and International Economy*, ed. K. Brunner and H. Meltzer, New York: Elsevier.

——— (1980), "Methods and Problems in Business Cycle Theory," *Journal of Money, Credit, and Banking*, 12(4), 696–715.

Luttwak, Edward (1999), *Turbo Capitalism: Winners and Losers in the Global Economy*, New York: Harper Collins.

Malkiel, Burton (1973; 2007), *A Random Walk Down Wall Street: The Time-Tested Strategy for Successful Investing (Revised and Updated)*, New York: W. W. Norton.

Mankiw, N. Gregory (1985), "Consumer Durables and the Real Interest Rate," *Review of Economics and Statistics*, 67(3), 353–62.

Mankiw, N. Gregory and Matthew Weinzierl (2006), "Dynamic Scoring: A Back-of-the-Envelope Guide," *Journal of Public Economics*, 90, 1415–33.

Manzi, Jim (2010), "Keeping America's Edge," National Affairs, http://national affairs.com/publications/detail/keeping-americas-edge, accessed 1 March 2010.

Marglin, Steven, and Juliet Schor (1990), *The Golden Age of Capitalism*, Oxford: Clarendon Press, Oxford.

Marmot, Michael (2005), *The Status Syndrome: How Social Standing Affects Our Health and Longevity*, New York: Holt Paperbacks.

McCain, John (2008), "John McCain's Florida Primary Speech," *New York Times*, 29 January.

McKean, Roland (1965), "The Unseen Hand in Government," *American Economic Review*, 55(3), 496–506.

Mehra, Rajnish, and Edward Prescott (1985), "The Equity Premium: A Puzzle," *Journal of Monetary Economics*, 15(2), 145–61.

Merton, Robert C. (1973), "Theory of Rational Option Pricing," *Bell Journal of Economics and Management Science*, 4(1), 141–83.

Mill, J. S. (2008), *Principles of Political Economy: And Chapters on Socialism (Oxford World's Classics)*, New York: Oxford University Press.

Minford, Patrick, and David Peel (1981), "The Role of Monetary Stabilization Policy under Rational Expectations," *Manchester School of Economics & Social Studies*, vol. 49(1), 39–50.

Minsky, Hyman (1975), *John Maynard Keynes,* London: Macmillan.

────── (1982), *Can "It" Happen Again?,* New York: M. E. Sharp.

────── (1986), *Stabilizing an Unstable Economy,* New Haven, CT: Yale University Press.

Mises, Ludwig, Murray N. Rothbard, Gottfried Haberler, and Friedrich A. Hayek (1996), *The Austrian Theory of the Trade Cycle and Other Essays,* Auburn, AL: Ludwig Von Mises Institute.

Mishel, Lawrence, Jared Bernstein, and Sylvia Allegretto (2006) *The State of Working America 2006/2007,* Washington, DC: Economic Policy Institute.

Modigliani, Franco, and Lucas Papademos (1975), "Targets for Monetary Policy in the Coming Year," *Brookings Papers on Economic Activity,* 1975(1), 141–65.

Montero, Alfred (1998), "State Interests and the New Industrial Policy in Brazil: The Privatization of Steel, 1990–1994," *Journal of Interamerican Studies and World Affairs,* 40(3), 27–62.

Moss, David (2002), *When All Else Fails: Government as the Ultimate Risk Manager,* Cambridge, MA: Harvard University Press.

Mueller, Dennis (1989) *Public Choice II,* Cambridge: Cambridge University Press.

Mulligan, Casey (2008), "An Economy You Can Bank on," *New York Times,* Oct 9, http://www.nytimes.com/2008/10/10/opinion/10mulligan.html?_r=2 &hp&oref=slogin, accessed 15 May 2010.

────── (2009), "Aggregate Implications of Labor Market Distortions: The Recession of 2008-9 and Beyond," NBER Working Paper No. 15681, National Bureau of Economic Research, Cambridge, MA.

Muth, John (1961), "Rational Expectations and the Theory of Price Movements," *Econometrica,* 29(3), 315–35.

Nairn, Bede (1989), *Civilising Capitalism: The Beginnings of the Australian Labor Party,* Melbourne: Melbourne University Press.

Nash, John (1951), "Non-cooperative Games," *Annals of Mathematics,* 54, 286–95.

New Economics Foundation (2009), "A Bit Rich: Calculating the Real Value to Society of Different Professions," http://www.neweconomics.org/publications/ bit-rich, accessed 12 February 2010.

Norvell, Scott (2001), "Rally around the Economy, as Well as Flag," Fox News, Sept. 17, at http://www.foxnews.com/story/0,2933,34378,00.html.

Palley, Thomas (1999), "Speculation and Tobin Taxes: Why Sand in the Wheels Can Increase Economic Efficiency," *Zeitschrift Fur Nationalokonomie,* 69(2), 113–26.

Phelps, Edmund (1968), "Money-Wage Dynamics and Labor-Market Equilibrium," *Journal of Political Economy,* 76(4), 678–711.

Phillips, A. William (1958), "The Relationship between Unemployment and the Rate of Change of Money Wages in the United Kingdom, 1861–1957," *Economica,* 25(4), 283–99.

Pigou, Arthur C. (1920), *The Economics of Welfare,* London: Macmillan.

Piketty, Thomas, and Emanuel Saez (2003), "Income Inequality in the United States, 1913–1998," *Quarterly Journal of Economics*, 118(1), 1–39.

―――― (2006), "The Evolution of Top Incomes: A Historical and International Perspective," *American Economic Review*, 96(2), 200–05.

Plosser, Charles (1989), "Understanding Real Business Cycles," *Journal of Economic Perspectives*, 3(3), 51–77.

Putnam, Robert (2001), *Bowling Alone: The Collapse and Revival of American Community*, New York: Simon & Schuster.

Quiggin, John (1982), "A Theory of Anticipated Utility," *Journal of Economic Behavior and Organization*, 3(4), 323–43.

―――― (1987), "Egoistic Rationality and Public Choice: A Critical Review of Theory and Evidence," *Economic Record*, 63(180), 10–21.

―――― (1993) *Generalized Expected Utility Theory: The Rank-Dependent Model*, Amsterdam: Kluwer.

―――― (1995), "Does Privatisation Pay?" *Australian Economic Review*, 110(2nd quarter), 23–42.

―――― (2003), "Privatisation," pp. 17–30, in *The Cambridge Handbook of the Social Sciences in Australia*, ed. I. Mcallister, S. Dowrick, and R. Hassan, Melbourne: Cambridge University Press.

―――― (2004), "The Unsustainability of U.S. Trade Deficits," *The Economists' Voice*, 1(3), Article 2.

―――― (2007), "The Risk Society: Social Democracy in an Uncertain World," Centre for Policy Development Occasional Paper No. 2, Sydney.

―――― (2009a), "Six Refuted Doctrines," *Economic Papers*, 28(3), 238–47.

―――― (2009b), "An Agenda for Social Democracy," Whitlam Institute Perspectives 1, University of Western Sydney.

―――― (2010), "Australia and the Global Financial Crisis," pp. 99–123, in *Goodby to All That*, ed., Robert Manne and David McKnight, Melbourne: Black Inc.

Rauchway, Eric (2009), "The Pony Chokers," http://edgeofthewest.wordpress.com/2009/02/02/the-pony-chokers/, accessed 15 February 2010.

RealtyTrac (2010), "Foreclosures Home News and Trends Center Press Room," http://www.realtytrac.com/ContentManagement/pressrelease.aspx?ChannelID=9&ItemID=5681&accnt=64847, accessed 28 January 2010.

Reinhart, Carmen, and Kenneth Rogoff (2009), *This Time Is Different: Eight Centuries of Financial Folly*, Princeton: Princeton University Press.

Ricardo, David (1817), *On the Principles of Political Economy and Taxation*. In *The Works and Correspondence of David Ricardo*, vol. 1, reprint ed., Piero Sraffa, with the collaboration of Maurice Dobb. Cambridge: Cambridge University Press, 1951.

Robinson, Joan (1932), *Economics of Imperfect Competition*, London: Macmillan.

Rumsfeld, Donald (2002), "Transcript of Press Briefing, February 12," http://www.defense.gov/transcripts/transcript.aspx?transcriptid=2636, accessed July 12, 2010.

Ryan, Paul (2009), "A Republican Road to Economic Recovery," *Wall Street Journal*, 2 March, http://online.wsj.com/article/SB123595257066605147.html.

Samuelson, Paul (1998), "Summing Up on Business Cycles: Opening Address," pp. 33–36, in *Beyond Shocks: What Causes Business Cycles*, Conference Series 42, ed. J. Fuhrer and S. Schuh, Boston: Federal Reserve Bank of Boston.

Samuelson, Paul (1948), *Economics: An Introductory Analysis*, New York: McGraw Hill.

———— (1965), "Proof that Properly Discounted Present Values of Assets Fluctuate Randomly," *Industrial Management Review*, 6(2), 41–49.

———— (1973), "Proof That Properly Discounted Present Values of Assets Vibrate Randomly," *Bell Journal of Economics*, 4(2), 369–74.

Samuelson, Paul, and William Nordhaus (2009), *Economics*, New York: McGraw-Hill/Irwin.

Samuelson, Paul, and Robert Solow (1960), "Analytical Aspects of Anti-inflation Policy," *American Economic Review*, 50(2), 177–94.

Sargent, Thomas, and Neil Wallace (1976), "Rational Expectations and the Theory of Economic Policy," *Journal of Monetary Economics*, 2(2), 169–83.

Sassoon, Donald (1998), *One Hundred Years of Socialism: The West European Left in the Twentieth Century*, London: New Press.

Schiff, Peter, and John Downes (2007), *Crash Proof: How to Profit from the Coming Economic Collapse*, New York: Wiley.

Setser, Brad and Nouriel Roubini (2005), "How Scary Is the Deficit? (with response from Levey and Brown)," *Foreign Affairs*, 84(4), 194–200.

Shackle, George (1952), *Expectations in Economics*, Cambridge: Cambridge University Press.

————. (1983), *The Years of High Theory: Invention and Tradition in Economic Thought, 1926–1939*, Cambridge: Cambridge University Press.

Shiller, Robert (1982), "Consumption, Asset Markets, and Macroeconomic Fluctuations," Carnegie-Rochester Series on Public Policy, 17: 203–38.

———— (1989), *Market Volatility*, Cambridge, MA: MIT Press.

———— (2000), *Irrational Exuberance*, Princeton: Princeton University Press.

———— (2003a), *The New Financial Order: Risk in the Twenty-first Century*, Princeton: Princeton University Press.

———— (2003b), "From Efficient Markets Theory to Behavioral Finance," *Journal of Economic Perspectives*, 17(1), 59–82.

———— (2008), *The Subprime Solution: How Today's Global Financial Crisis Happened, and What to Do About it*, Princeton: Princeton University Press.

Shlaes, Amity (2007), *The Forgotten Man: A New History of the Great Depression*, London: Jonathan Cape.

Shonfield, Andrew (1984), *In Defence of the Mixed Economy*, Oxford: Oxford University Press.

Shulman, David (1992), "The Goldilocks Economy: Keeping the Bears At Bay," Salomon Brothers strategy paper.

Silverman, B. (1998), "The Rise and Fall of the Swedish Model—Interview with Swedish Economist Rudolf Meidner," *Challenge*, January–February, http://findarticles.com/p/articles/mi_m1093/is_n1_v41/ai_20485334/, accessed 28 February 2010.

Smith, Adam (1776), *The Wealth of Nations* (1976 ed.), Raleigh NC: Hayes Barton Press.

Smith, Adam (George Goodman), (1968), *The Money Game By "Adam Smith,"* New York: Random House.

Solow, Robert (1966; 1992), "Comments (response to Friedman's Comments on Solow's paper, The Case against the Case against Guideposts)," pp. 248–51, in *Price Controls*, ed. H. Rockoff, Aldershott, UK: Elgar.

Sowell, Thomas (2005), "Liberals and Class: Part II," http://www.jewishworld review.com/cols/sowell060905.asp, accessed July 12, 2010.

——— (2010), *Intellectuals and Society*, New York: Basic Books.

Sperling, Gene (2005), "How to Refloat These Boats," *Washington Post*, 18 December.

Stiglitz, Joseph E. (2010), *Freefall: America, Free Markets, and the Sinking of the World Economy*, New York: W. W. Norton.

Stock, James H., and Mark W. Watson (2002), "Has the Business Cycle Changed, and Why?" NBER Working Papers No. 9127, Cambridge, MA: National Bureau of Economic Research.

Strebel, Paul (1980), "A Contract Hysteresis Model of Inflation and Unemployment," *Southern Economic Journal*, 46(4), 1167–74.

Sullivan, Theresa, Elizabeth Warren, and Jay Westbrook (2006), "Less Stigma or More Distress: An Empirical Analysis of the Extraordinary Increase in Bankruptcy Filings," *Stanford Law Review*, 2 (November), 257–72.

Summers, Lawrence (2006), "The Great Liberator," *The New York Times*, 19 November.

Sumner, Scott (2010), "Defending the Indefensible," http://www.themoney illusion.com/?p=3773, accessed July 12, 2010.

Surowiecki, James (2005), *The Wisdom of Crowds: Why the Many Are Smarter Than the Few and How Collective Wisdom Shapes Business, Economies, Societies and Nations*, New York: Anchor.

Sweeney, Joan, and Richard Sweeney (1977), "Monetary Theory and the Great Capitol Hill Baby Sitting Co-op Crisis: Comment," *Journal of Money, Credit, and Banking*, 9(1), 86–89.

Taleb, Nassim (2007), *The Black Swan: The Impact of the Highly Improbable*, New York: Random House.

Taylor, John (1993), "Discretion versus Policy Rules in Practice," *Carnegie-Rochester Conference Series on Public Policy*, 39, 195–214.

Temin, Peter (1991), *Lessons from the Great Depression (Lionel Robbins Lectures)*, Cambridge, MA: MIT Press.

Thaler, Richard, and Cass Sunstein (2009), *Nudge: Improving Decisions about Health, Wealth, and Happiness*, New Haven, CT: Yale University Press.

Tobin, James (1958), "Liquidity Preference as Behavior toward Risk," *Review of Economic Studies*, 25(1), 65–86.

———— (1980), "Stabilization Policy Ten Years After," *Brookings Papers on Economic Activity*, 1980(1), 19–78.

———— (1978), "A Proposal for Monetary Reform," *Eastern Economic Journal*, 4(3–4), 153–59.

———— (1992), "Tax the Speculators," *Financial Times*, 12 December, 7T.

Tversky, Amos, and Daniel Kahneman (1992), "Cumulative Prospect Theory: An Analysis of Attitudes towards Uncertainty and Value," *Journal of Risk and Uncertainty*, 5(3), 297–323.

United Nations (2010), "Gini Coeffcent—Factsheet," http://www.scribd.com/doc/328232/United-Nations-Gini-Coefficient, accessed 28 January 2010.

Vickrey, William (1993), "The Other Side of the Coin," *American Economist*, 37(2), 5–17.

von Neumann, John and Oskar Morgenstern (1944), *Theory of Games and Economic Behavior*, Princeton: Princeton University Press.

Wade, Robert (1990), *Governing the Market: Economic Theory and the Role of Government in East Asian Industrialization*, Princeton: Princeton University Press.

Wakker, Peter (2010), *Prospect Theory*, Cambridge: Cambridge University Press.

Walras, Léon (1877, reprinted 1954), *Elements of Pure Economics* (Reprints of Economics Classics), Cambridge, Mass.: Harvard University Press.

Wanniski, Jude (1978), *The Way the World Works: How Economists Fail and Succeed*, New York: Basic Books.

Wikipedia (2010), "A Rising Tide Lifts All Boats," http://en.wikipedia.org/wiki/A_rising_tide_lifts_all_boats, accessed 28 January 2010.

Wilkinson, Richard, and Kate Pickett (2009), *The Spirit Level: Why More Equal Societies Almost Always Do Better*, London: Allen Lane.

Williamson, John (1990), "What Washington Means by Policy Reform," pp. 7–33, in *Latin American Adjustment: How Much Has Happened?* ed. J. Williamson, Washington, DC: Institute for International Economics.

Wilper, Andrew et al. (2008), "A National Study of Chronic Disease Prevalence and Access to Care in Uninsured US Adults," *Annals of Internal Medicine*, 149(3), 170–76.

Woodford, Michael (2009), "Convergence in Macroeconomics: Elements of the New Synthesis," *American Economic Journal: Macroeconomics*, 1(1), 1–23.

Woodward, Bob (2001), *Maestro: Greenspan's Fed and the American Boom*, New York: Simon & Schuster.

Yergin, Daniel and Joseph Stanislaw (2002), *The Commanding Heights: The Battle for the World Economy*, New York: Free Press.

Zywicki, Todd (2005), "Institutions, Incentives, and Consumer Bankruptcy Reform," *Washington & Lee Law Review*, 149–90.

INDEX